POSTCARD HISTORY SERIES

# *Owensboro*

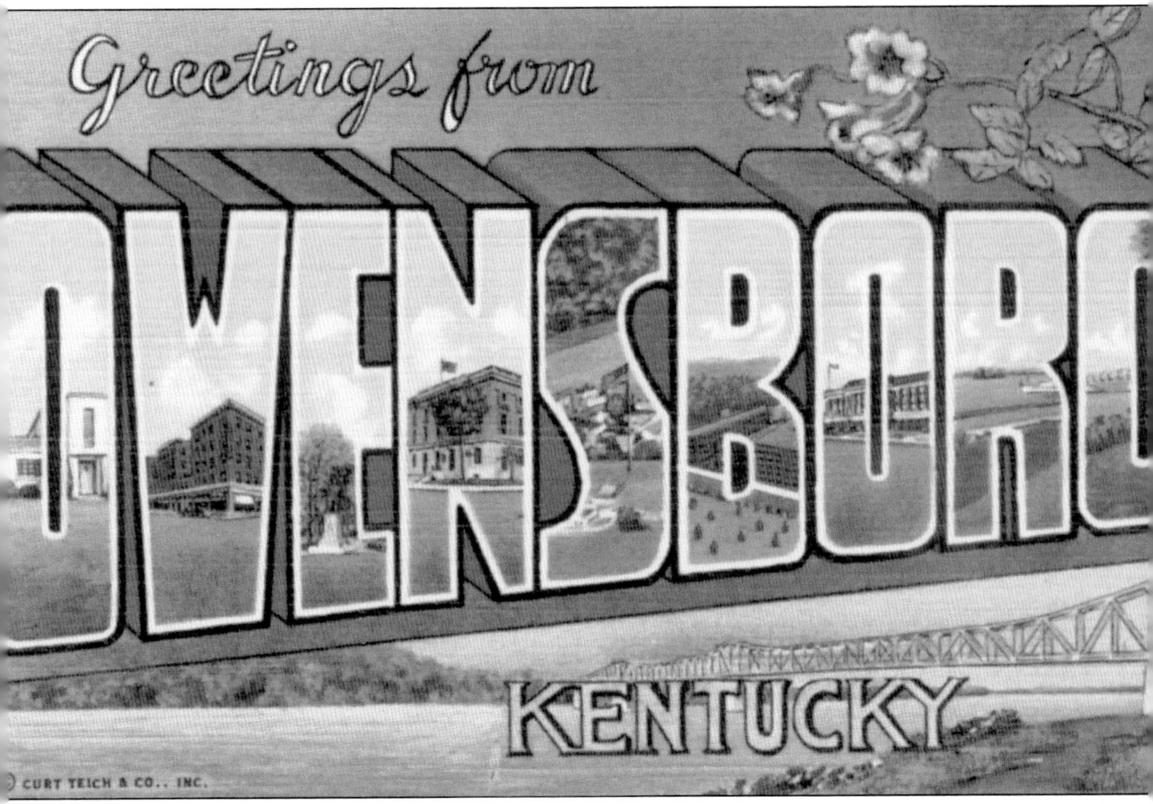


The Owensboro postcard above was produced by the famous Curt Teich and Company of Chicago, Illinois. This printer mass-produced postcards from 1898 to 1972. The individual letters serve as windows through which local images can be seen: O—WOMI Radio station, W—the Hotel Owensboro, E—the Court House Square, N—U.S. post office, S—Glenmore Distilleries, B—Ken-Rad Corporation, O—Owensboro High School, R—Dam 46, O—the Owensboro Bridge.

**On the Front Cover:** This postcard is one of at least 10 postcards of Union Station. The original brick-and-stone building was completed in 1906 at 1035 Frederica Street with a tile roof. It united three railroad companies under one roof: the Louisville and Nashville Railroad, the Louisville, Henderson, and St. Louis Railroad, and the Illinois Central Railroad. A two-story building addition, not shown, was constructed in the 1930s. (Author's collection.)

**On the Back Cover:** This postcard captures the opening of Mills Drugs and Candy Store at 220 West Third Street in 1914. The photograph centers on children, with east-falling shadows indicating an afternoon event. Note the women looking out the second-floor windows, just above the streetlamp. On this day, druggist Thomas W. Mills gave whistles to local kids with the help of Tom Jr., his son. Mills, his wife Sara, and their family lived at 1018 1/2 East Fourth Street. (Author's collection.)

POSTCARD HISTORY SERIES

# *Owensboro*

*Terry Blake and David Edds Jr.*

ARCADIA
PUBLISHING

ISBN 978-0-7385-4427-4

Published by Arcadia Publishing
Charleston, South Carolina

Printed in the United States of America

Library of Congress Catalog Card Number: 2006939386

For all general information contact Arcadia Publishing at:
Telephone 843-853-2070
Fax 843-853-0044
E-mail sales@arcadiapublishing.com
For customer service and orders:
Toll-Free 1-888-313-2665

Visit us on the Internet at www.arcadiapublishing.com

*This book is dedicated to our loving and patient wives, Carol and Sandy.*

# Contents

# Acknowledgments

I am grateful to Dan King, Kentucky Wesleyan College's library director, for first introducing me to Owensboro postcards in 1973. I recall the vivid postcard images Mr. King showed me of the many fine houses along south Frederica Street. "This can't be Owensboro," I reacted in fascination. Mr. King was quick to share, in vivid detail, the location of each building prior to its being razed. These postcards represented to me windows into Owensboro's past. From that moment, I began a never-ending quest to find other "windows" into our past through collecting local antique postcards and photographs of Owensboro and Daviess County, Kentucky.

When David Edds Jr., marketing manager for the Owensboro–Daviess County Tourist Commission, approached me about the concept for this book, I was happy to work with him. I had contemplated writing a book on this topic for many years. He found this wonderful publisher, Arcadia Publishing, and together we agreed to direct all author proceeds from this book to the Owensboro Area Museum of Science and History.

All the postcards used for this book came from my personal collection. David and I wrote the text from a wide variety of sources, listed in the bibliography. We'd like to thank my wife, Carol; David's wife, Sandy; his father, David; museum director Kathy Olson; and writer/historian Keith Lawrence for providing editing and proofreading assistance.

# Introduction

Every U.S. community has some form of photographic documentation through the advent of the "penny postcard." Owensboro, Kentucky, is no exception. Numerous real photographs and lithographic images have been made of Owensboro and Daviess County. Approximately 300 images are known to exist of commercial-grade local postcards, and perhaps many more of these historic documents remain preserved in attics, trunks, and living spaces yet to be discovered by this generation. Each offers a window into the past through which we may glimpse the city's history.

This book shows an Owensboro unfamiliar to most and unrecognizable to many. Through these postcards, we are able to imagine this city's earliest settlements high on the Ohio River's yellow banks and see the growth of this community. Many of these postcards tender the only remaining images of some of the city's most historically important places, which have succumbed to demolition, neglect, and a disregard for the values of our past.

Everything starts with the river. It delivered the community's first settlers and continues to fuel industrial growth for the area. Long before the U.S. Interstate Highway System, the Ohio River was the nation's primary east-west transportation artery. Owensboro was a popular river port, shipping agricultural products such as tobacco and whiskey. The river was both generous and destructive. The great floods of 1913 and 1937 brought devastation to the community's low-lying areas. Dam 46 was later constructed in an effort to control this mighty force of nature.

Owensboro has long been Western Kentucky's premier marketplace and industrial center. Businesses of all types have prospered in this thriving river town. The city's governmental center was the Court House Square, with Second Street, also known as Main Street, serving as the retail hub until the 1970s. Banks, restaurants, service stations, and department stores, as well as other businesses, offered shoppers a full range of goods and services. The community manufactured a wide range of products including bourbon, wagons, vacuum tubes, and buggies for many years.

Churches tell us much about this community. Three religious organizations existed even before Daviess County was founded on June 1, 1815, and while the first church in 1808 was Methodist, the majority of the new congregations to follow were Baptist and Catholic. These congregations built magnificent houses of worship throughout the city and county. Postcards allow us the opportunity to see these churches as they were and learn more about the people who built them.

Schools have been a symbol of pride for this community since the early 1800s. One-room, privately supported schoolhouses occupied settlements throughout the county, and more than 2,000 children were enrolled in Daviess County schools by 1850. Parochial schools were organized by the Catholic Church in 1849, and the Owensboro Public Schools were opened in 1871. Since 1820, Owensboro has been a seat of higher learning, offering a variety of small colleges.

Great cities have great parks. Owensboro established its first park along the river when it organized in 1815. It is now known as Smothers Park. Dr. James H. Hickman, in his first term as mayor, led the city's purchase of a 23.75-acre plot outside town that is now known as Legion Park. Chautauqua Park was privately developed in 1901 in the Seven Hills area east of town. After financial difficulties, the city purchased the 31-acre property in 1916.

Hotels and motels make a substantial impression on community visitors. They reflect a city's prosperity and hospitality. The city has had a succession of fine hotels beginning with the Planter's Hotel, then the Rudd Hotel, the Hotel Owensboro, Gabe's Tower Inn, and the Executive Inn Rivermont. One can also follow a community's development by studying the location and life cycle of smaller hotels and motels. This can best be illustrated by the rise and decline of the Triplett Street area.

Public places say much about a community's past. Keen observers of these postcards will note the buildings that are featured with pride and the clues they give about the people who built them. Consider the progressive statement of a small town in the 19th century that privately builds an 1,800-seat theater to stage the great shows of the day. Notice the conservative nature of the courthouse's architecture and the city's use of an old used building for its city hall. Note the compassion of a community that continuously reinvests in the health care of its citizens and has the foresight to build a municipal utility for a growing city.

The people presented in these few postcards reflect only a small sample of this community's population, but they provide an important window into the past. Notice the pride bursting from the cooper's faces, the Owensboro Business College student's fashion styling, the Sunday school class's purposeful passion, and the marching band's commitment in spite of the storm clouds gathering.

The houses people build and occupy tell a lot about a community. Fine homes built as single-family residences evolve over time into boarding houses, schools, dormitories, and fraternal organizations. Neighborhoods developed for residential needs evolve to accommodate commercial and academic growth.

The surrounding communities contribute much to the cultural and economic development of a city. It is unfortunate that Owensboro's surrounding communities were not better represented by postcards, but the available examples tell us much. Through these documents, we are able to see Mount St. Joseph for over a century.

The objective of this book is to present a window into our past through the use of postcards of Owensboro, Kentucky. It is not meant to be all-inclusive but simply reflect some of the changes within the city.

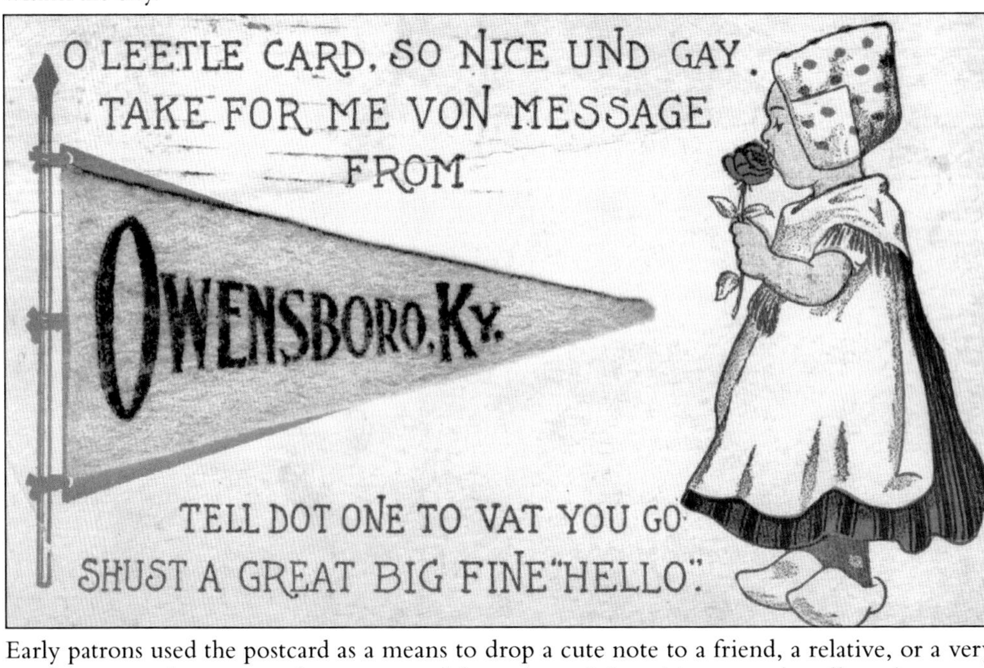


Early patrons used the postcard as a means to drop a cute note to a friend, a relative, or a very special person. A return card was expected from the recipient. Many people collected postcard images in albums for display and conversation at family gatherings. Almost every family had a photo album, but postcards allowed people to collect top-quality images of their community and others around the world. The postcard above depicts a little Dutch girl presenting her Owensboro message to the lucky recipient.

# *One*

# The Ohio River

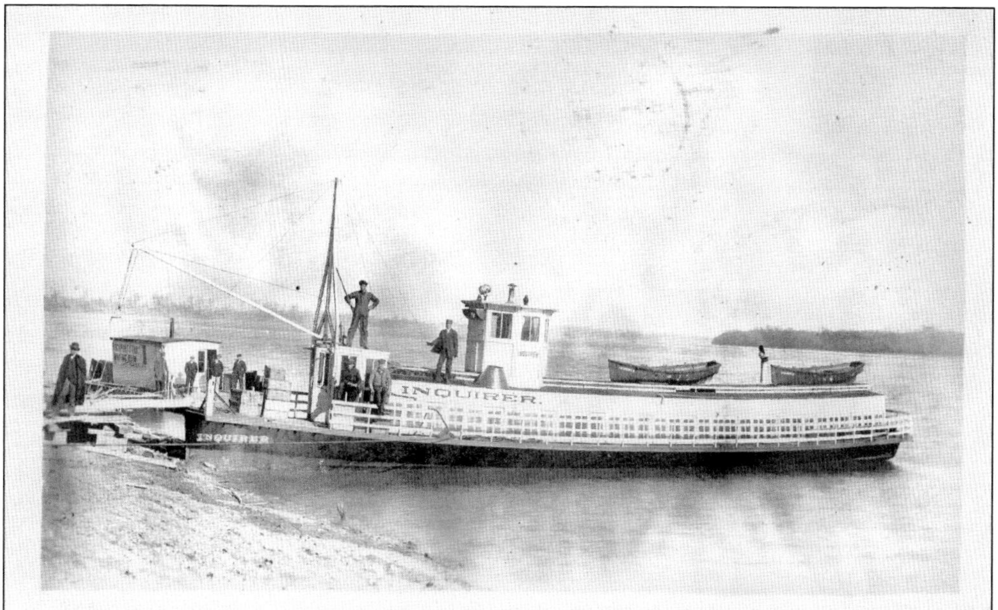


The *Inquirer* was a water taxi that ran on the Ohio River daily between Kentucky's Owensboro and Indiana's Rockport and Evansville. The Rounds brothers owned the Owensboro Ferry Company, which managed a fleet that included the towboat *Sabrina* and the gasoline yachts *Messenger, Margaret R., Ben R.,* and *Inquirer.* In 1910, the *Inquirer* was listed with a speed of 12 miles per hour upstream and 17 miles per hour downstream with a 90-foot hull, 15-foot beam, and 3-foot draft. The boat was powered by a 3-cylinder, 4-cycle engine with a 10-inch bore and a 10-inch stroke. The engine ran at 350 revolutions per minute with a 39-inch-diameter propeller.

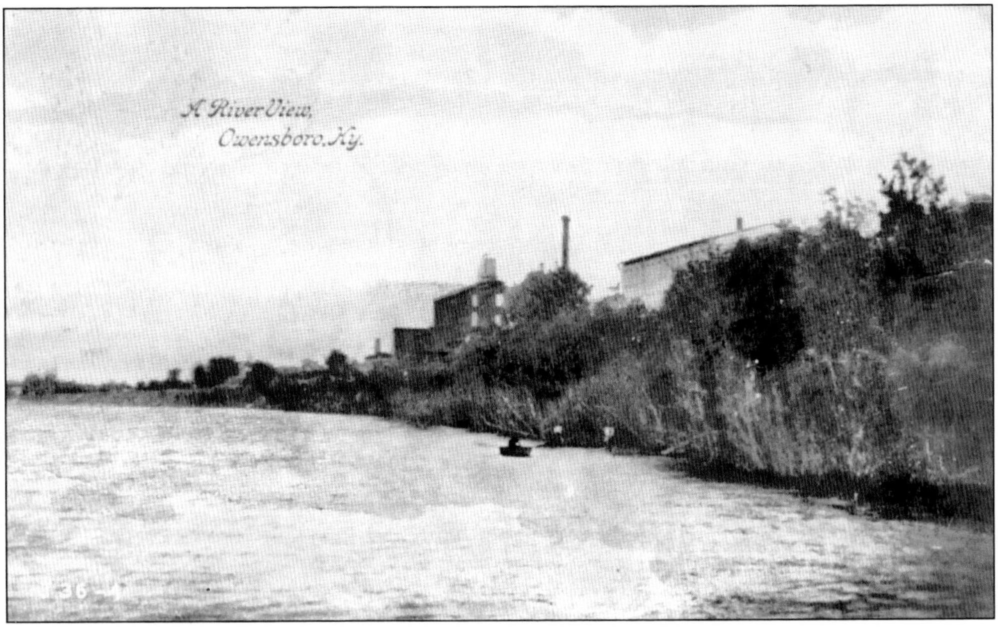


This is a very early view taken from the river and looking upstream toward present-day Glover Cary Bridge. The first building on the right is A. T. Harris Tobacco Stemmery, which sat at what today is the main entrance to the RiverPark Center. The tall stack was the boiler flue for the Charles Broeker and Company Flower Mill and Elevator, located between Lewis (now J. R. Miller Boulevard) and Crittenden Streets. The postcard below shows a similar view of the Ohio River and its bank but presents a much more romantic view of what the river was used for by those seeking the hand of a young lady in Owensboro.

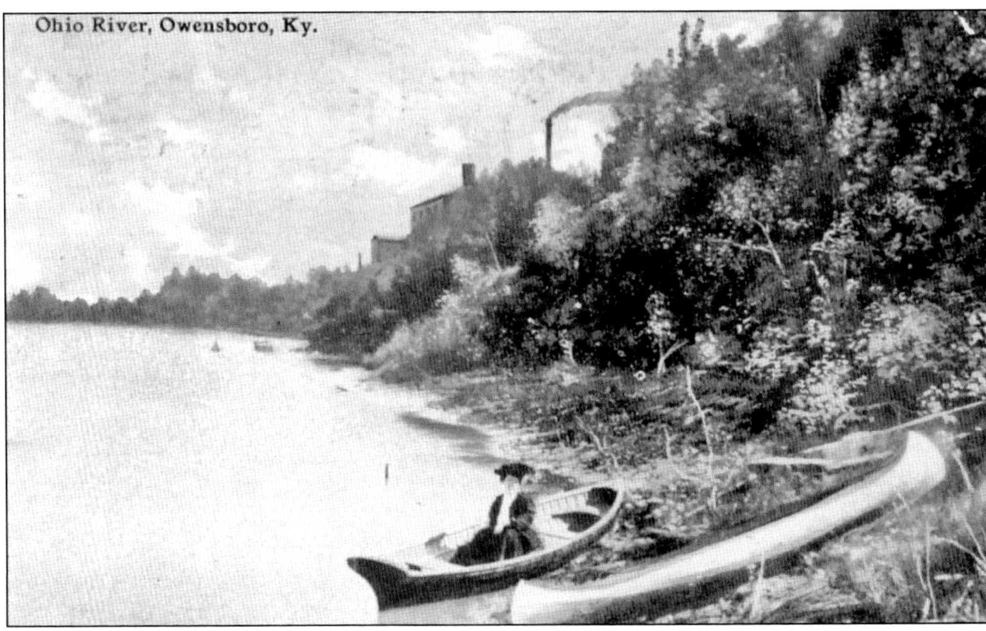

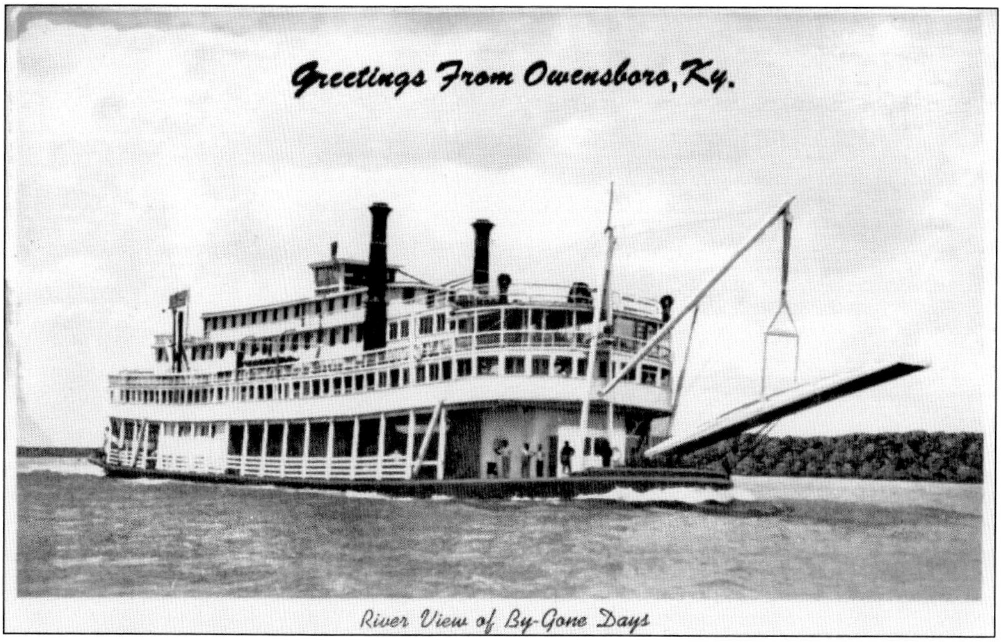


The postcard above is of *Gordon C. Green*, one of the last paddlewheel steamboats to cruise the Ohio and Mississippi Rivers. Built in 1923 in Jeffersonville, Indiana, the boat appeared in the famous movies *Steamboat around the Bend*, *Gone with the Wind*, and *The Kentuckian*. She sank in St. Louis, Missouri, in 1967. The postcard below is of the same boat in Owensboro.

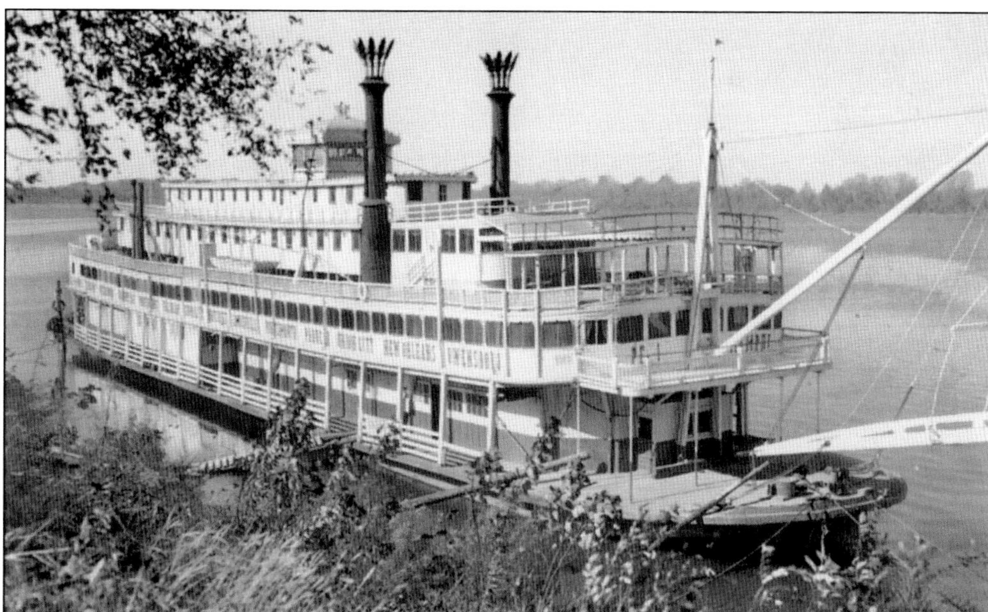

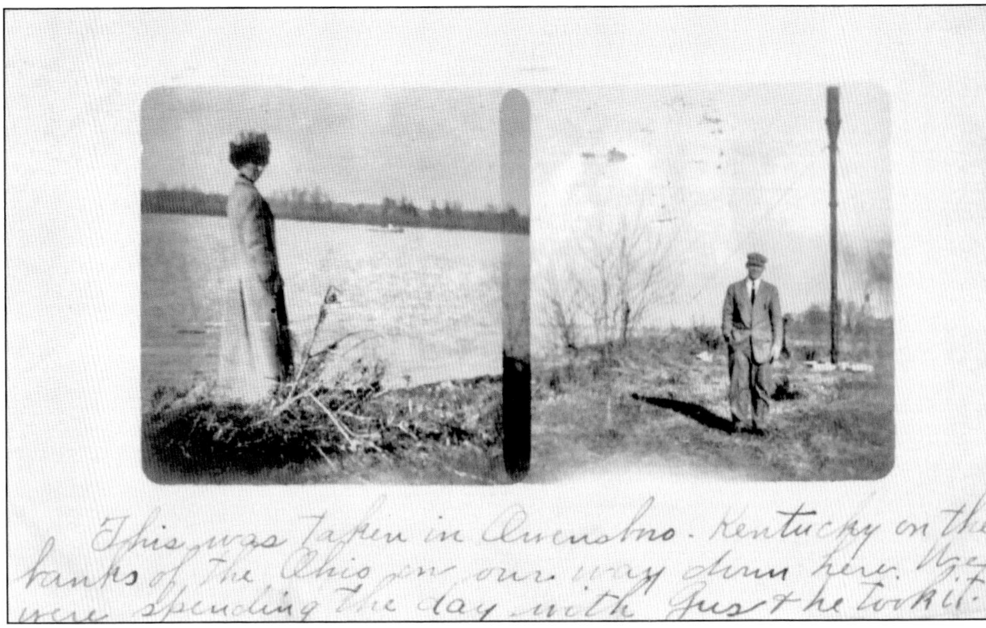

This is a 1912 real-photo postcard addressed to Miss Anna Burgman of Logansport, Indiana, and reads: "This was taken in Owensboro Kentucky on the banks of the Ohio on our way down here. We were spending the day with Gus and he took it." Note the overlap of this double-exposure shot. This postcard reflects the skills of an early photographer. The postcard below shows another view of boating on the Ohio River, although the boating part may be questionable.

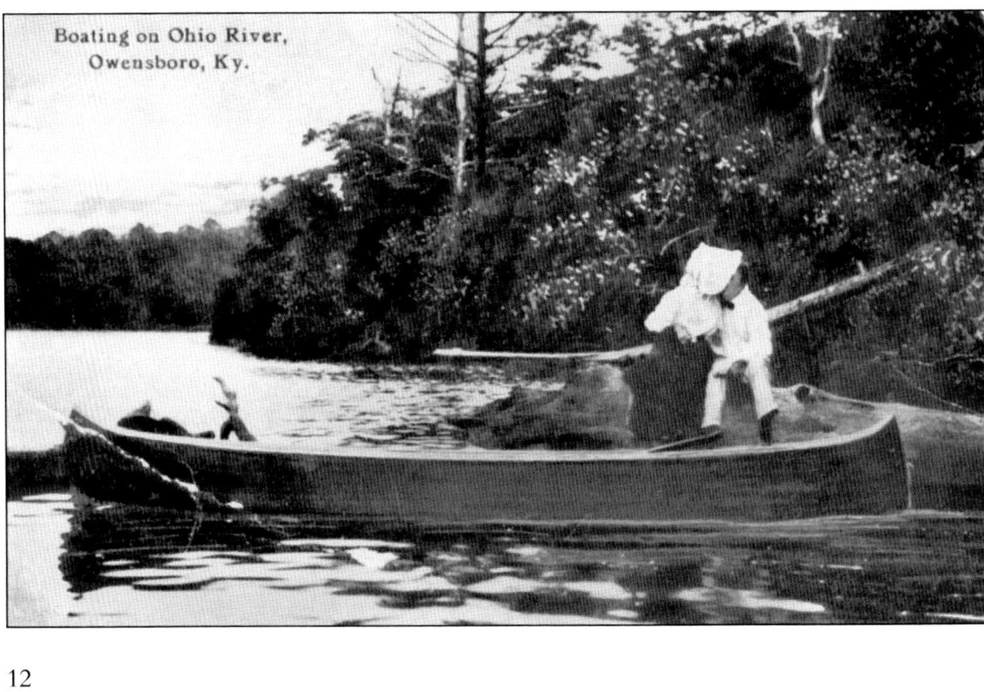

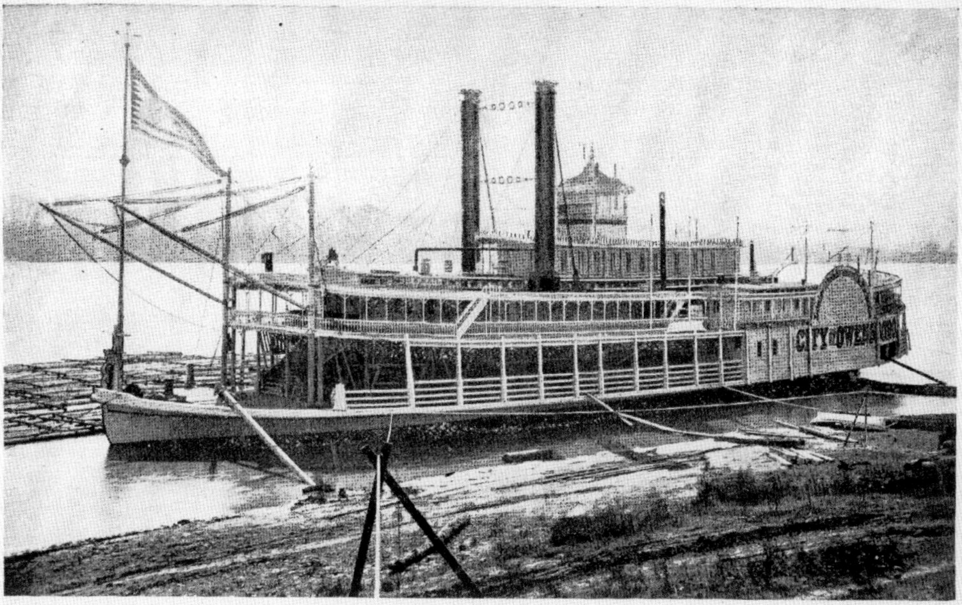

"CITY OF OWENSBORO," IN THE LOUISVILLE AND EVANSVILLE TRADE, OHIO RIVER.

The postcard above captures the riverboat called *City of Owensboro.* Howard Shipyard of Jeffersonville, Indiana, built the 240-foot-long boat in 1883 to travel between Evansville, Indiana, and Louisville, Kentucky. The 1940s postcard below shows the towboat steamer *Charles T. Campbell* docked at the Owensboro wharf. A new owner changed her name in 1947 to the *John J. Rowe*, and it was changed again in 1955 to the *Orco.*

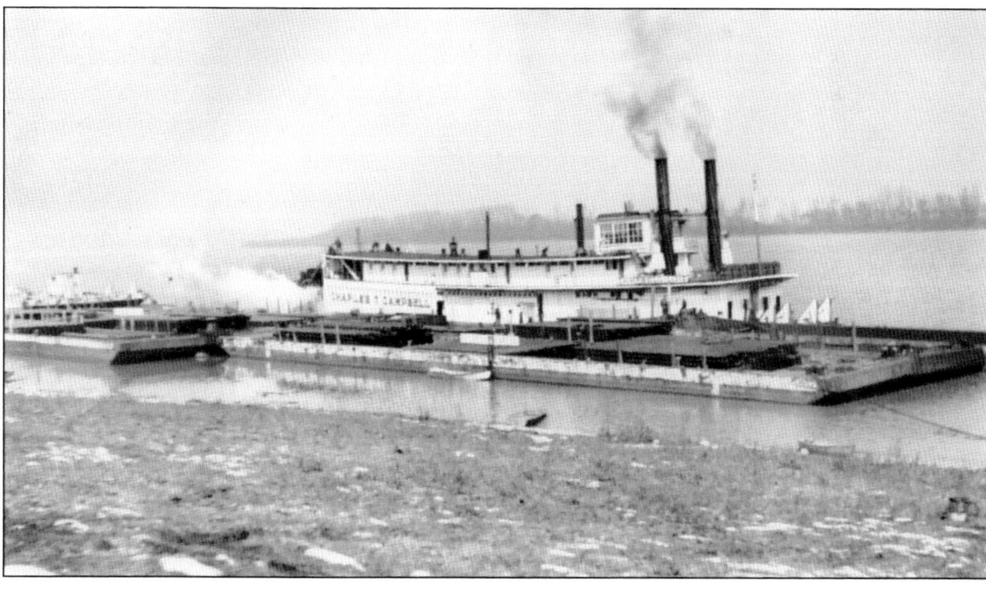

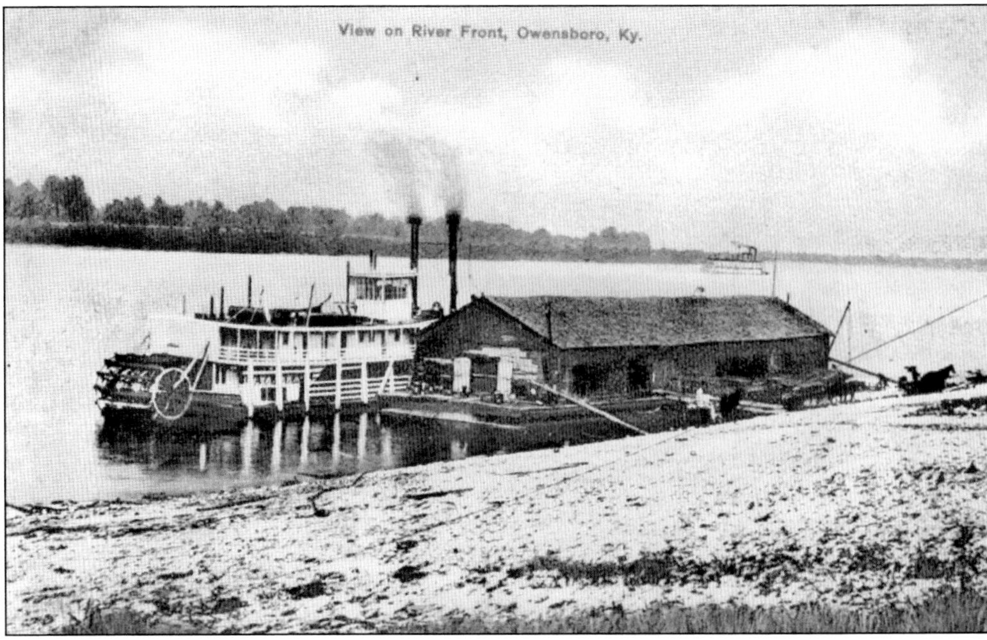


The wharf landing was located at the foot of Frederica Street. The barge-like platform served as a waiting and departure point for patrons ferrying up and down the Ohio River. This is where one would go to catch the packet boats ferrying passengers and freight by water.

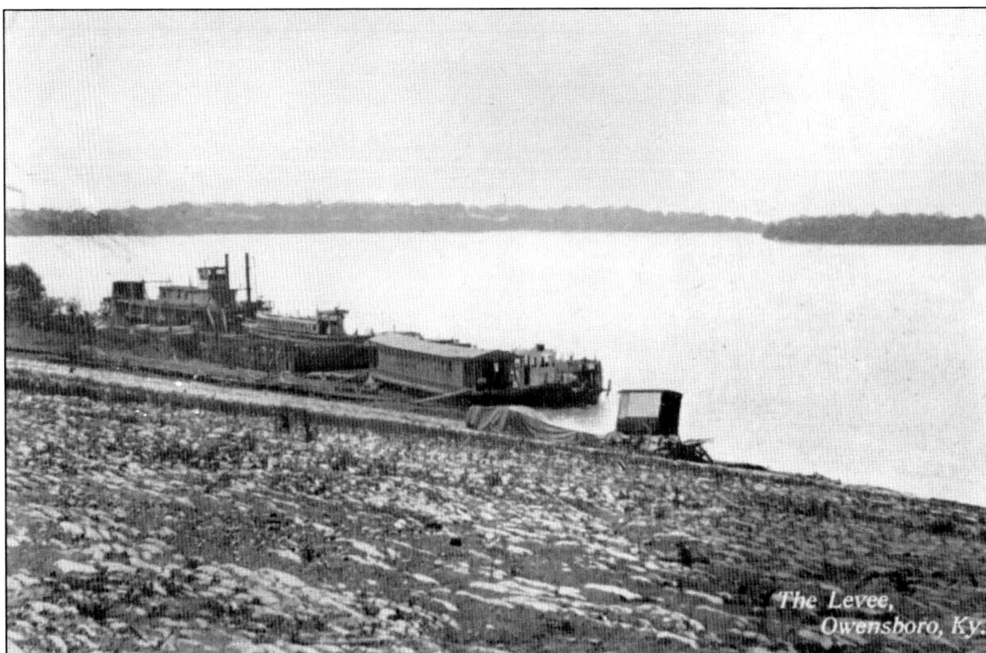


The Levee is the floating building in the center of this 1910 postcard. It served as Owensboro's front door, greeting passengers arriving and departing by riverboats, known as packet boats, from the 1840s to the 1920s. Notice on the right of the postcard the undertaker's hearse awaiting its passenger. The first boat to the Levee's left is the passenger ferryboat *Inquirer.*

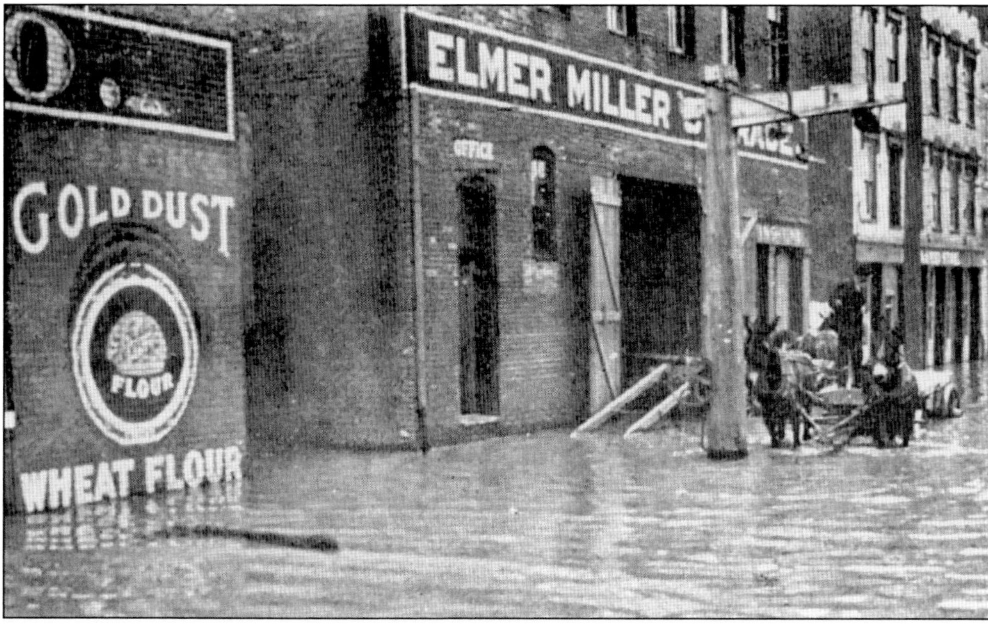


The rare early postcard above is of the 1913 Ohio River flood at the Elmer Miller Storage facility on First Street. This flood reached the corner of Main and St. Ann Streets, eclipsing the 1884 flood high-water mark by four inches. The postcard below is of the boat dock facility at the wharf landing looking west down the Ohio River during the flood of 1913. The building on the photograph's left edge sits on the southwest corner of First and St. Ann Streets, site of the present-day 100 St. Ann Building. The photograph was taken from the upper level of the Grand Theater, located on the southeast corner of St. Ann and First Streets.

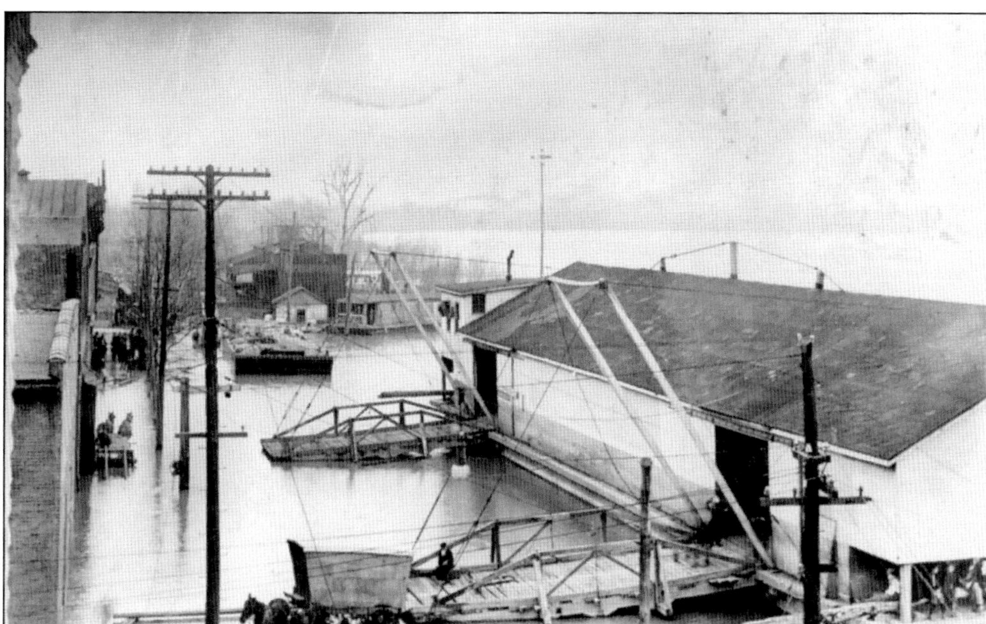

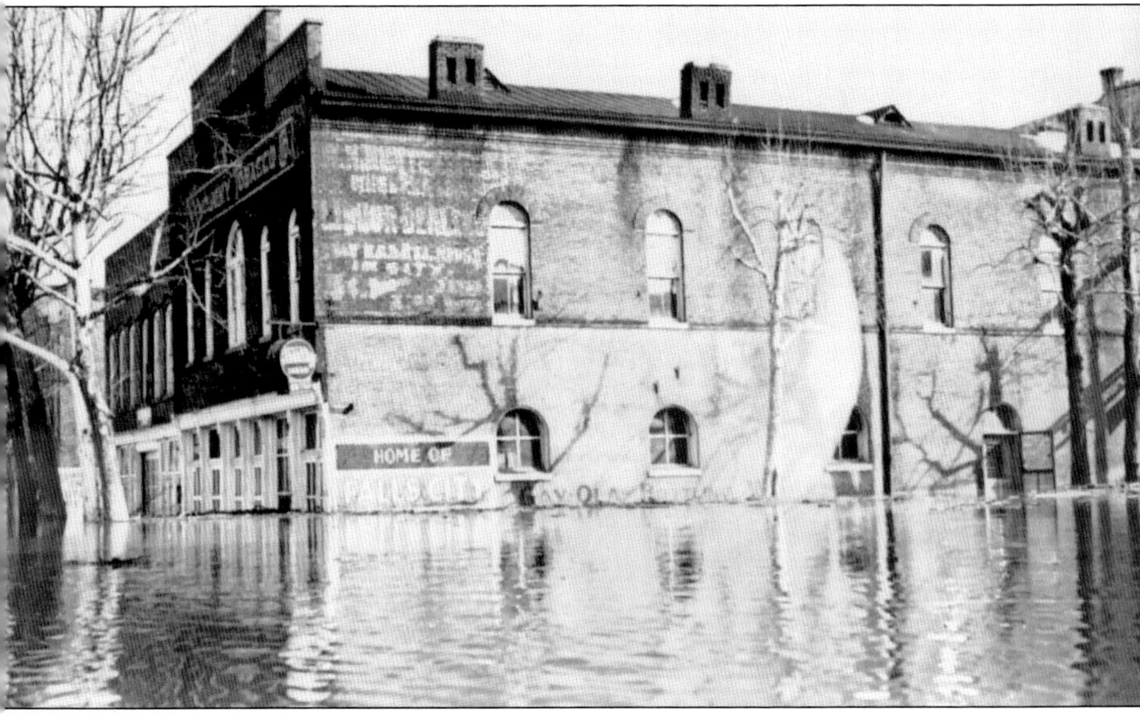


The photo postcard above shows the Ohio River level during the "Great Flood" of 1937. The building shown was located on the southeast corner of First and Frederica Streets. The Kentucky Tobacco Company name is faintly visible on the building's upper front. In 1937, the river crested at Owensboro at 54.85 feet, nearly 6 feet higher than the previous record set in 1913. While water stood on Main Street and filled store basements, most of the city sitting high on the riverbanks was spared the devastation inflicted on lower-lying areas.

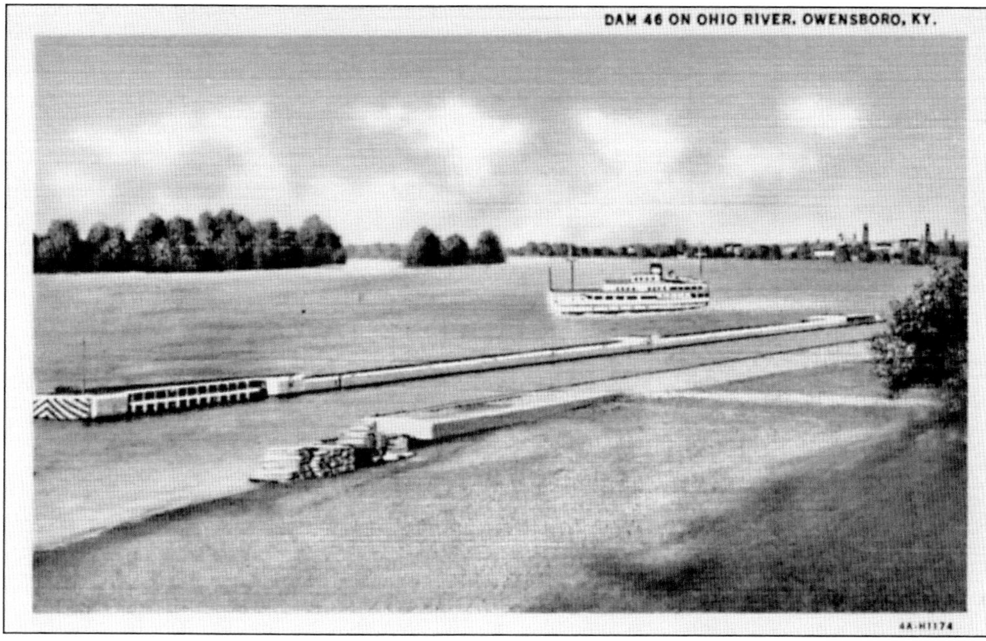


Ohio River Dam 46 was located on the city's west side at present-day English Park. The lock was 110 feet wide and 600 feet long with a 900-foot-wide navigable boat pass. The total width of the lock and dam was 2,630 feet including the abutment on the Indiana shoreline. It is interesting to note that the 1916 charts and drawings for the Ohio River site selected for Dam 46 show that it was planned to be upstream, east of the city between Owensboro and Rockport, Indiana, with the lock being on the north bank. The photograph below shows the locks of Dam 46 under construction. The project was completed in 1926 at a cost of $3.5 million.

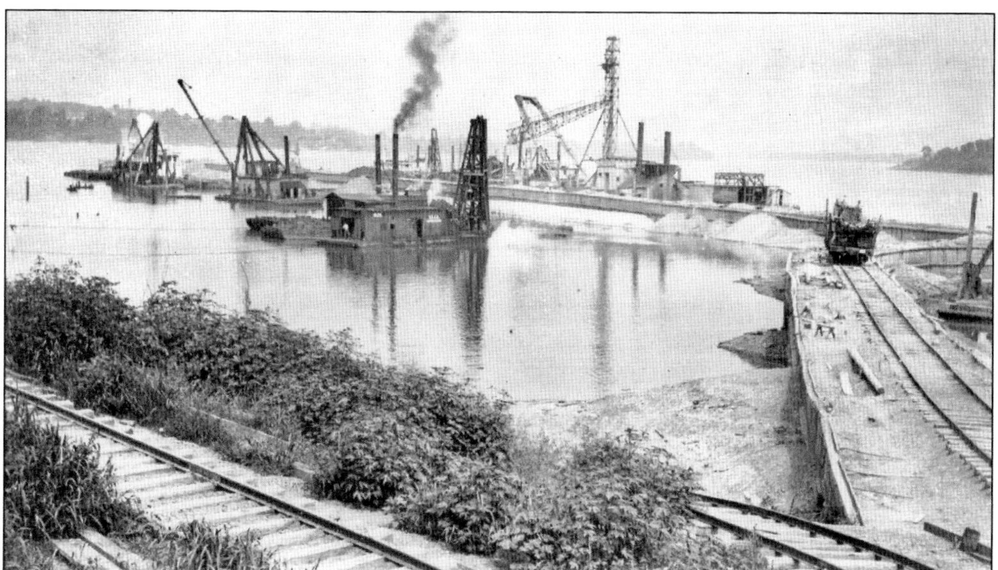

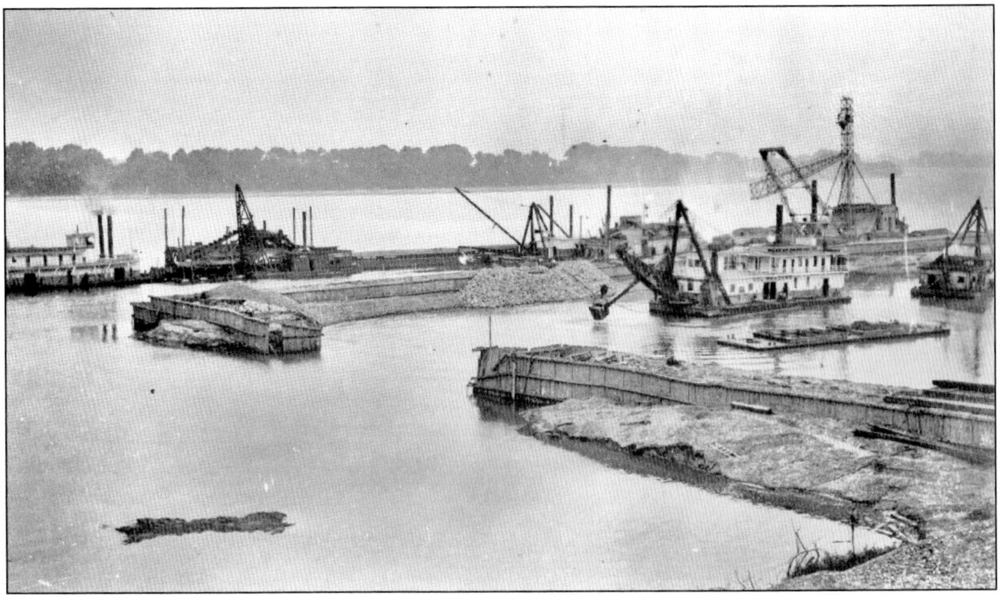

The above photograph taken around 1924 from atop the riverbank looks out over the construction of Ohio River Dam 46 Locks. Notice the crane rig floating in the river in the top right. The photograph below looks back at the same construction from atop that crane. The sloped riverbank in the background became part of the Peter B. English Park after the dam's demise in 1975. The federal government donated the dam's 11-acre site, located one mile west of downtown Owensboro, to become a unique public area. The city park was named for English, who served the Corps of Engineers for 50 years, 16 as lockmaster.

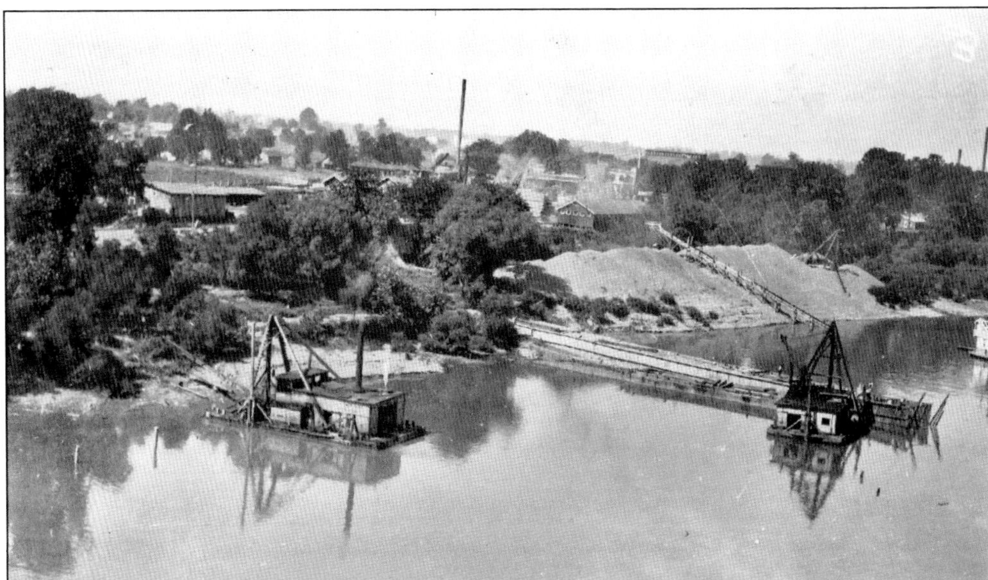

## *Two*

# BUSINESS AND INDUSTRY

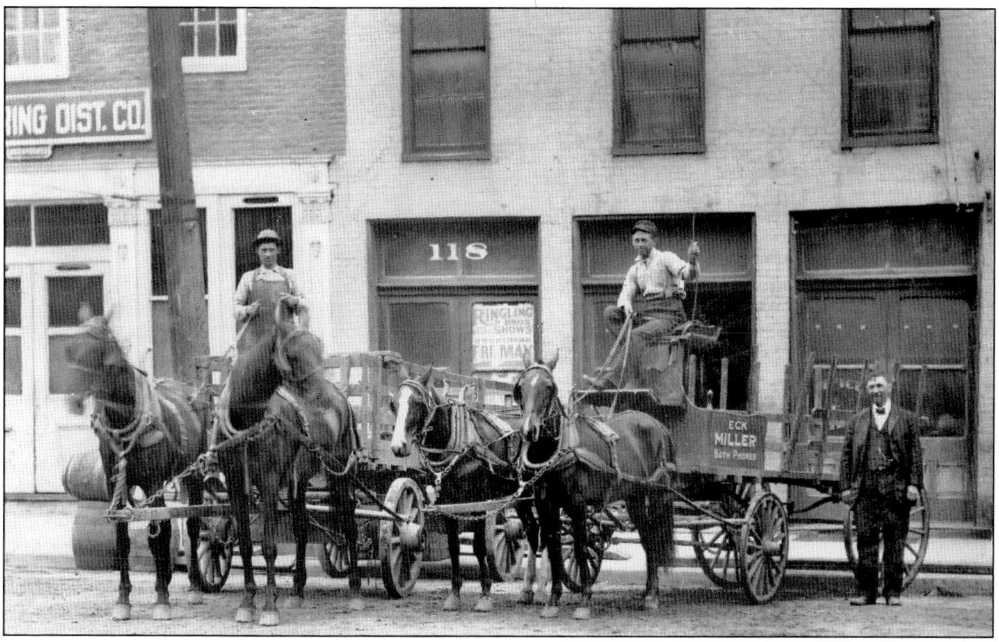


Eck Miller Contract Company hauled construction materials for Owensboro's building trades. Established in 1905, the company had its first office at 118 Frederica Street. This building pictured above was on Frederica's west side just off First Street, on the current site of the State Office Building. Standing to the right is company president Eck Miller, who lived on south Frederica Street with his wife, Eunice. The driver in the center is unidentified, but the driver on the left is John Ferguson of Rockport, Indiana. Note the Ringling Brothers Circus poster in the window. This company grew, and by 1960, Eck Miller's moving and storage division served customers nationwide as an Allied Van Line agent. Its office and warehouse at 1125 Sweeney Street was destroyed by a major fire in 1973.

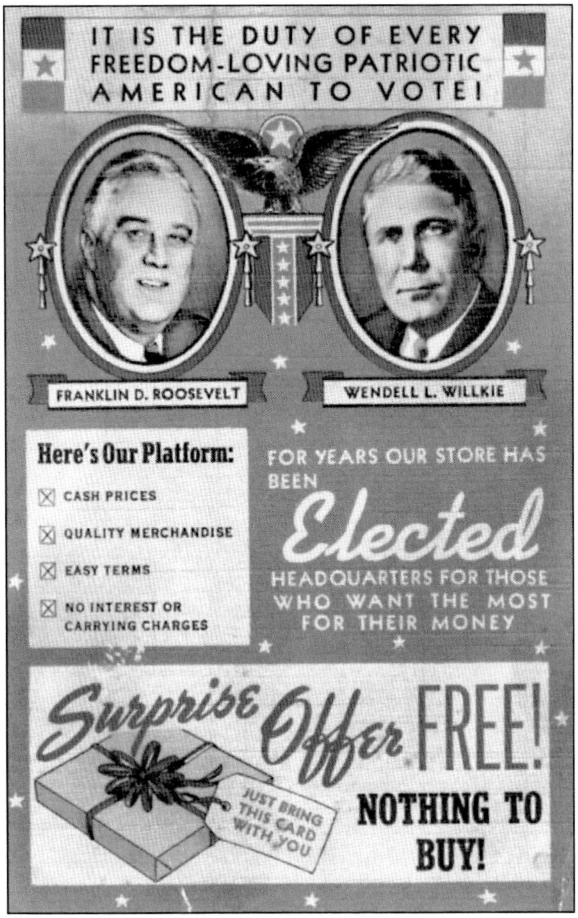


The postcard was also used to specifically target individuals with products, services, and politics. This was one of the earliest systems used for target marketing. This 1940 Owensboro advertisement was addressed to William Lonzo Porter of 1207 Hathaway Street, City. The Union Store was located at 109 West Second Street and was managed by John J. Newman. The store advertised clothing for the entire family with generous credit terms.

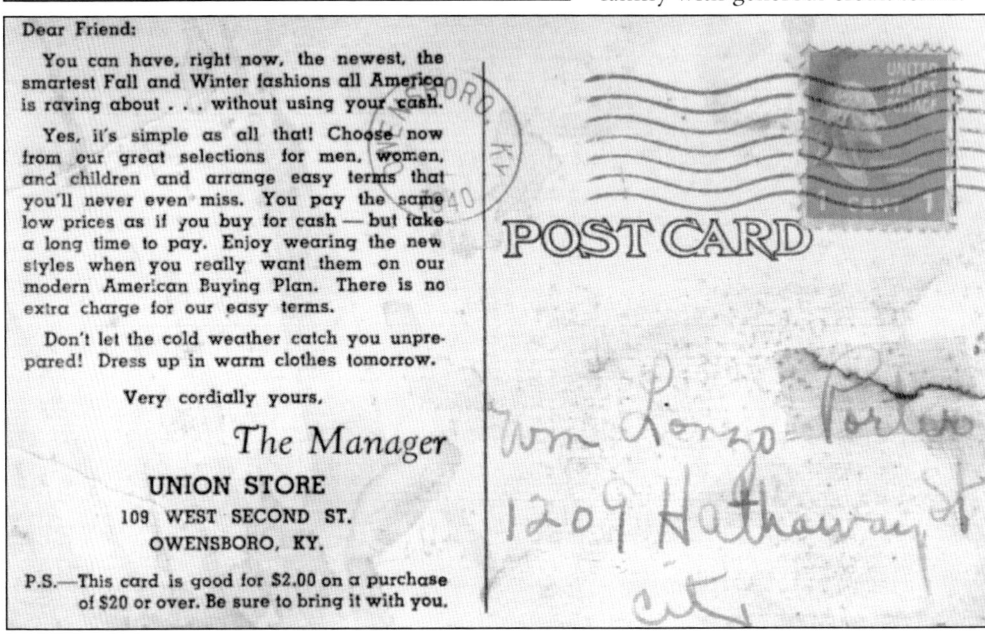

Dear Friend:

You can have, right now, the newest, the smartest Fall and Winter fashions all America is raving about . . . without using your cash.

Yes, it's simple as all that! Choose now from our great selections for men, women, and children and arrange easy terms that you'll never even miss. You pay the same low prices as if you buy for cash — but take a long time to pay. Enjoy wearing the new styles when you really want them on our modern American Buying Plan. There is no extra charge for our easy terms.

Don't let the cold weather catch you unprepared! Dress up in warm clothes tomorrow.

Very cordially yours,

*The Manager*

UNION STORE
109 WEST SECOND ST.
OWENSBORO, KY.

P.S.—This card is good for $2.00 on a purchase of $20 or over. Be sure to bring it with you.

POST CARD

Wm Lonzo Porter
1209 Hathaway St
City

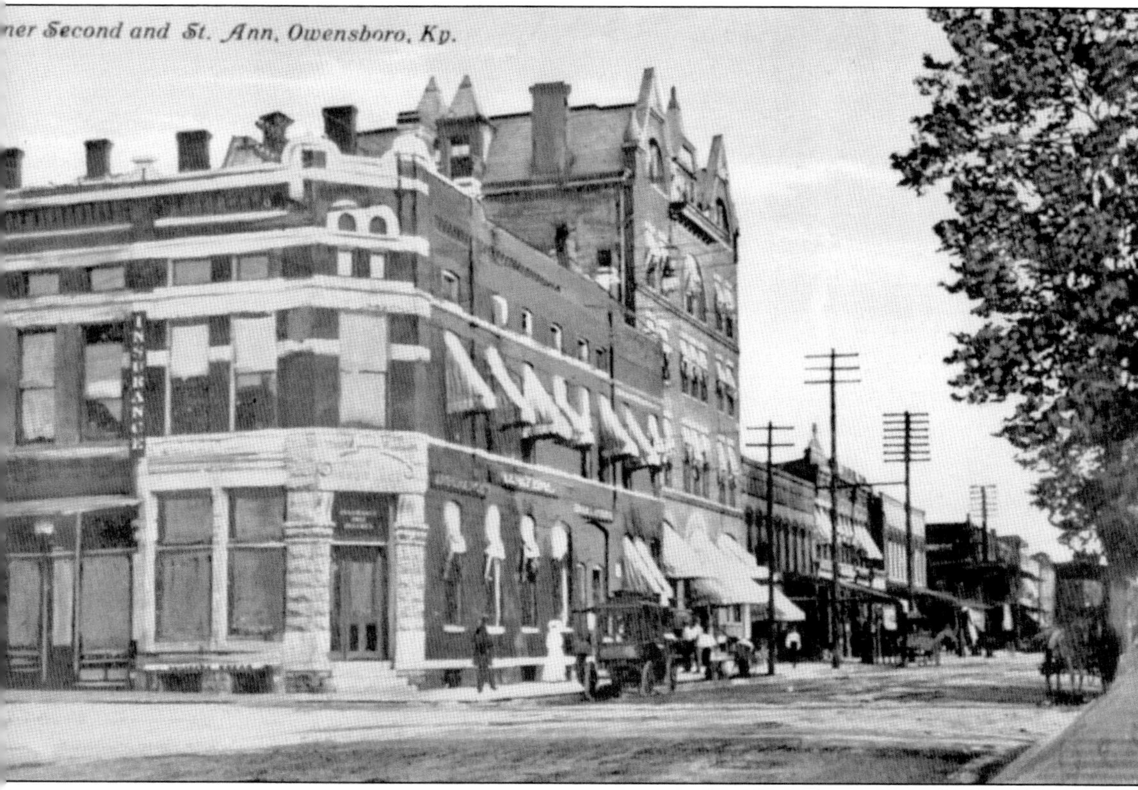


The 1909 postcard above shows the Bank of Commerce on the southeast corner of Second and St. Ann Streets. This building was constructed in 1888 on a former city hall site and was best remembered as the home of Walgreens drugstore. It was torn down in the early 1990s to create a parking lot. The tall building just behind the bank facing St. Ann Street is the Rudd Hotel. It was demolished after a fire in 1973. While the Masonic Temple was later built in 1912 on this eastern block of the Court House Square, many of the other buildings seen here still remain with new facades. Note the horse-drawn vehicles at both sides of the street.

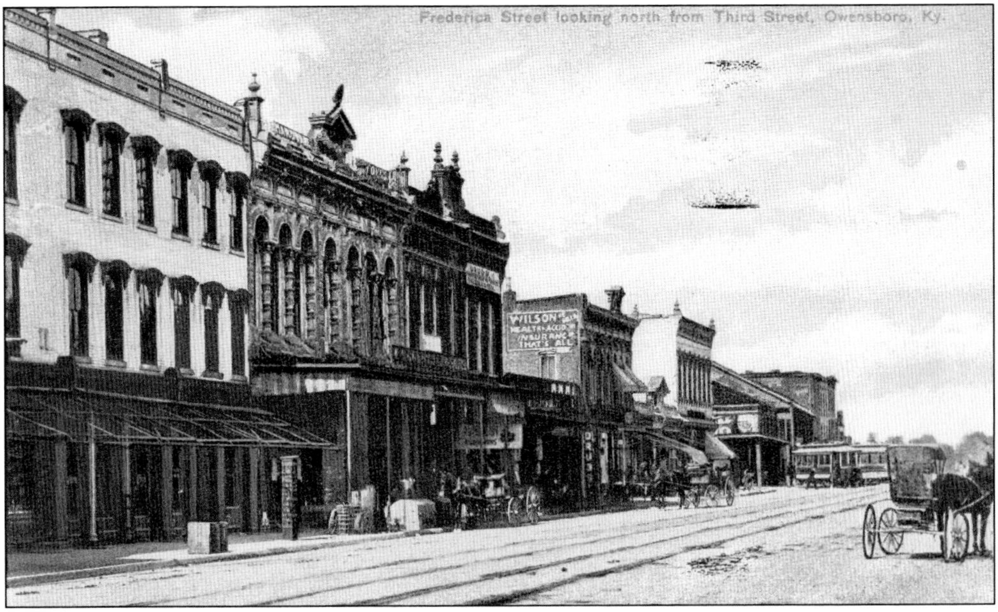


These postcards show the same block of Frederica Street between Second and Third Streets. The top 1909 view looks north toward the Ohio River with the Planter's Hotel on the left on the northwest corner of Third and Frederica Streets. Planter's Hotel, built in 1846, was Owensboro's first major hotel. Jenny Lind, the "Swedish Nightingale," was once reportedly a guest there. Notice the horse-drawn buggies and trolley car turning the corner. For this west-side block of the Court House Square, much has changed. Many of these buildings were razed to make room for the construction of the imposing four-story Owensboro National Bank building, completed in January 1969. The bank is now known as BB&T. The postcard below looks south down Frederica from Second Street. This view shows a large number of trees on the courthouse lawn.

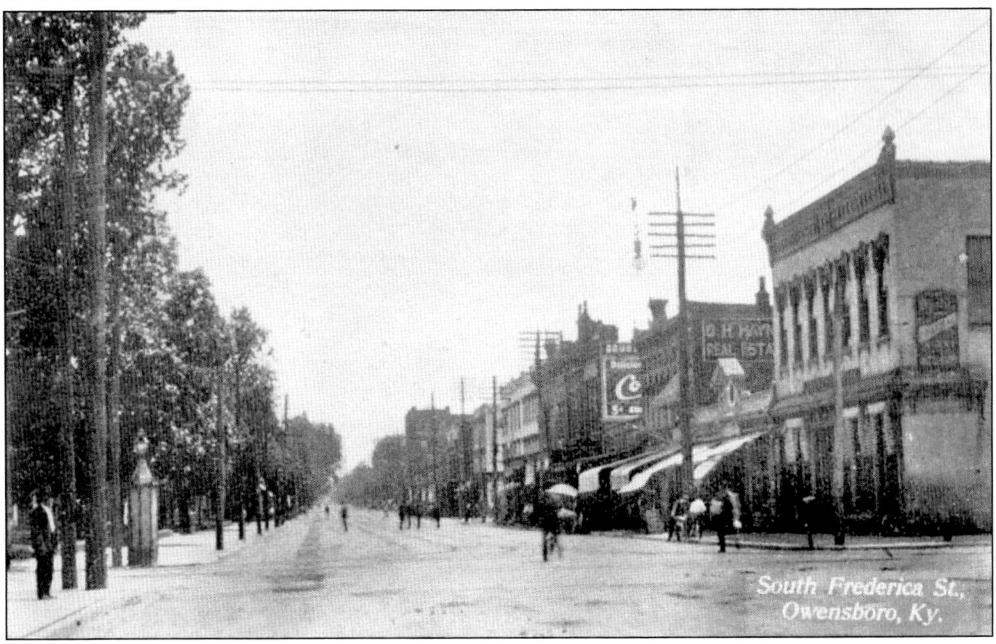

In 1900, the Daviess County Bank and Trust Company constructed this building at 114 West Third Street. The pediment over the central entry pavilion, monumental columns, stone window surrounds, and roofline balustrade all serve as important elements to identify this building as an example of Classical Revival architecture. This style adheres to the principles set forth by the Paris Beaux Arts educational program for many American-trained architects. The building's architect is currently unknown. The postcard below represents an advertising format used by the U.S. National Bank. It projects an image of security, trust, and honesty. The verses paint an analogy of the tortoise beating the hare. These cards were distributed to customers, friends, and relatives for their own personal use.

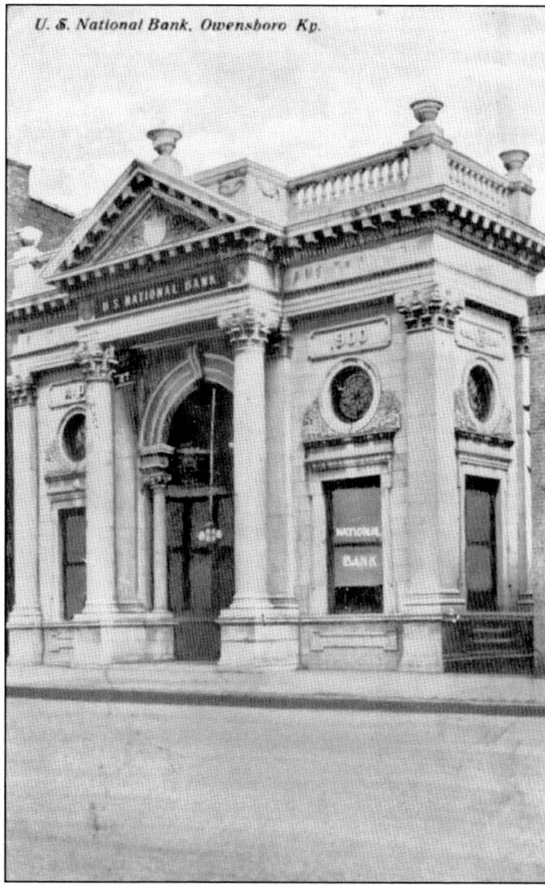


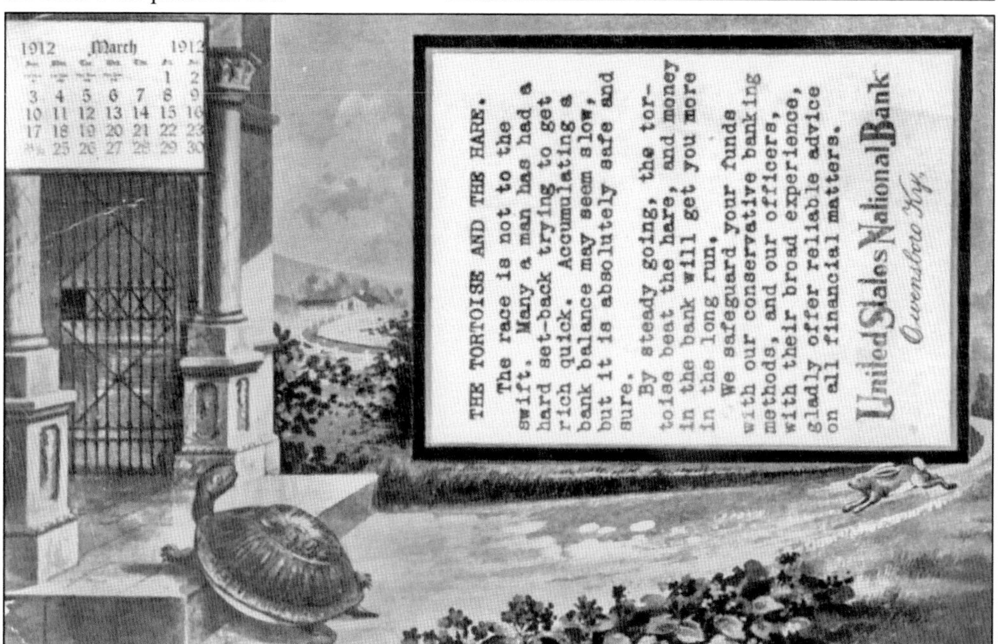

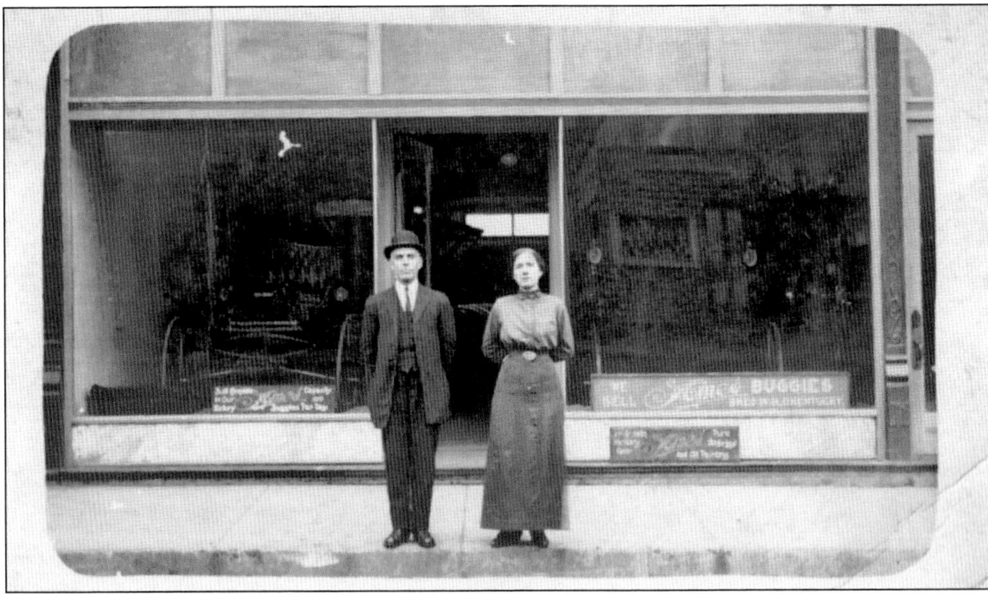

Frederic A. Ames opened a carriage repair shop on the southeast corner of Third and St. Elizabeth Street in 1887. A native of Washington, Pennsylvania, Ames enjoyed building new buggies in his spare time. The business grew to be among the top carriage builders in the nation by 1920. When the last buggy was completed in June 1926, over 300,000 buggies, carriages, and spring wagons were estimated to have been manufactured by Ames. The real-photo postcard shows Mr. and Mrs. B. S. Chambers of Dixon, Kentucky, in front of the downtown Owensboro headquarters. The sign in the window reads, "We sell Ames Buggies bred in old Kentucky."

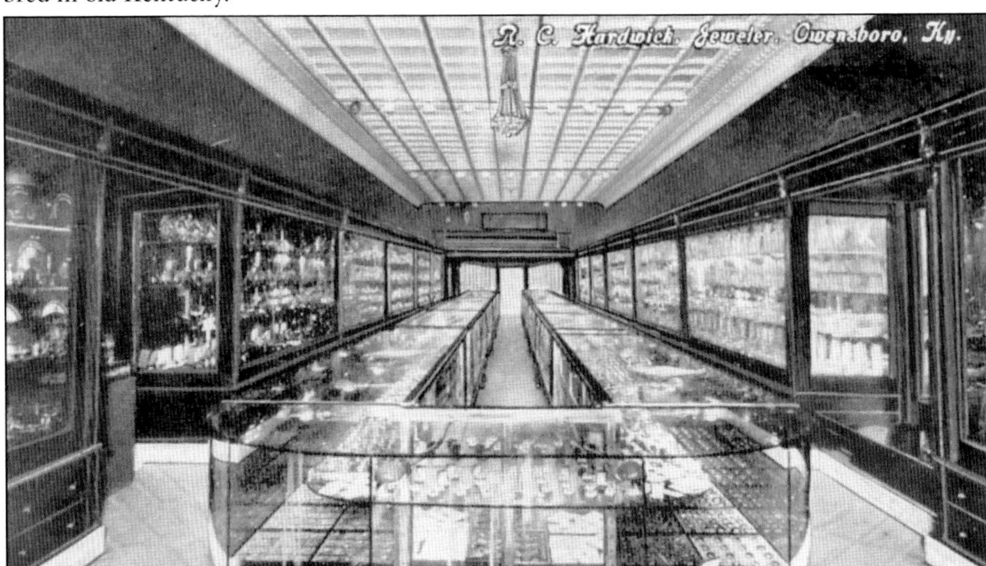


R. C. Hardwick Jewelers was located at 120 East Second Street, site of the present-day Daviess County Judicial Center. The 1911 postcard above proudly projects a shop filled with glass display cases full of fine silver, crystal, and jewelry. Owner Richard C. Hardwick was an optician and jeweler who fabricated specialty products such as pocket watches.

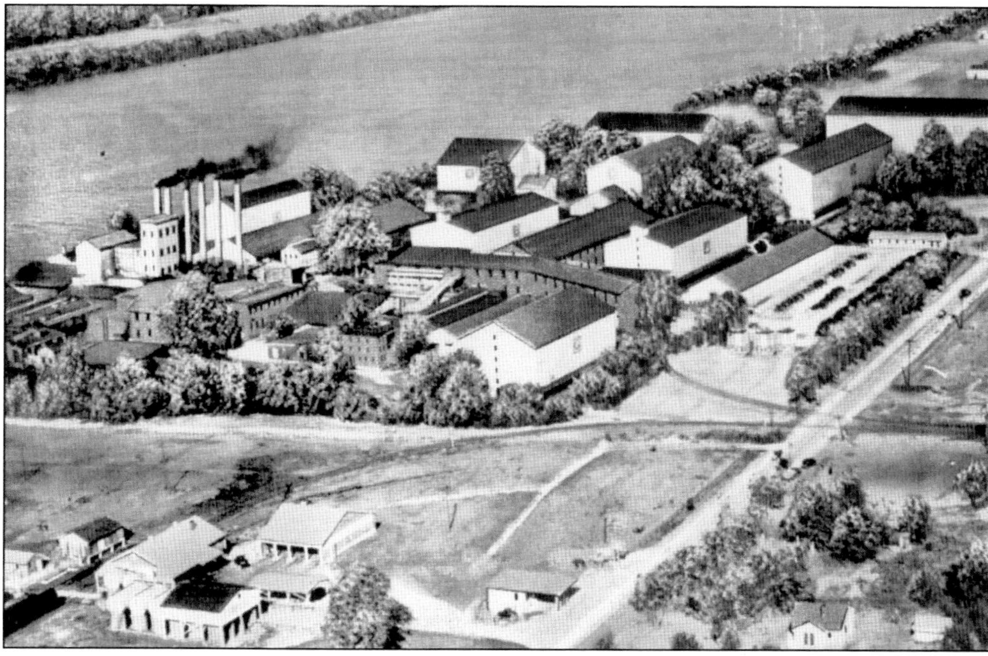

The postcard above is of the Glenmore Distillery in about 1945. James Thompson emigrated from Northern Ireland in 1871 and later purchased this distillery from Richard Monarch in 1901. Thompson named the facility after the Glenmore Castle in Ireland. During Prohibition, Glenmore Distillery was one of only a few companies allowed to produce medicinal whiskey. The postcard at right was used to solicit customers from the medical field, like dentist Charles C. Urie from Greeley, Colorado. Today this facility is known as Barton Brands, Ltd., and is still located on East Fourth Street just west of the Highway 60 bypass.

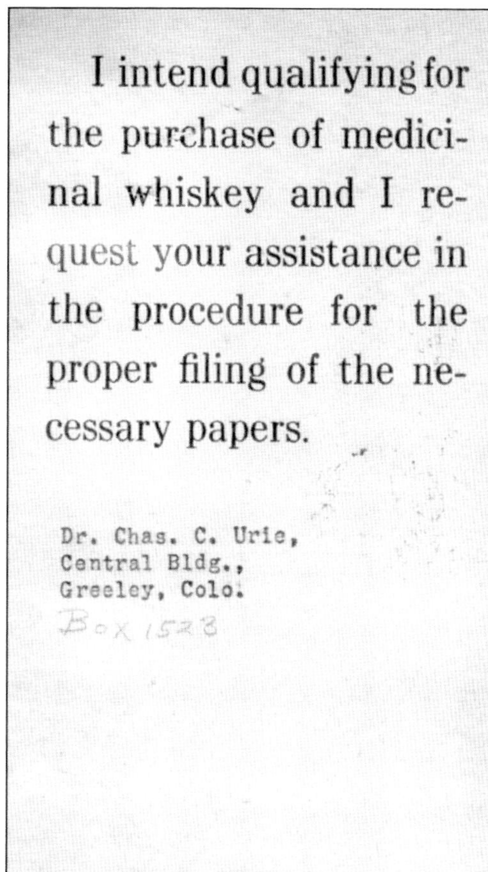

I intend qualifying for the purchase of medicinal whiskey and I request your assistance in the procedure for the proper filing of the necessary papers.

Dr. Chas. C. Urie,
Central Bldg.,
Greeley, Colo.
Box 1528

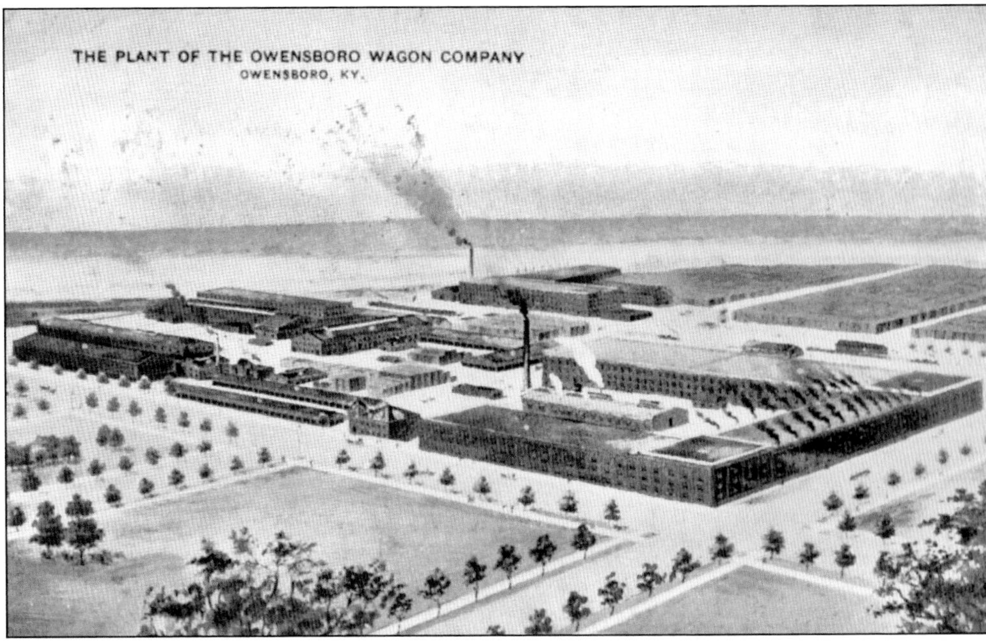


Owensboro Wagon Company began in 1883 on the east side of Leitchfield Road, north of Fourth Street. The above 1910 postcard shows the vast size of this manufacturing plant, which produced 6,000 wagons a year. Longtime Owensboro mayor Dr. J. H. Hickman was an original officer, and Josh T. Griffith was the company president for many years. One hundred wagons per day, like the one pictured below, were produced with signs on the sides and back that simply read, "The Owensboro." As the city's largest manufacturing plant, employing up to 250 men, the company produced wagons for various functions and loading conditions.

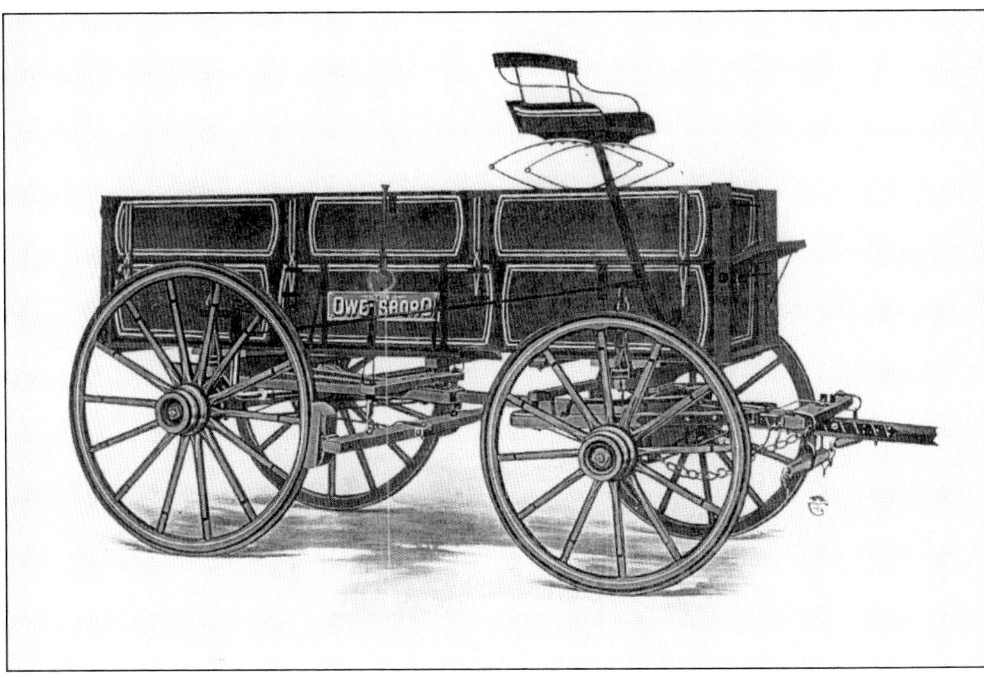

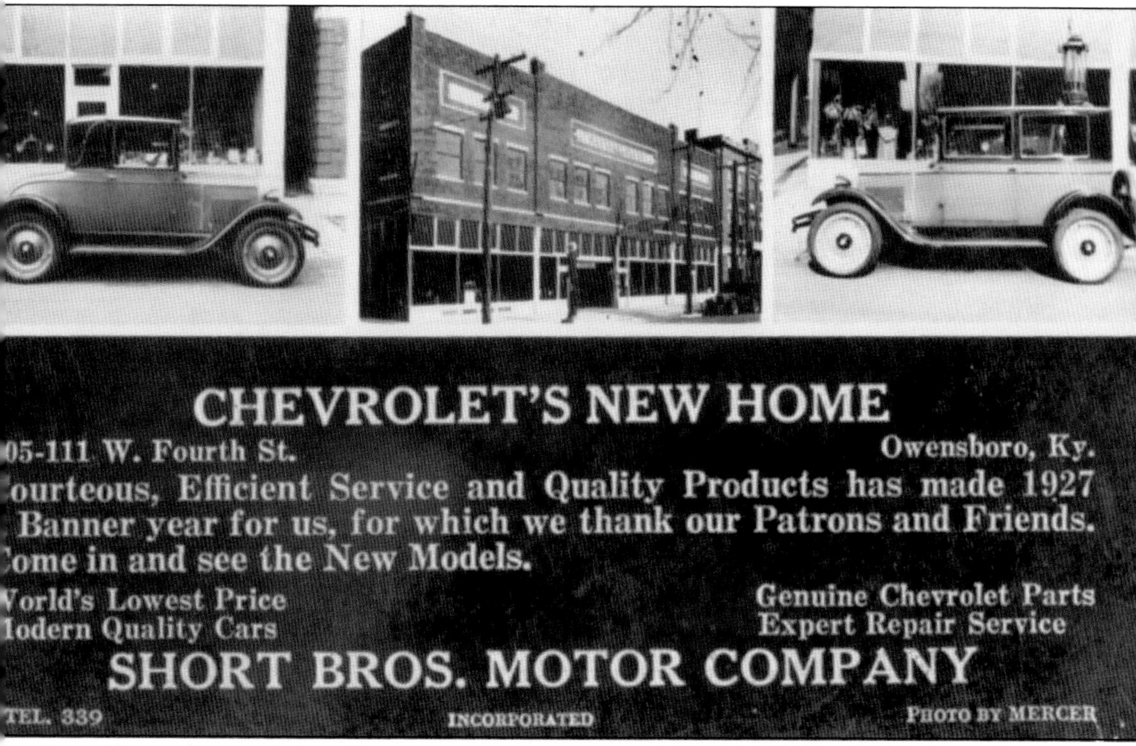


Percy Short, along with his siblings Kelley and H. L., founded Short Brothers Motor Company in Owensboro in 1920. In the above 1927 postcard, Short Brothers Motor Company was located on the northeast corner of Fourth and St. Ann Streets, site of the present-day Old National Bank parking lot. Short Brothers Motor Company went on to become Don Moore Chevrolet Cadillac and Auto Mall. The two pictured automobiles are believed to be 1928 Chevrolets, with a rumble-seat coupe on the left and a two-door sedan on the right.

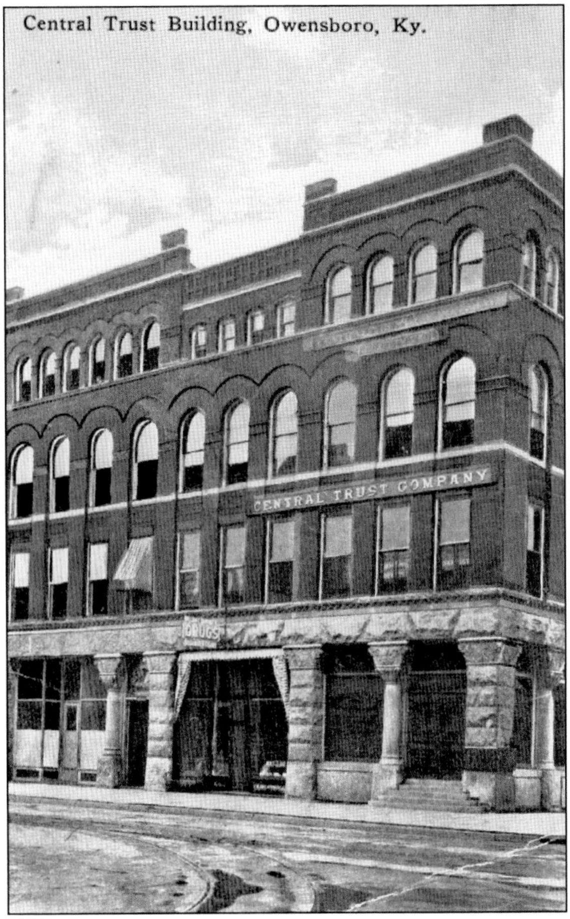


The Central Trust Company building was constructed in 1891 on the southwest corner of Fourth and Frederica Streets. This building, pictured to the left, has since been demolished, and the site currently provides parking for Steve Jones Chrysler. The 1926 postcard below shows a wider-angle view of the bank looking southward down Frederica Street. Other adjacent buildings visible are the Bleich and Empress Theaters. Druggist W. E. Danhauer and "the Kodak finisher who gives satisfaction," Arthur Lee May, published the postcard. The Danhauer Drug Company remains in business today at 330 Frederica Street. Note that the three buildings visible at the end of the block still stand today.

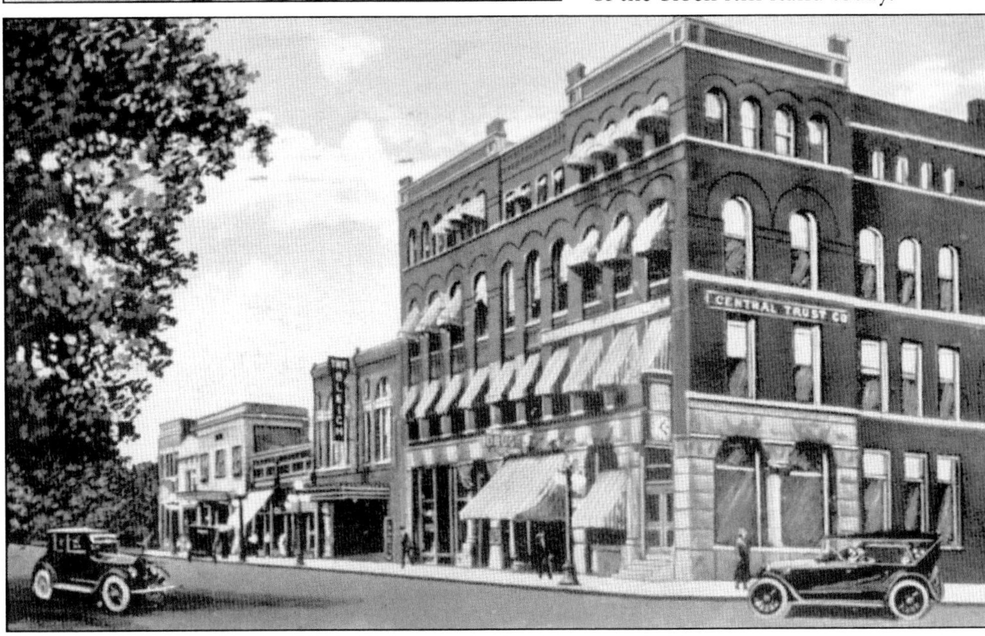

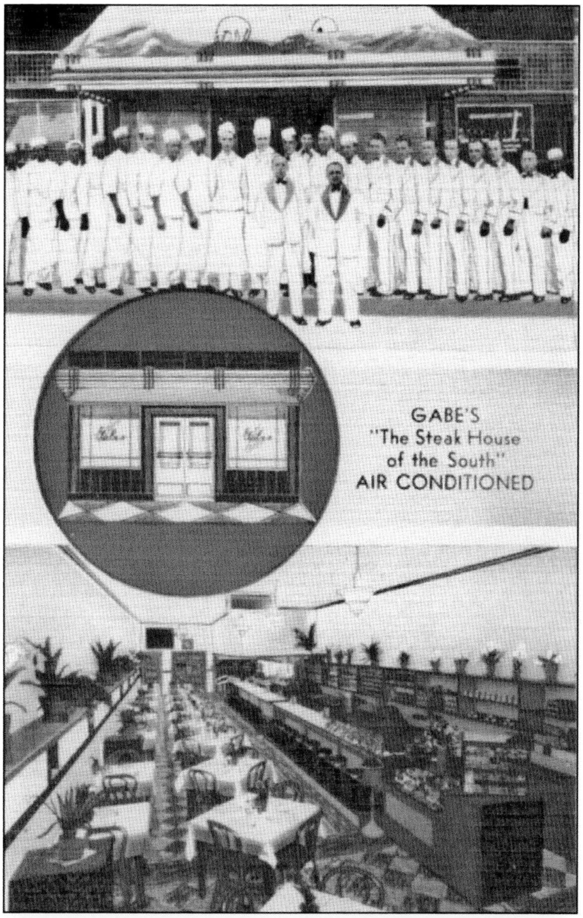


Gabe's Restaurant was first located on the west side of Frederica Street between Third and Fourth Streets. Proclaimed "The Steakhouse of the South," Gabe's was Owensboro's best-known restaurant. Not only was owner Gabe Fiorella a very colorful and friendly person, he was much attuned to the importance of advertisement. In these two postcards, the art deco era was reflected, making effective use of bright colors to grab viewer attention. The top card projects service, comfort, and style while the bottom postcard, with the all-black night scene, was an unusual design but stylistically consistent with the 1940s and 1950s.

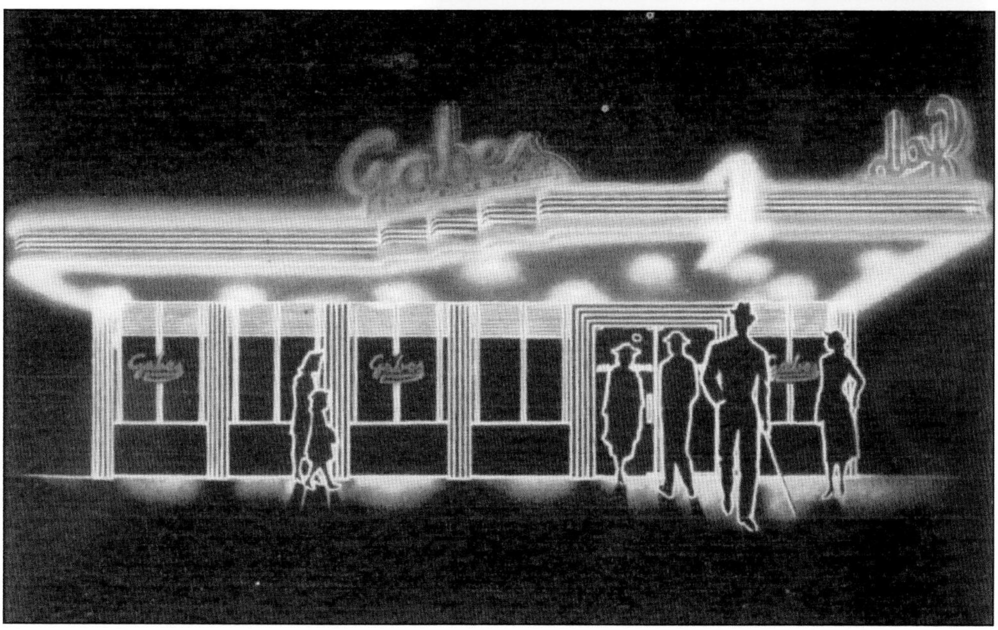

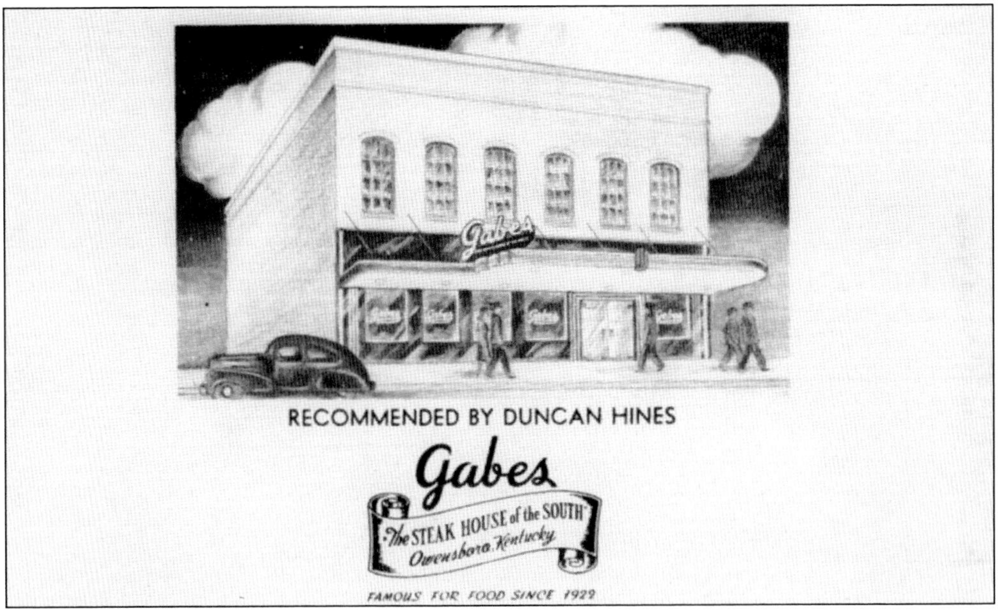


Gabriel Fiorella began providing food service in downtown Owensboro in 1919 from a homemade lunch cart he called the "Little Seal." He opened Gabe's Restaurant, portrayed in the postcard above, at 324 Frederica Street three years later. The foldout postcard below presents Gabe's extensive offerings for dining, lounging, and banquets. It was proclaimed to be a place "where Southern hospitality is still the fashion" and was a recommendation of Duncan Hines.

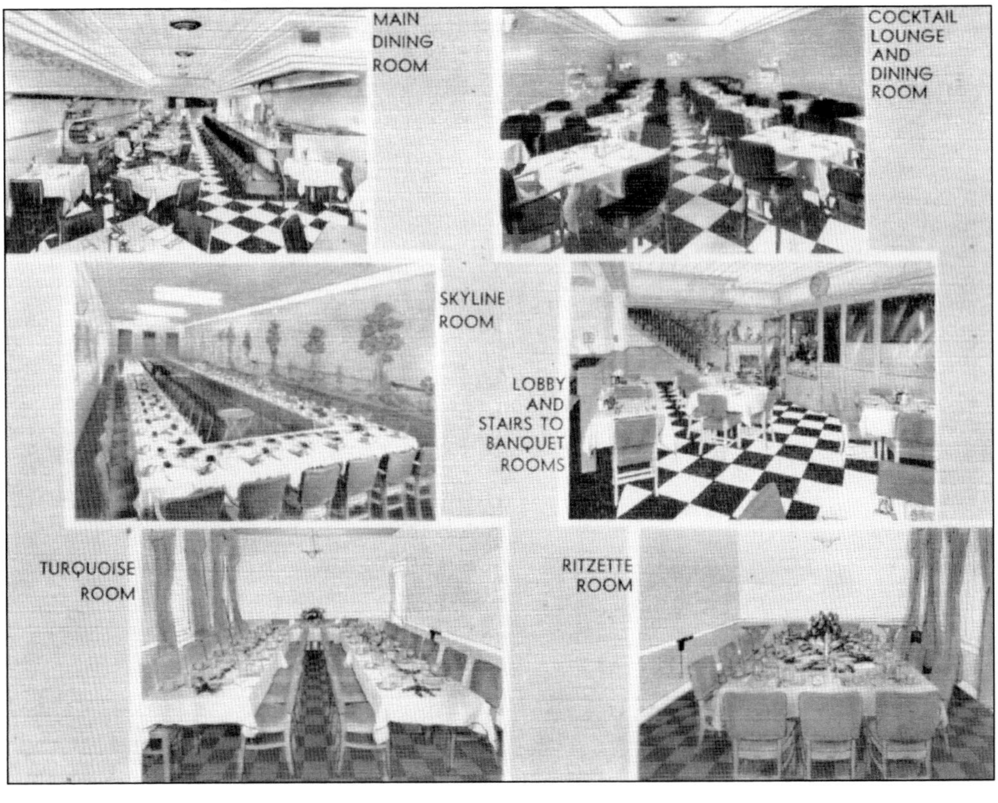

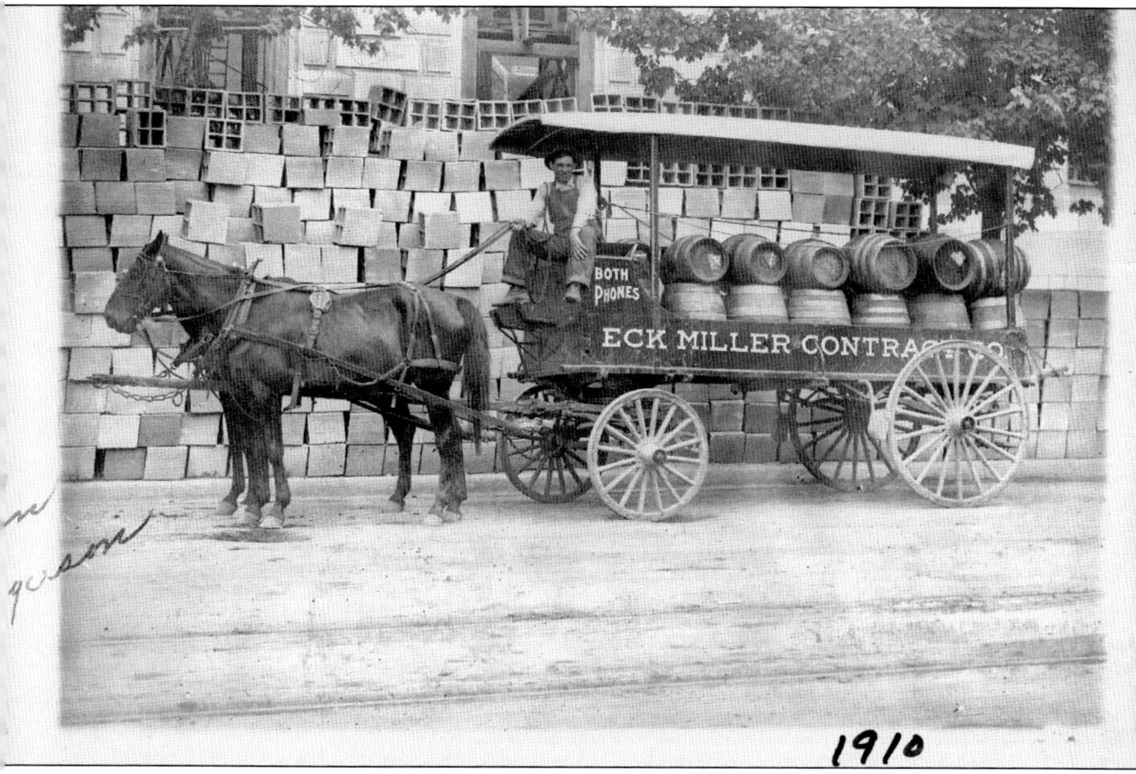


The postcard above shows an Eck Miller Contract Company wagon delivering mortar-filled barrels in 1910. The mortar was produced by F. W. Cook Brick Company of Evansville, Indiana. Behind the wagon team are stacks of clay tiles ready for construction of the Federal Post Office Building at 401 Frederica Street. The heavy hauler wagon pictured was equipped with larger 18-spoke rear wheels, rather than the standard 14-spoke variety, and smaller front wheels, allowing easier steering through deep dirt-road ruts. It is unclear whether this is an Owensboro Wagon Factory product. John Ferguson of Rockport, Indiana, drove this wagon for Eck Miller.

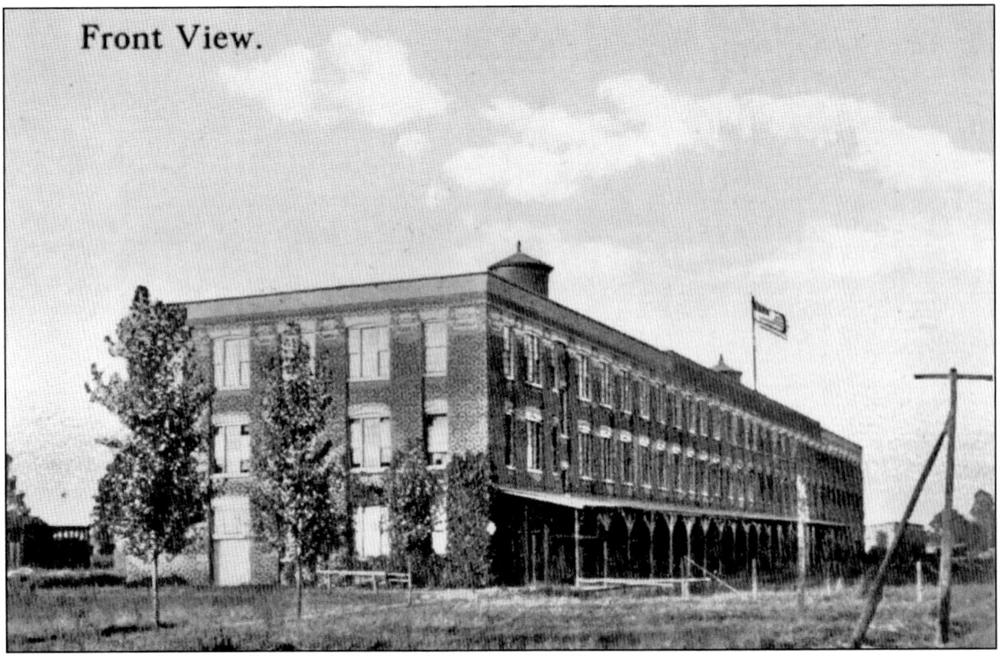


The east-end building above was constructed in 1905 for the Hickman-Ebbert Wagon Company. That business lasted just a few years. Then the property at 931 Wing Avenue at the railroad tracks became the home of the Universal Stenotype Company, which printed letterheads, stationery, and business forms. In 1912, the company president was W. S. Ireland, who must have been very proud of the shipment featured below. The Murphy Chair Company became the building's next tenant in 1917. That business evolved into Murphy-Miller Chair Company in 1961 and later into the present-day Hon Company.

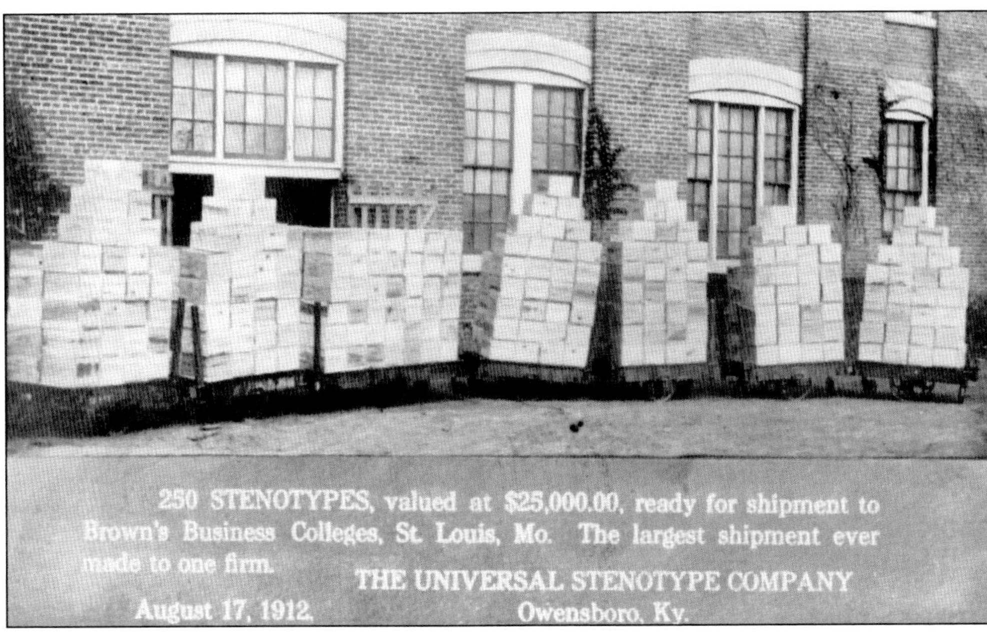

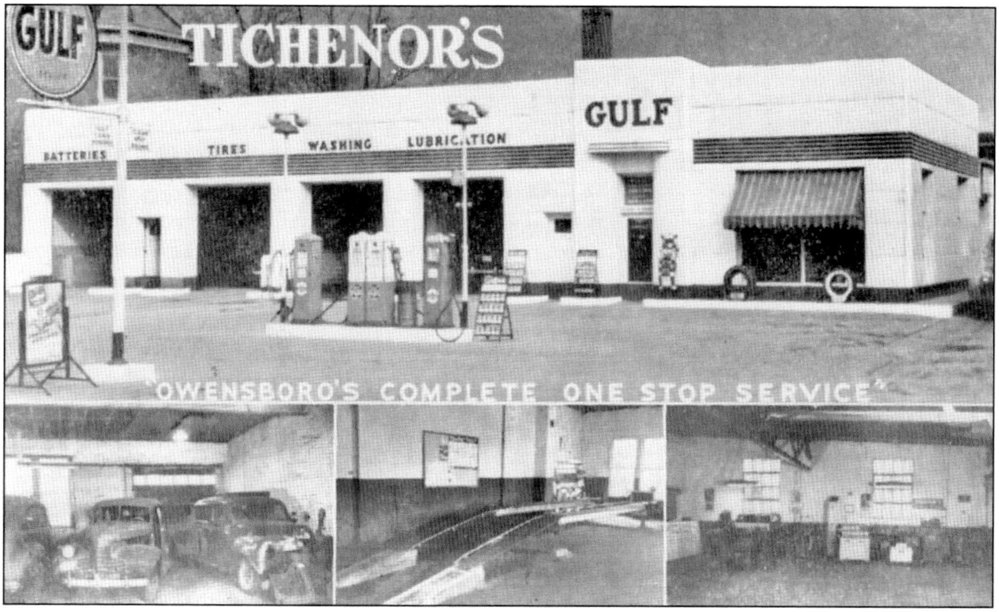


Tichenor's Gulf service station was located at 919 Frederica Street. A review of the early Sanborn maps of Owensboro shows some form of service station was at one time or another located on almost every block of the downtown area. This site still houses a convenience store with fuel pumps.

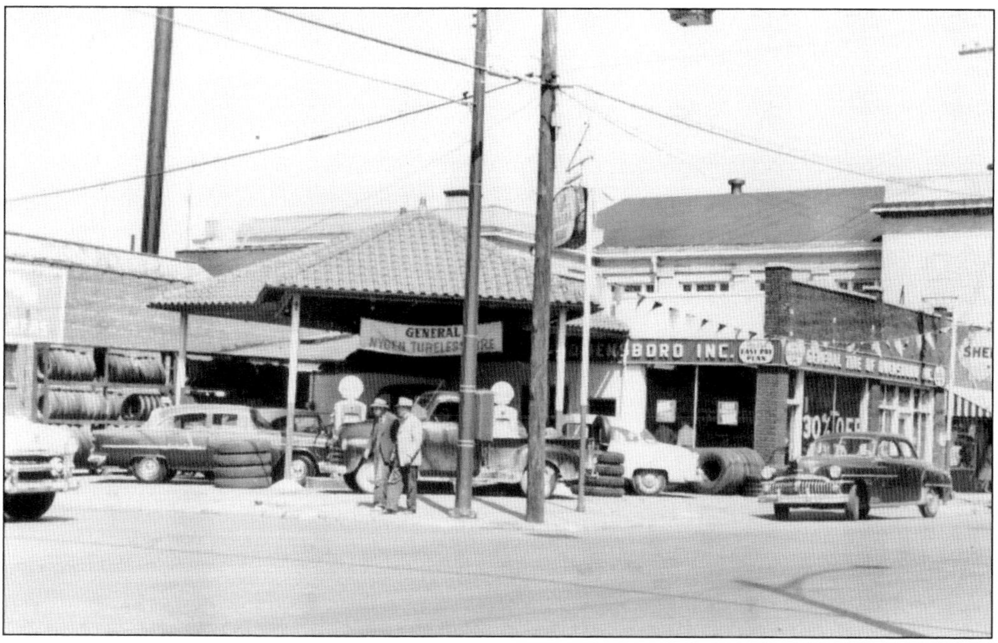


General Tire, located at the northeast corner of Third and Daviess Streets, went on to become the present-day Bowen Tire Company. The First Baptist Church roofline and west wall are identifiable in the background. This photograph was taken in the late 1950s, before the church purchased and developed this entire city block.

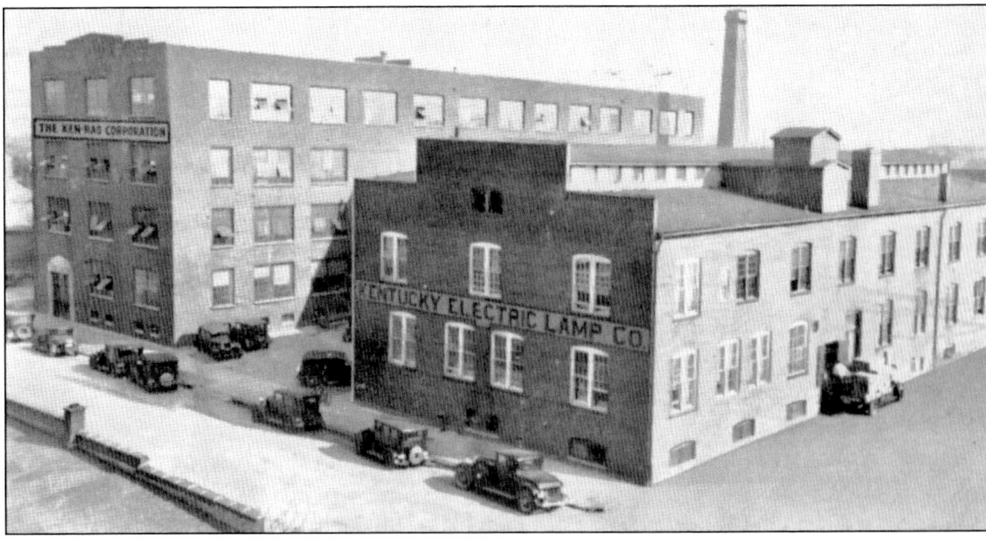


Kentucky Electrical Company was founded in 1899. Roy Burlew purchased the plant in 1918 for $55,000 and began Ken-Rad Corporation. The postcard above looks southeast at the Ken-Rad Tube and Lamp Corporation, with over 2,600 employees. In 1945, Burlew sold the Ken-Rad Tube Plant to General Electric for $5.5 million and later the lamp plant to Westinghouse for $1.6 million. The postcard below looks southwest at the complex of buildings at 316 East Ninth Street, which covered one entire city block. Writer Glenn Hodges shared this bit of history in an October 3, 1999, *Messenger-Inquirer* article: "Roy Burlew's Ken Rad plant in Owensboro supplied the light bulbs that illuminated the first night game in major league baseball history" at Crosley Field because "the Owensboro company had provided tubes for the Crosley family radio station WLWL in Cincinnati, Ohio."

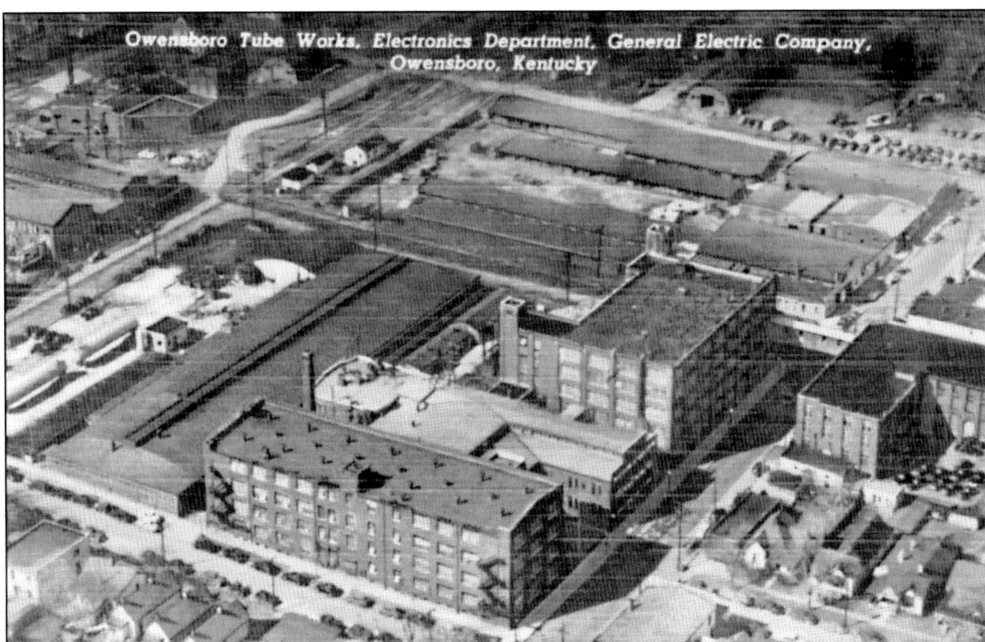

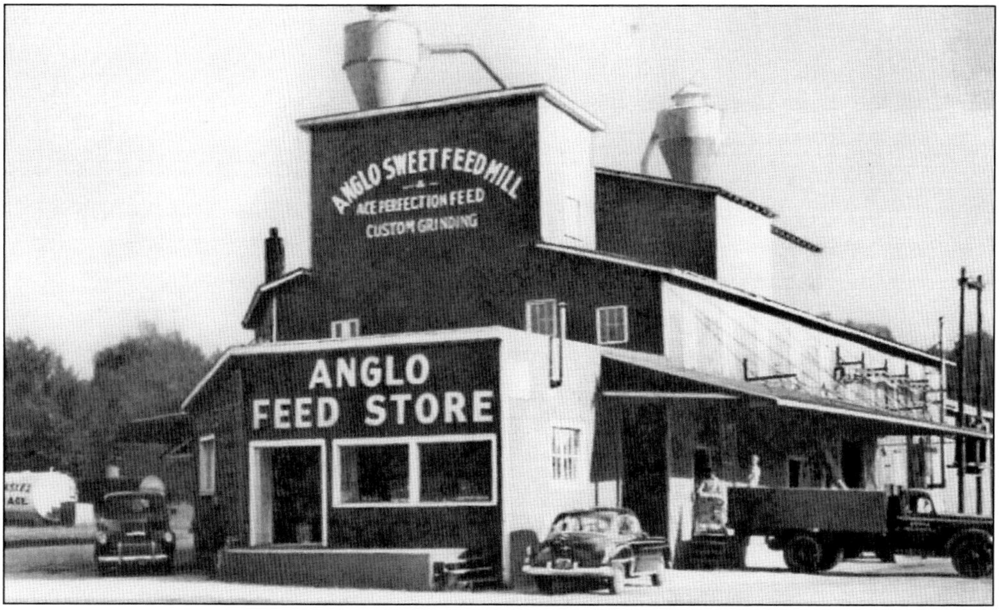


The Anglo American Mill Company produced sweet feed at 1500 East Eighteenth Street. The company organized in 1908 and flourished for 30 years. Most communities across the country had a small local mill that processed local grains. Anglo American utilized a special European-designed machine called the Marvel Flour Mill and used the inexpensive advertising postcard below to encourage other small feed mills across the country to purchase this special machine. This location is now the site of Kentuckiana Animal Clinic Professional Service Corporation (PSC).

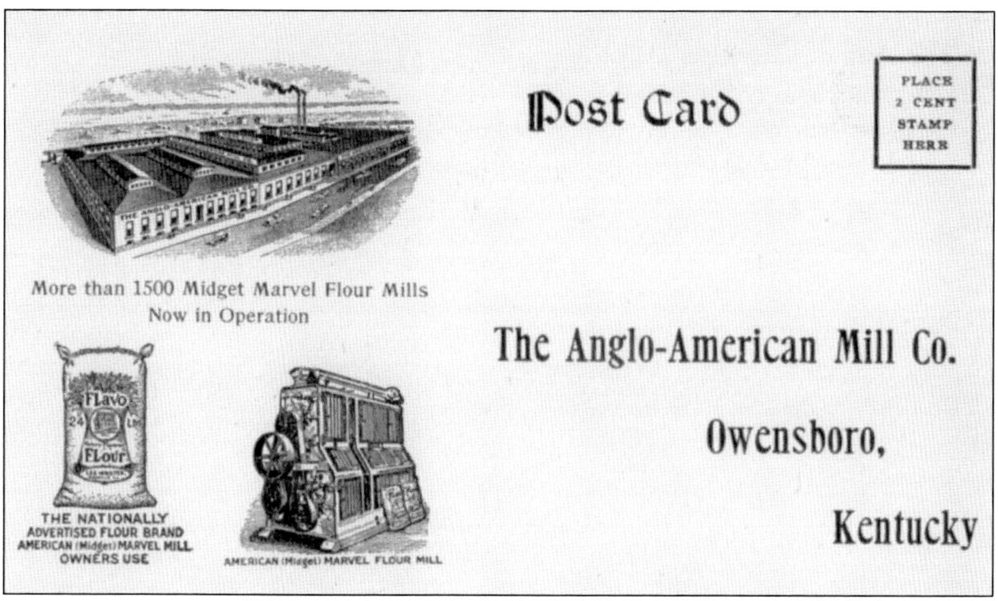

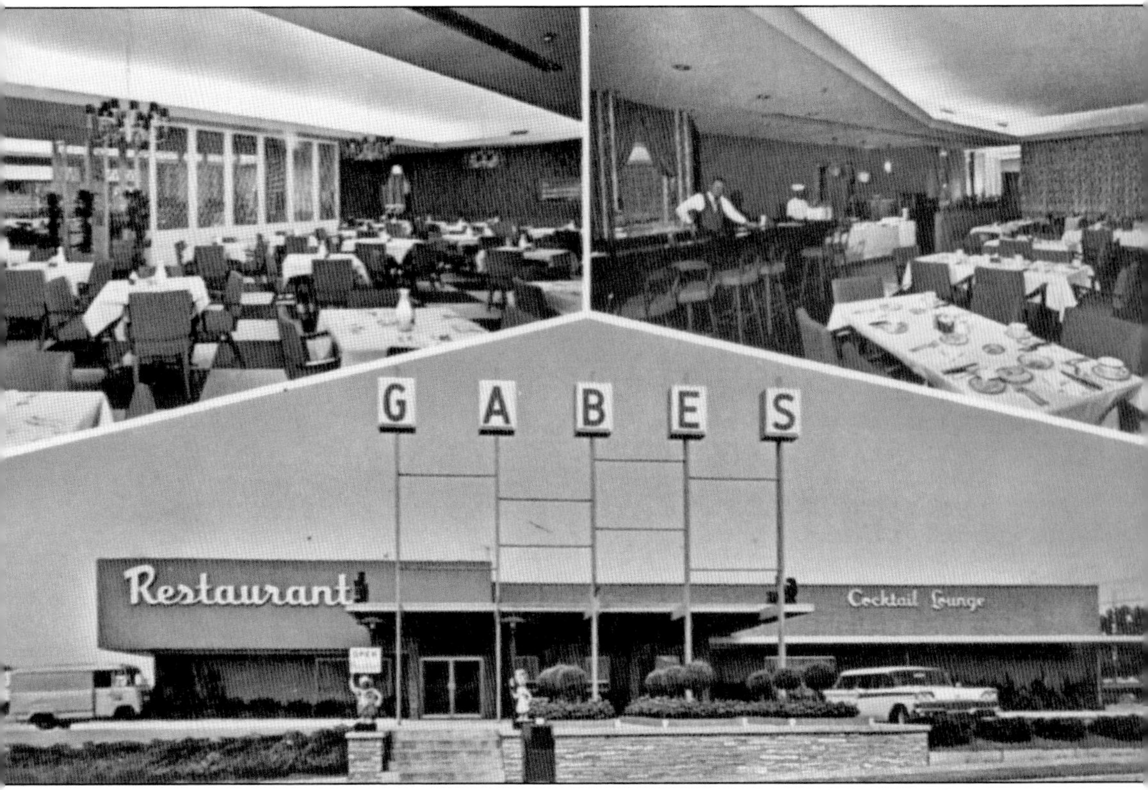


The new Gabe's Restaurant on the southwest corner of Eighteenth and Triplett Streets was truly revolutionary upon opening in 1959. Anchoring the Gabe's Shopping Center complex, the "Steakhouse of the South" included a main dining room and lounge on the main level and large party rooms in the basement, as depicted in the above postcard. A small Gabe statue greeted visitors entering from the street, and a large canopy protected guests dropped off at the main entrance. This 1959 shopping center development touting "lots of parking spaces" was the first serious challenge to downtown's retail dominance. Gabe's Motor Inn, a 13-story hotel, was added in 1963. While the shopping center and tower remain today, this landmark restaurant building was replaced by a gas station in the early 1990s.

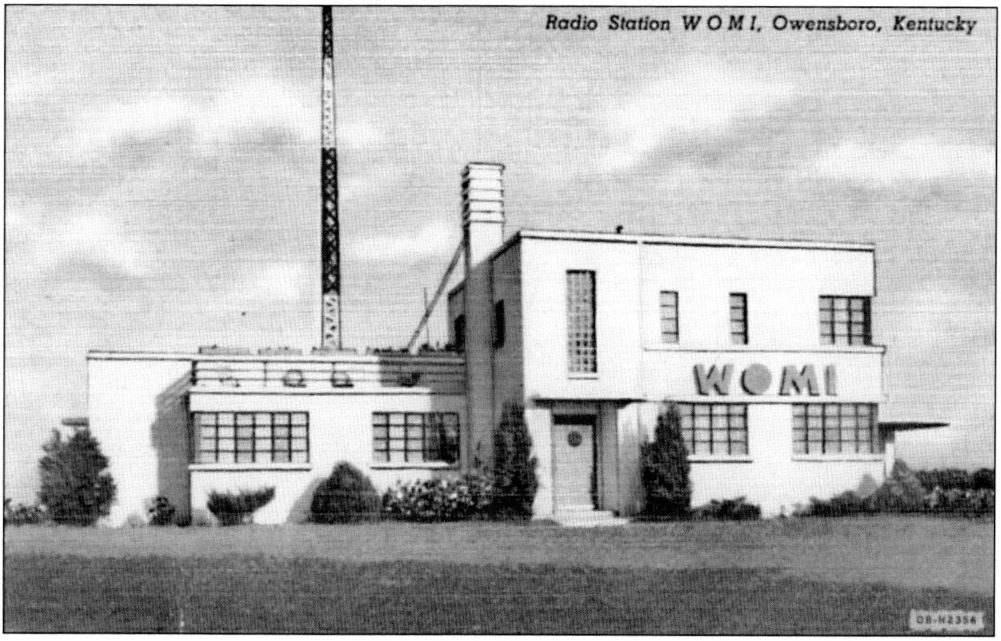


WOMI went on the air on February 7, 1938, live from the Hotel Owensboro. The station's call letters stood for its founder, the Owensboro *Messenger-Inquirer.* The International-style building pictured above was the brainchild of architect Walter Scott Roberts, who designed it to resemble a radio with the station tower's shadow forming the sweeping hand of the dial. The building, located on the southeast corner of Frederica and Byers Avenue, was replaced in 1985 with the present WOMI building. The postcard below is of the radio station WVJS, which became Owensboro's second radio station on November 27, 1947. Similarly, this station's call letters also reflect its founder, V. J. Steel. This 1950s building still stands on the north side of scenic U.S. Highway 60 West.

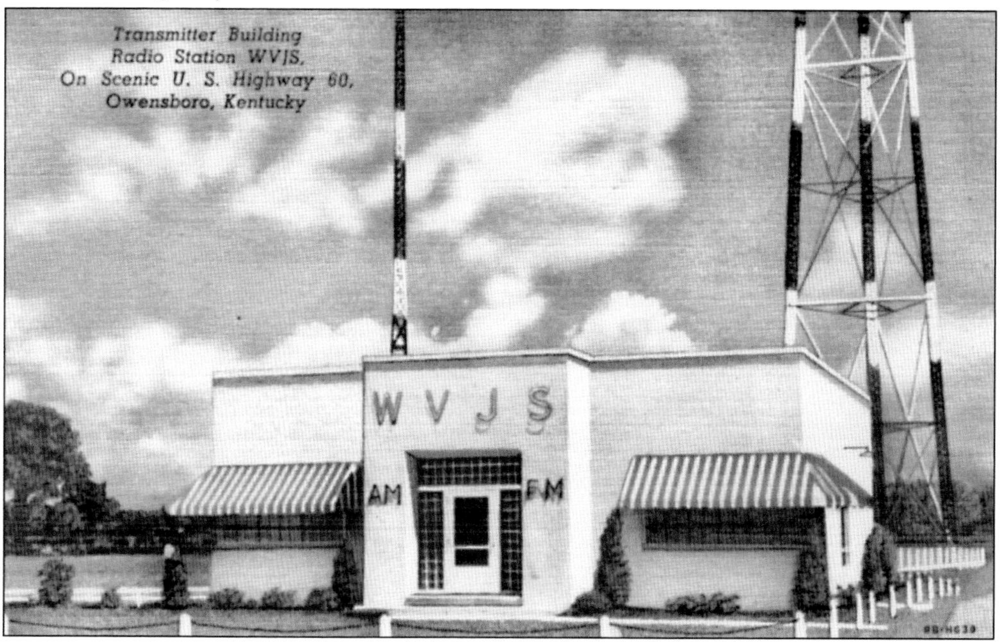

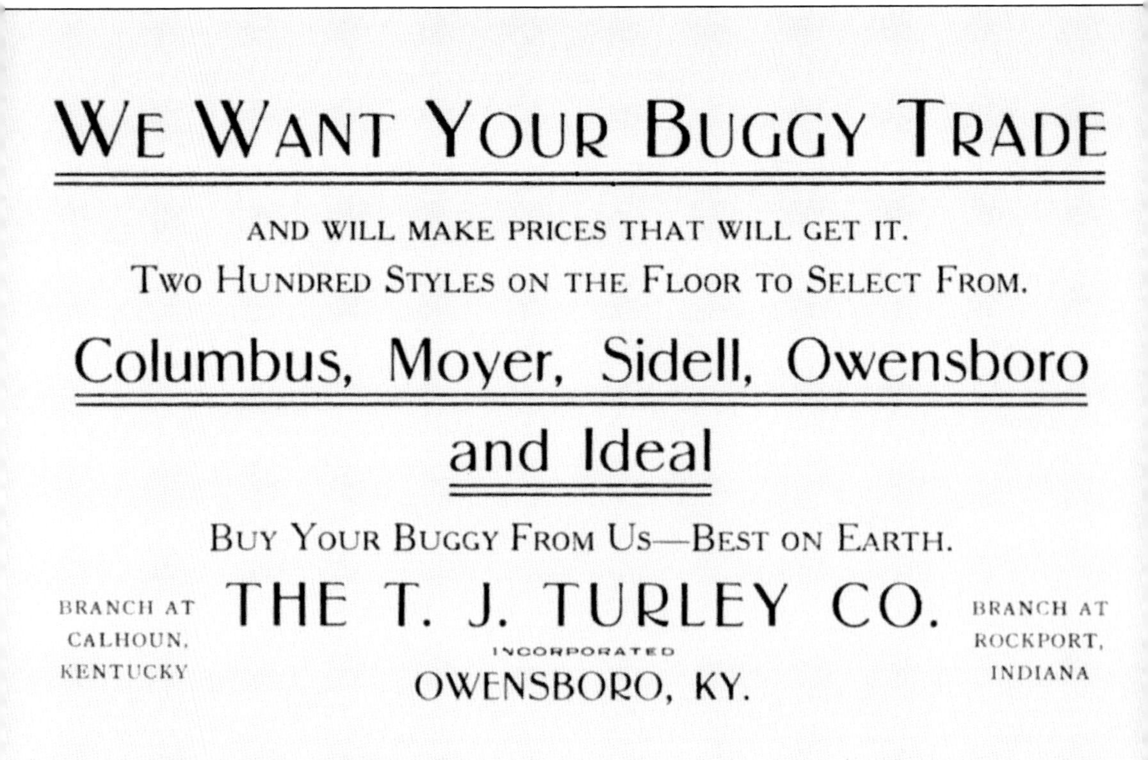


The postcard above is from a well-known business whose president, Thomas J. Turley, and wife, Nannie, lived on south Frederica Street. The business sold wholesale farm implements, seeds, and buggies. Edgar Turley managed the buggy department. Please note: the "south Frederica" above is not simply for the name of the local street, but actually a reference to an area of town beyond the end of the business district on Frederica Street. Socially the south Frederica area could be compared to the present-day Griffith Avenue, as it was renowned for its stately homes.

# *Three*

# Churches

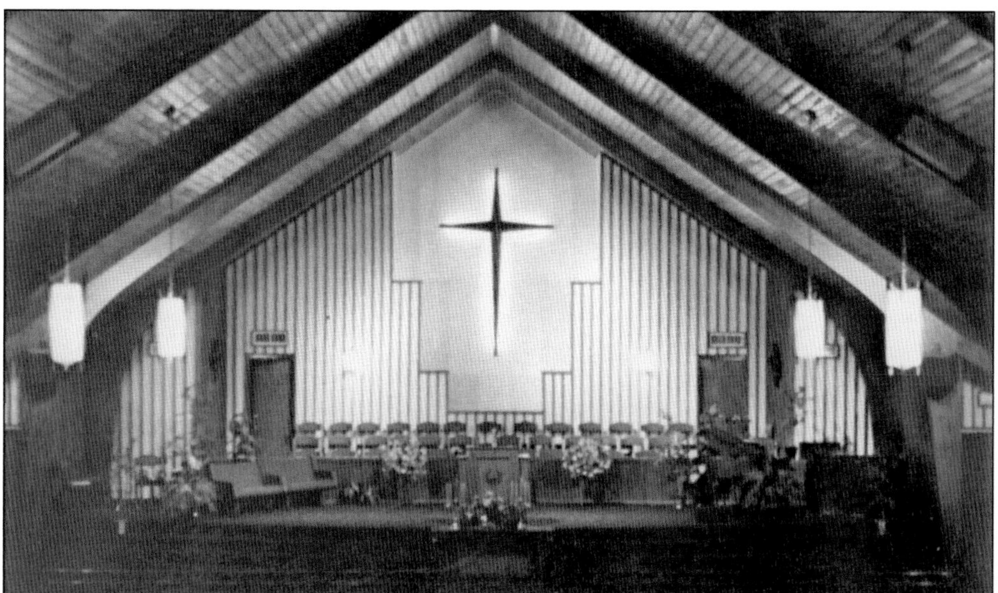

A postcard shows the interior of Good Shepherd Church, located at 3031 Bittel Road. This is a 1970s view of the first worship space. A new and much larger sanctuary was constructed in the 1980s along with a Christian school and day care facility.

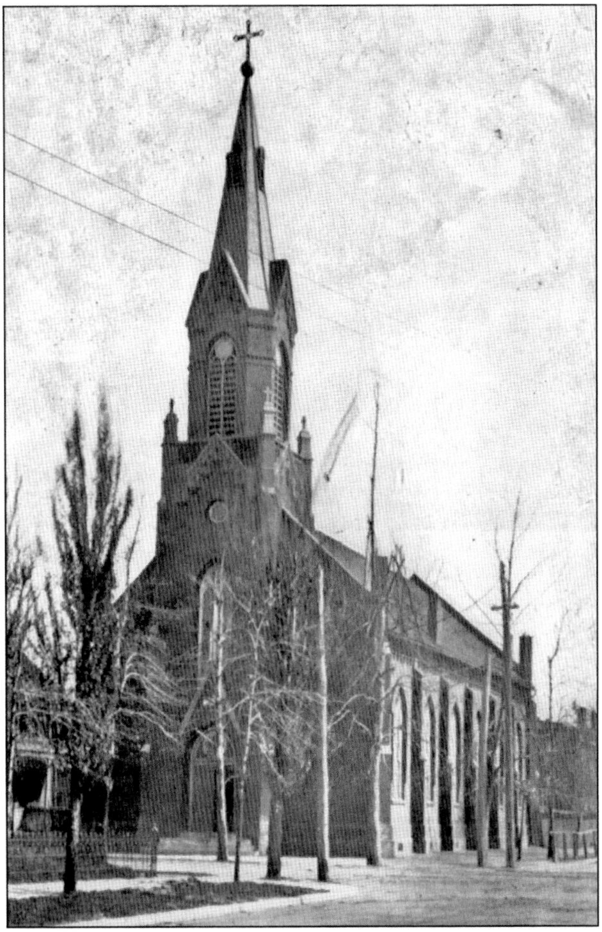

St. Joseph Catholic Church was completed in 1883 on the southeastern corner of Fourth and Clay Streets for a German-speaking congregation. The church measured approximately 40 feet in width by 100 feet in length and was the city's best example of Victorian Gothic architecture. The postcard below, dated 1914, is a rare real-photo postcard of the church's interior. When the building was razed in 1989, the 16 beautiful stained-glass windows were donated to the Owensboro Museum of Fine Art. Originally crafted by internationally recognized German American glassmaker Emil Frei (1867–1941), these treasures were carefully restored and mounted in special 25-foot light towers to create a unique Stained Glass Gallery for the museum.

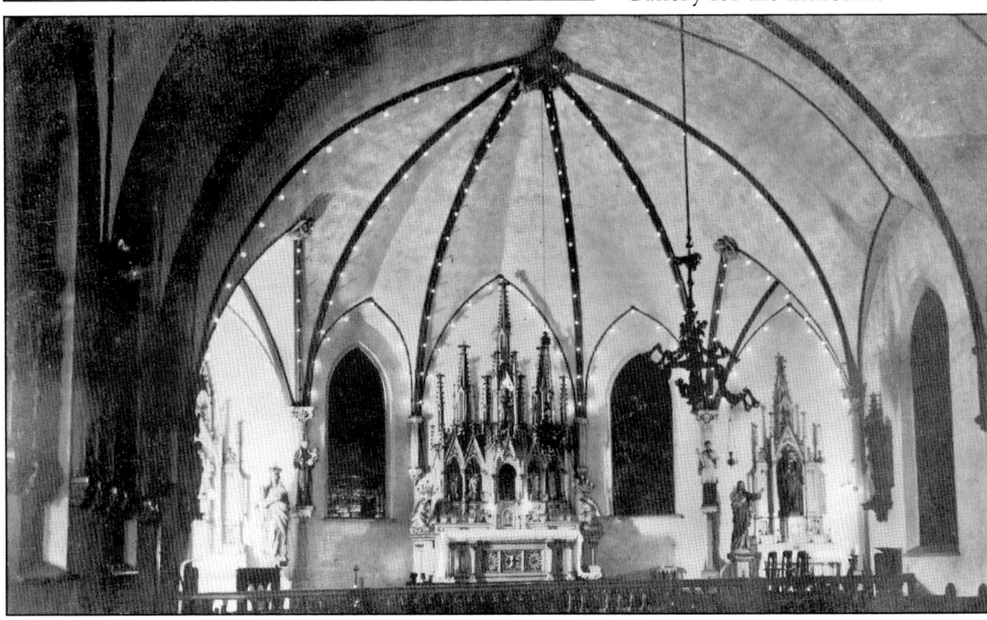

Seven Hills Baptist Church was one of the earliest missions seeded in the Chautauqua community. Pictured at right is the original building constructed in 1902 at 1717 Alexander Avenue under the leadership of Third Baptist Church. An educational wing was added across the rear in 1949, and the current sanctuary, pictured below, replaced the old one in 1957. The Seven Hills–Chautauqua area was an early planned community outside of the city of Owensboro. In 1910, within this community, there was a park, public library, public school, several factories, and numerous private homes.

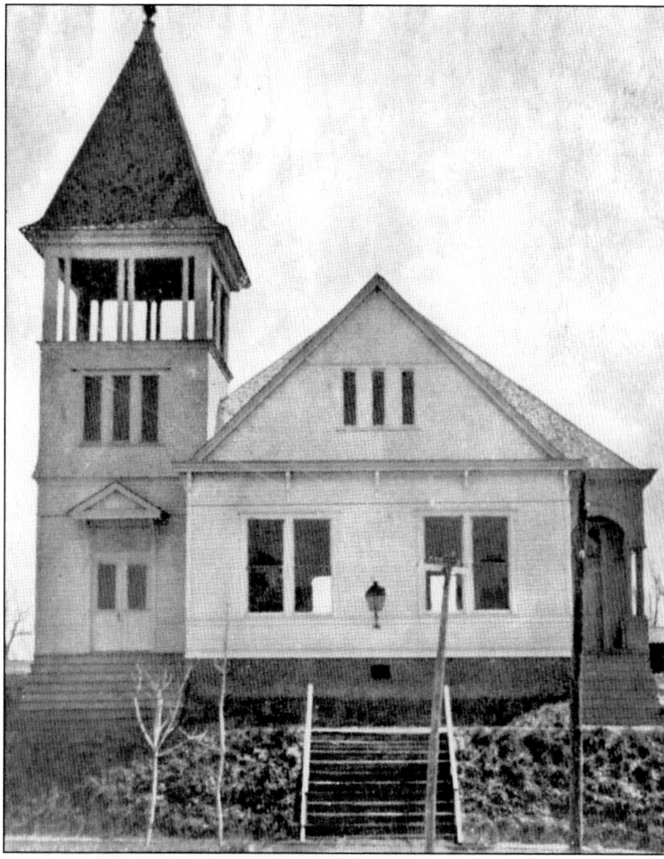

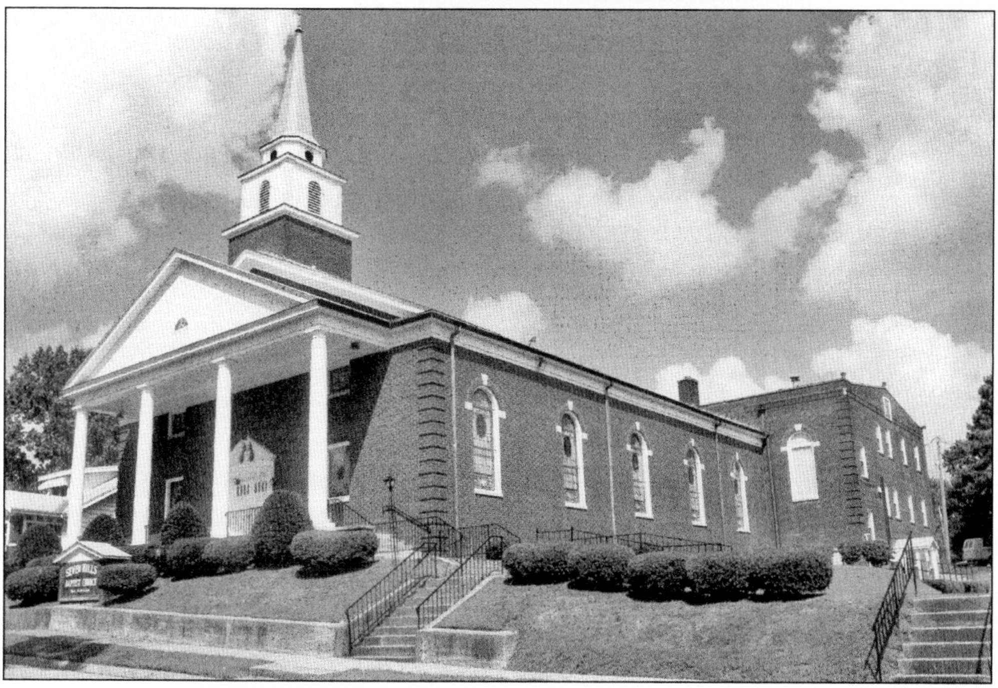

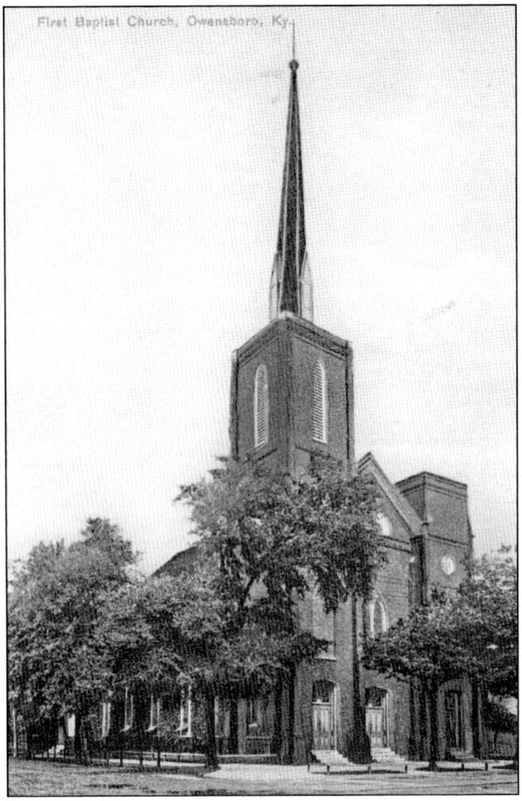


First Baptist Church organized in 1834. Its first building was located on Water Street, also known as First Street and Veteran's Boulevard. The top postcard shows the congregation's second building, constructed in 1860. It was located on the southwest corner of Third and Lewis Streets, also known as J. R. Miller Boulevard. The building faced due east, the traditional exposure for most churches at the time. The belief was that Christ would return from the east, so graves and religious edifices were aligned eastward ready for his return. This traditional design element has since lost favor. Below is an illustration of the church's interior auditorium as presented in the City of Owensboro's 1982 *A Brief General Outline of Its Past, Present and Future.* This building was razed in 1923 to make way for the present building.

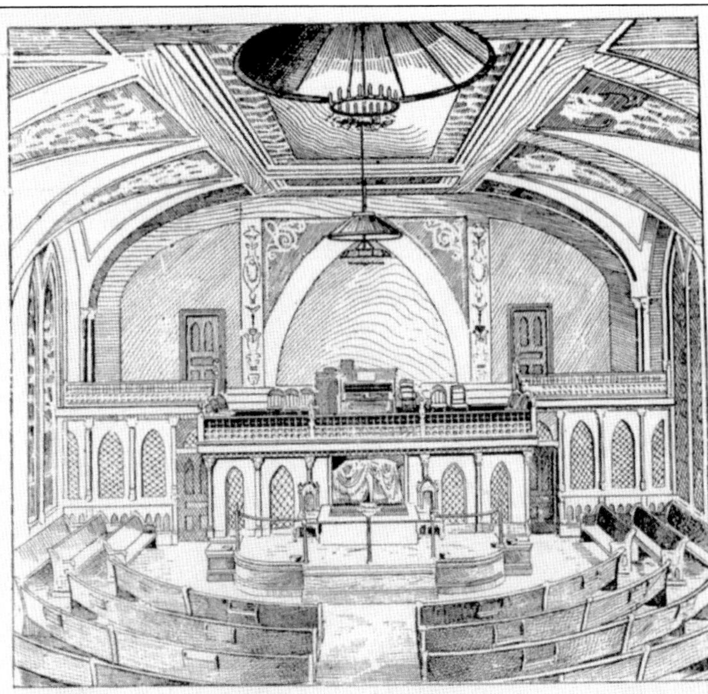

INTERIOR FIRST BAPTIST CHURCH.

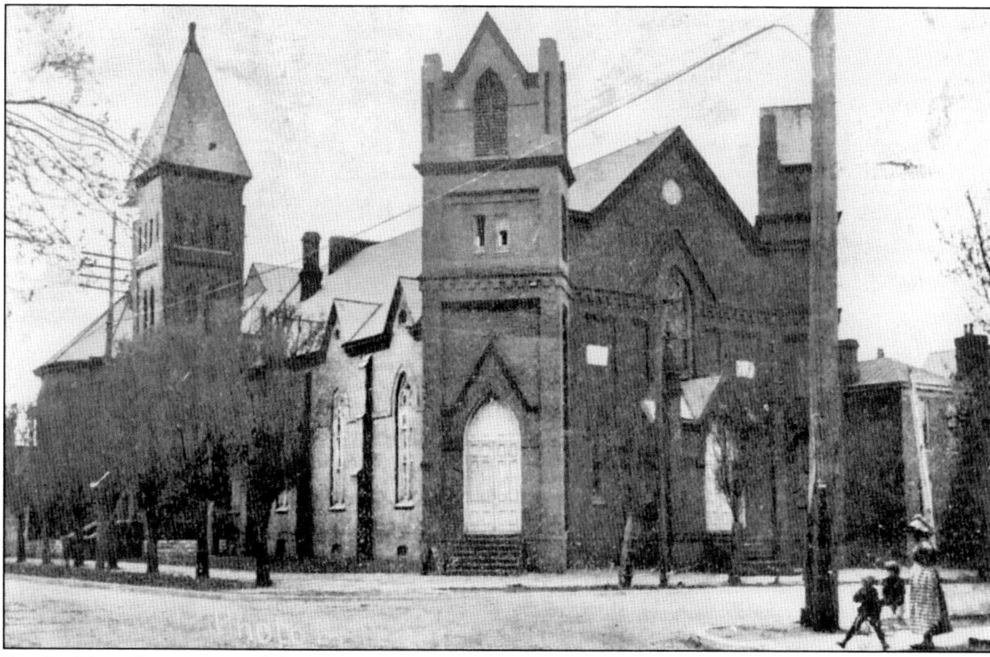

Settle Chapel was named for Dr. Henry Clay Settle, who served the Owensboro congregation from 1877 to 1881. This Methodist congregation first organized locally in 1836. This building, completed in 1880 on the northeast corner of Fourth and Daviess Streets, was designed in a Gothic style by Boyd and Brickly of Evansville, Indiana.

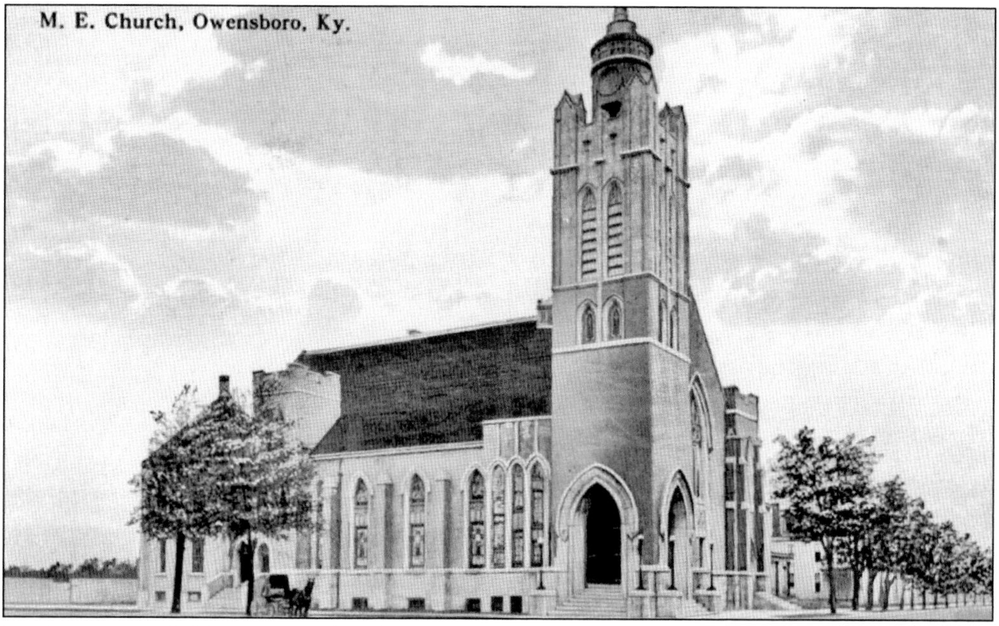


Settle Memorial Methodist Church was constructed in 1907 on the former Settle Chapel site. The figures in the stained glass were painted by Louis Millet, nephew of the famous French impressionist Jean Francoise Millet. The English Gothic architecture style was again employed by designer Brinton B. Davis. This Louisville architect was also a major influence for developing many early buildings on the Western Kentucky University campus.

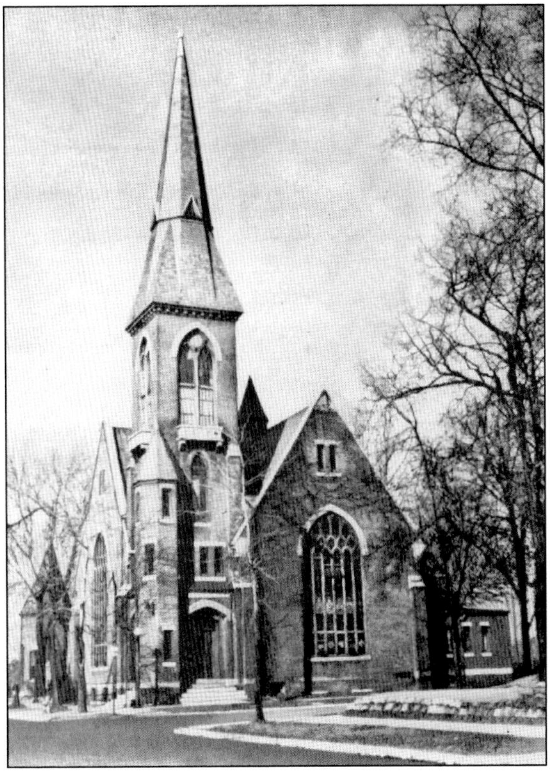

In 1870, the Southern Assembly completed a lecture hall on Fourth Street. The photograph at the left shows the new worship center completed at the northwest corner of Fourth and Crittenden Streets in 1884. The building burned sometime in the late 1950s or early 1960s.

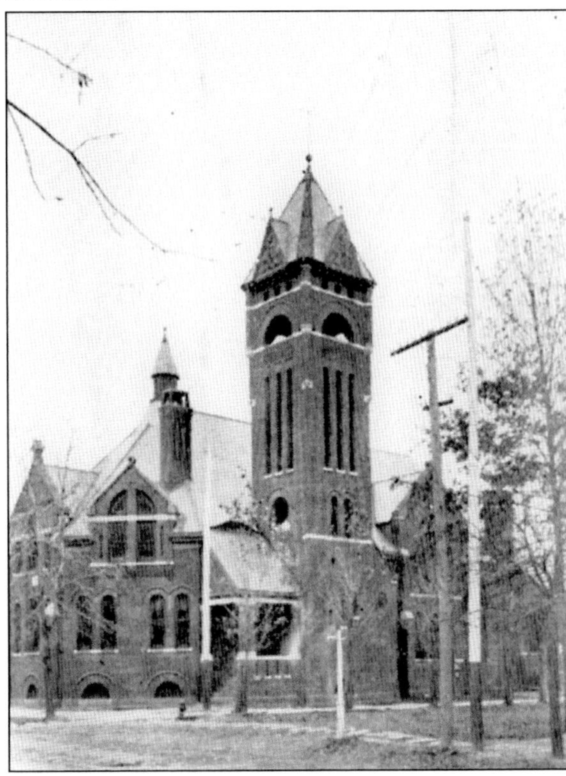

Completed in 1891, the First Presbyterian Church was located on the northeast corner of Seventh and Frederica Streets. William A. Mercer made this photograph about 1903. In 1947, this building was purchased by Brescia College and converted into a library, assembly room, and additional classrooms. The church building was later razed to make room for the Brescia College Science Building construction in 1968.

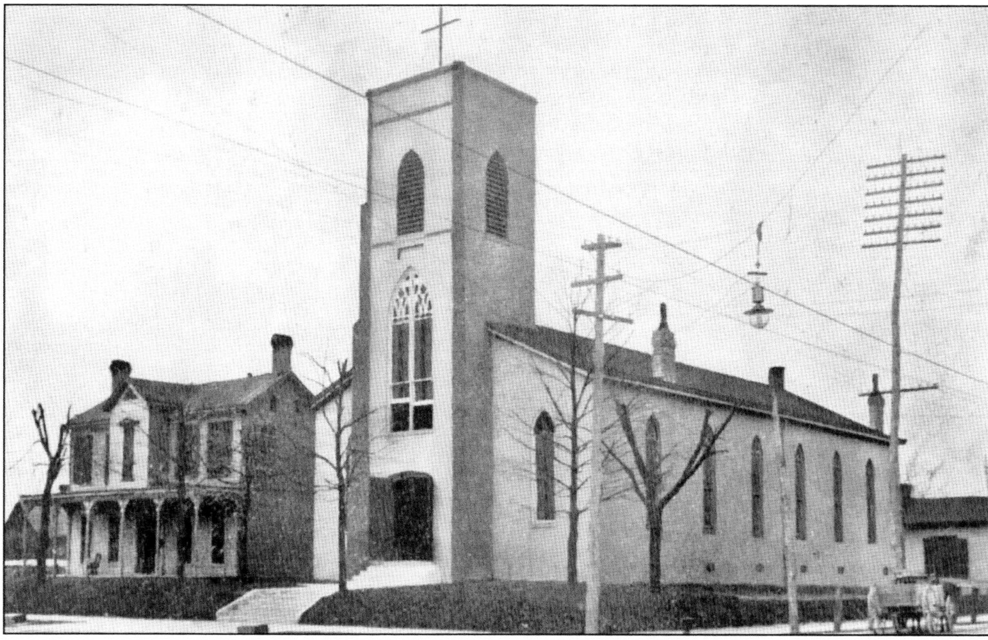

St. Stephen's Catholic Church began in 1839 under founding pastor Rev. John C. Wathan. St. Stephen's constructed its first church building on the southwest corner of Second and Cedar Streets in 1842. This site is currently the home of Don Moore Cadillac's showroom. As shown above, the church's building had 12 stained-glass windows flanking the sanctuary and a three-level bell tower along with an east exposure, all reflecting early traditional symbolism of the religious order. The postcard below shows an earlier view of the congregation's second church building, erected in 1924 at 614 Locust Street, with the original bell tower roof and the steps leading directly out of the church. This second building, like the first, faced east awaiting Christ's return. The Romanesque design was drawn under the watchful eye of Louisville architect Frederick T. Erhart.

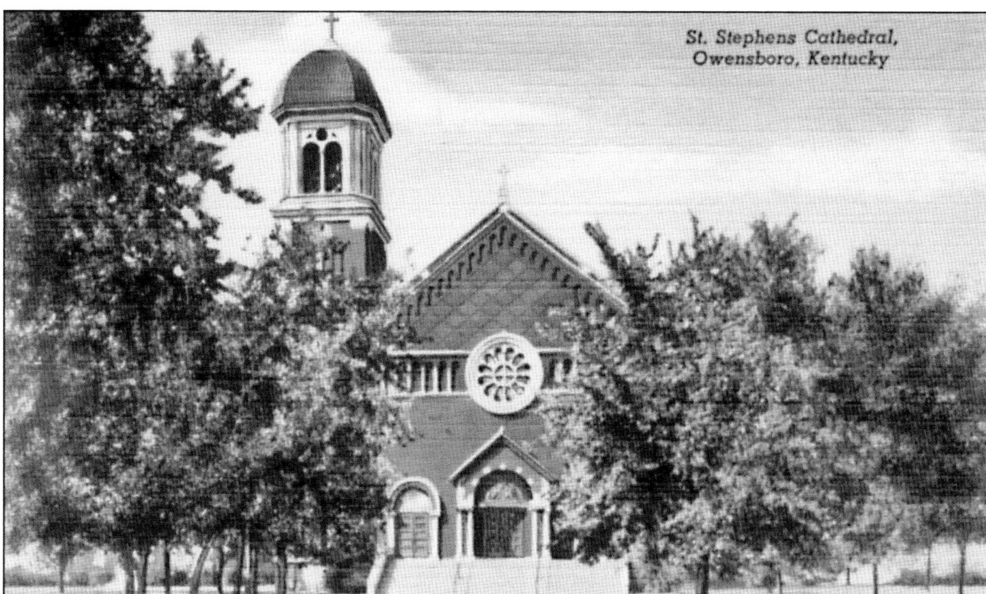

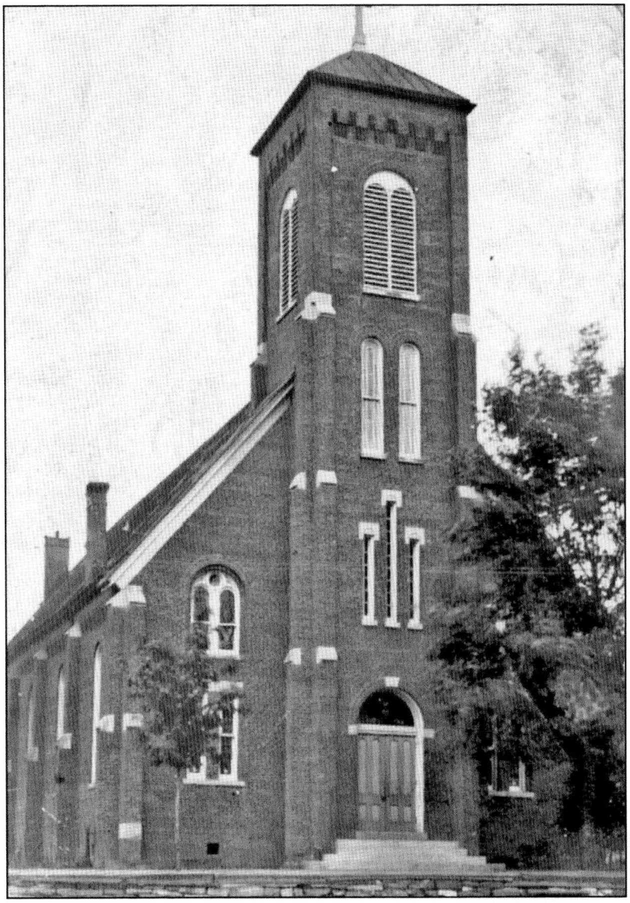

St. William's Catholic Church of Knottsville, Kentucky, was organized in 1887 following a meeting of the local clergy and laity. The result of the meeting was the formation of the St. William's Parish. The symbolic cornerstone for St. William's was set in 1888 for the subdued Romanesque Revival design. The building was later remodeled in 1968.

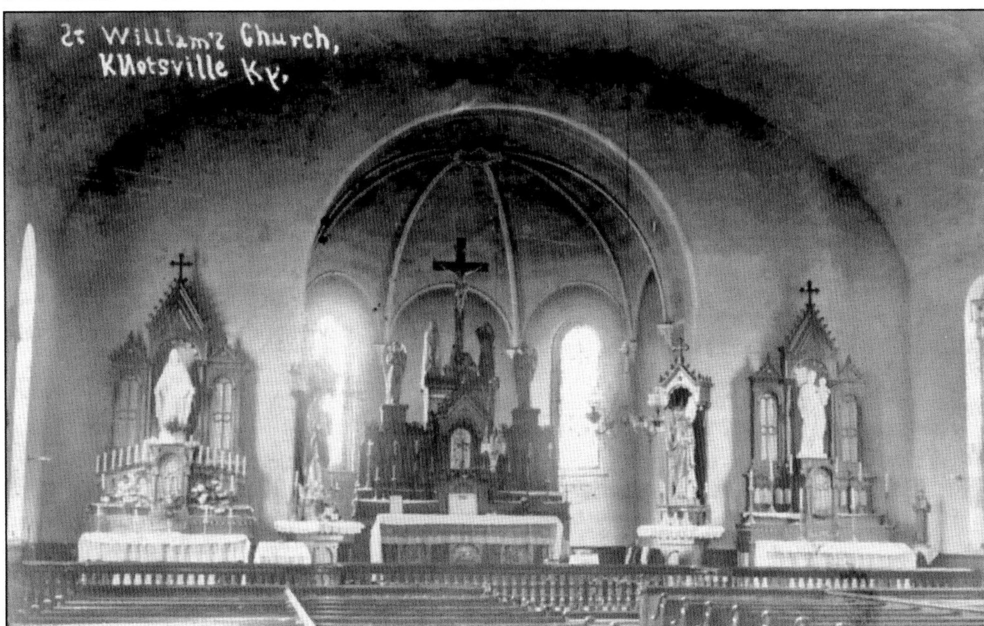

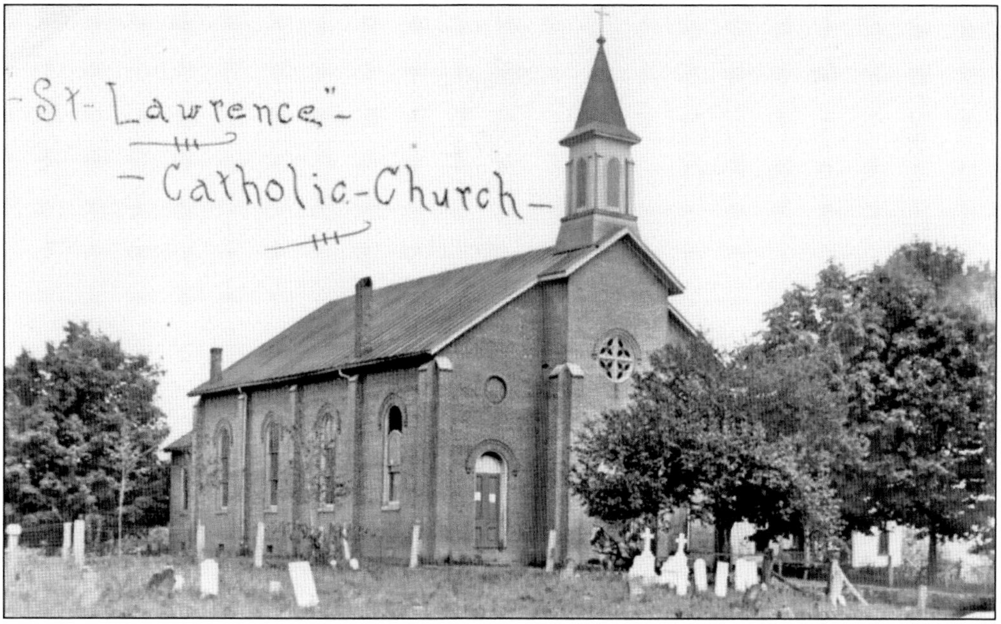


St. Lawrence of Knottsville is the oldest Catholic church in Daviess County. The present building was constructed in 1872 as a replacement for an older brick structure built in 1839. The real-photo postcard is postmarked October 11, 1910.

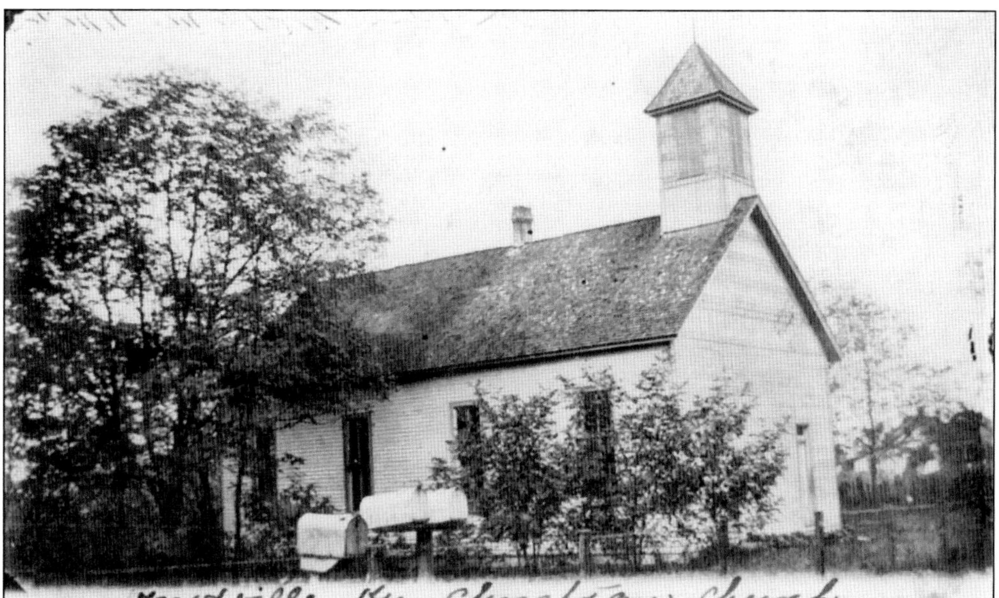

Not much is known of this early Christian church of Knottsville in eastern Daviess County.

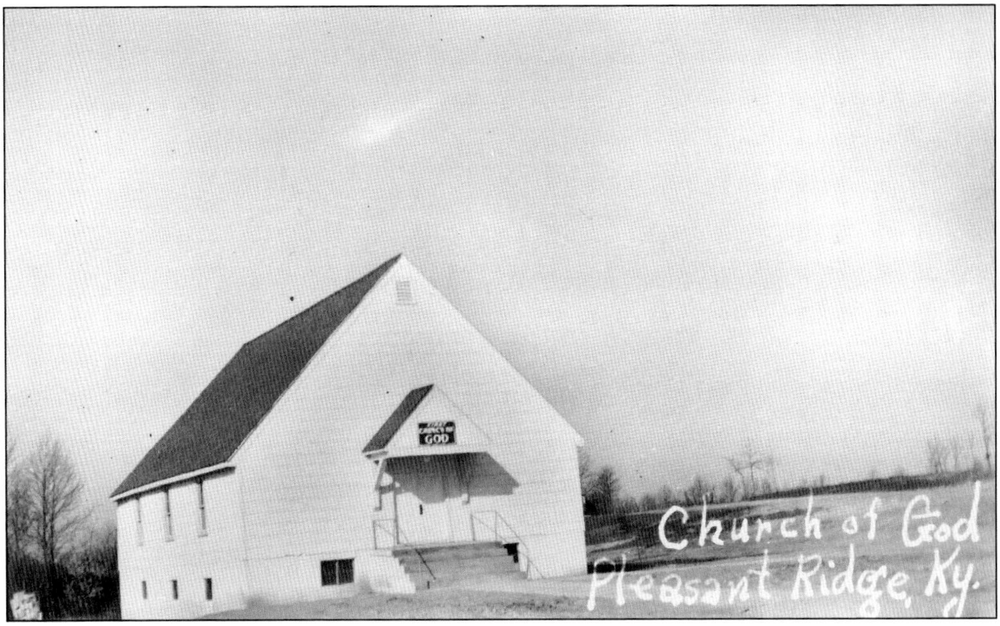


The Church of God at Pleasant Ridge was located just east of U.S. Highway 231 at the Ohio and Daviess County line.

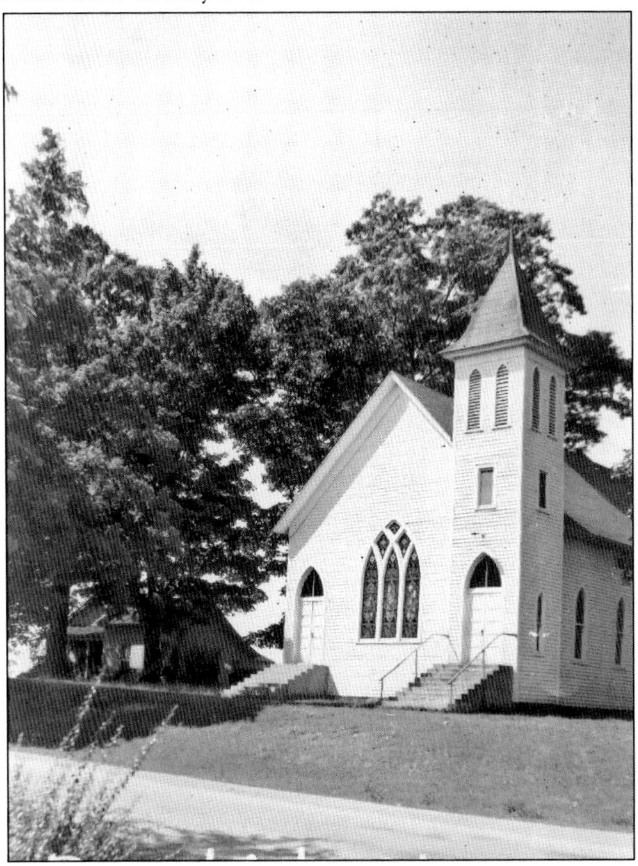

This is a real-photo postcard of Pleasant Ridge Baptist Church. The congregation first organized in 1892, and this building was erected in 1906. An educational wing was added in the 1950s, and the church's brick veneer came sometime in the 1980s.

# *Four*

# SCHOOLS

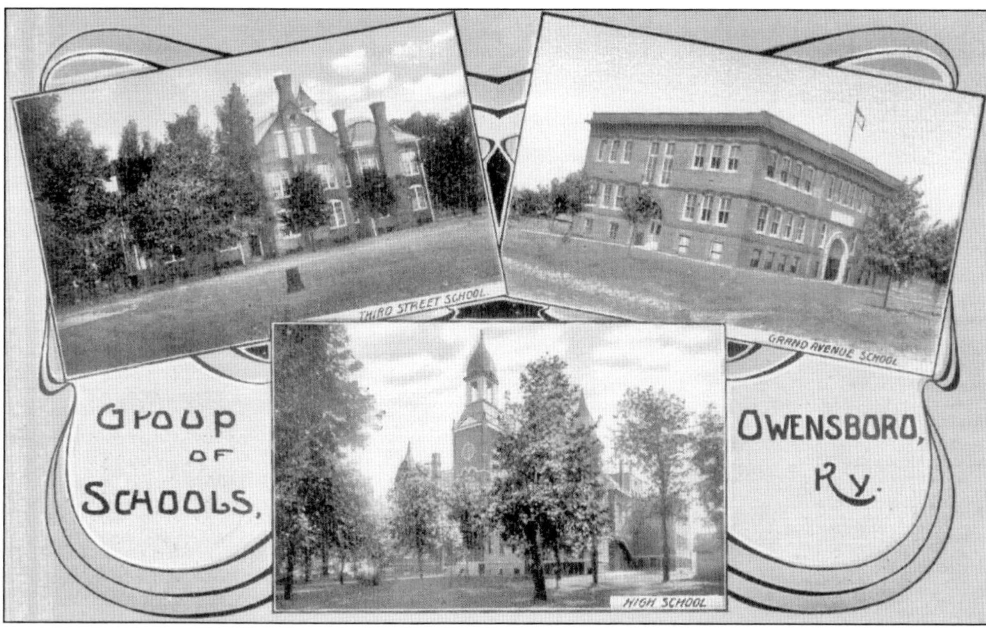


These three Owensboro Independent School System buildings are long retired but wonderfully recorded on this 1920s postcard. The Third Street School building on the left was built in 1886, was razed to construct the new Sears, Roebuck, and Company building in 1950, and is now the home of Wax Works Video Works at 325 East Third Street. The high school building pictured in the center was built in 1892 and became a junior high in 1924. The school board later sold the building, and it is now known as the Mid-Town Office Building at 920 Frederica Street. The Grand Avenue School on the right, later known as Emerson Elementary, was built in 1908 and razed in 1972 to make room for the construction of the city school system's central office.

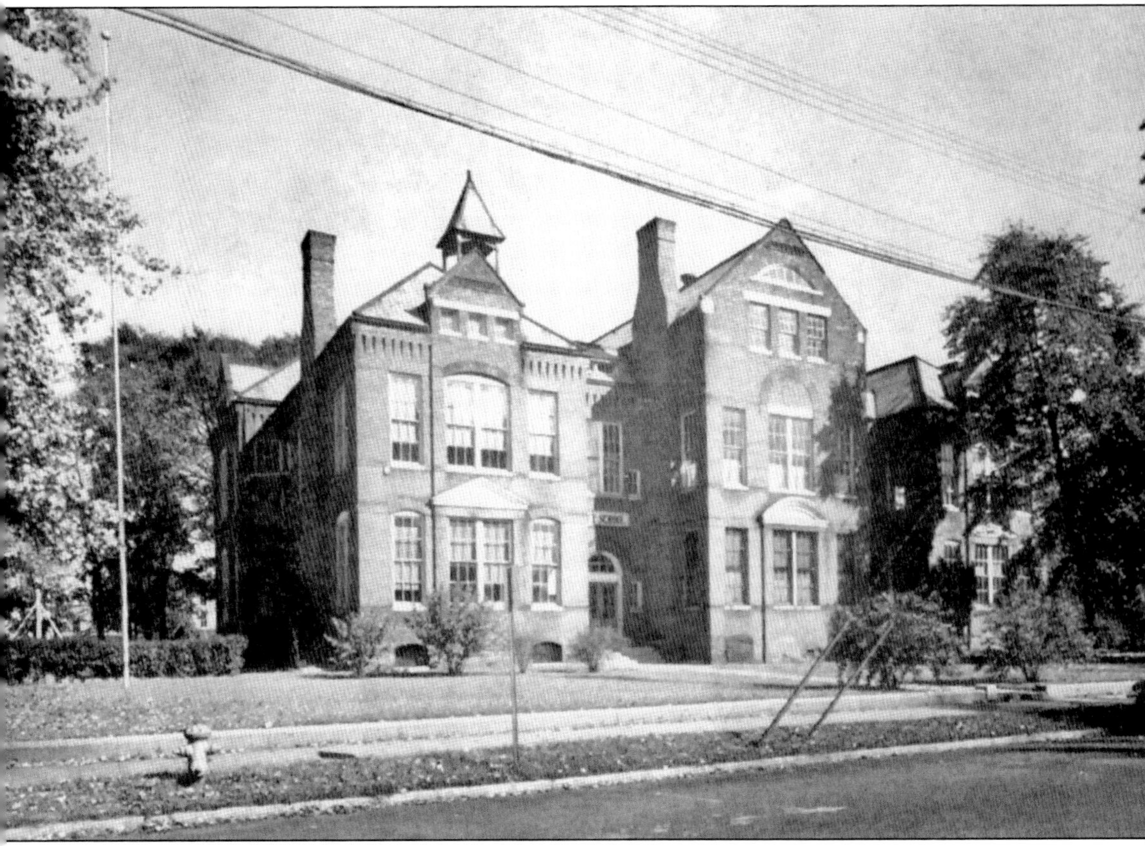

The George Washington Elementary School is pictured above. In 1871, the Owensboro Public School system ordered that a school be built in each of the city's two wards. For an upper ward school, the school board purchased the Baptist College property on June 5, 1871, for $12,000. The seminary building was located on the northeast corner of Third and Lewis Streets, now known as J. R. Miller Boulevard. The facility was known for a long time as the Third Street School before being named for the first U.S. president. On December 15, 1886, the new $18,500 Washington School building pictured above replaced the old college structure at the same Third Street location. In 1949, the school burned and was razed to make way for a new Sears, Roebuck, and Company building in 1950, and the site is currently the home of Wax Works Video Works.

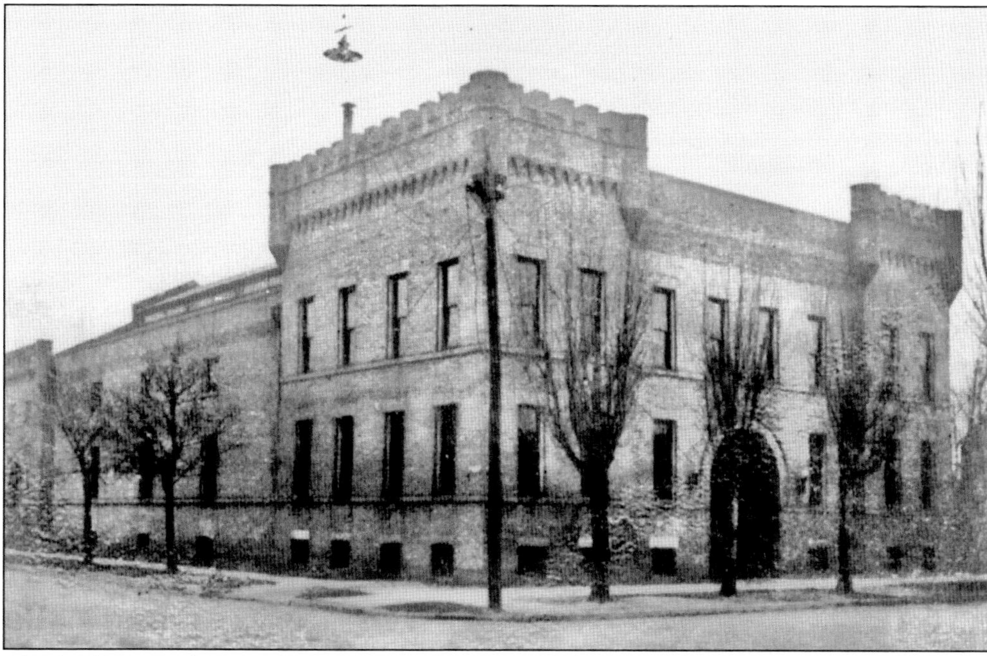

This building on the northwest corner of Third and Cedar Streets saw a variety of tenants. Built as the Owensboro Armory, it provided a home for Daviess County High School when this photograph was taken in 1923 and later sheltered Owensboro Ice Cream and Dairy Products, better known as Velvet milk. This building at 230 Cedar Street was razed in 1991.

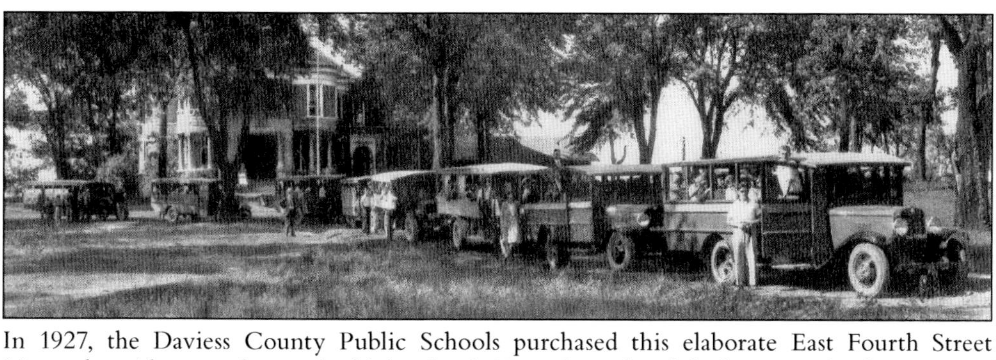

In 1927, the Daviess County Public Schools purchased this elaborate East Fourth Street Monarch residence to house the high school. Note the style of the buses in the front yard of this 1932 photograph. While the home section of the building was razed in 1960 to make room for a gym, the remaining facility continues to educate students today as the Daviess County Middle School.

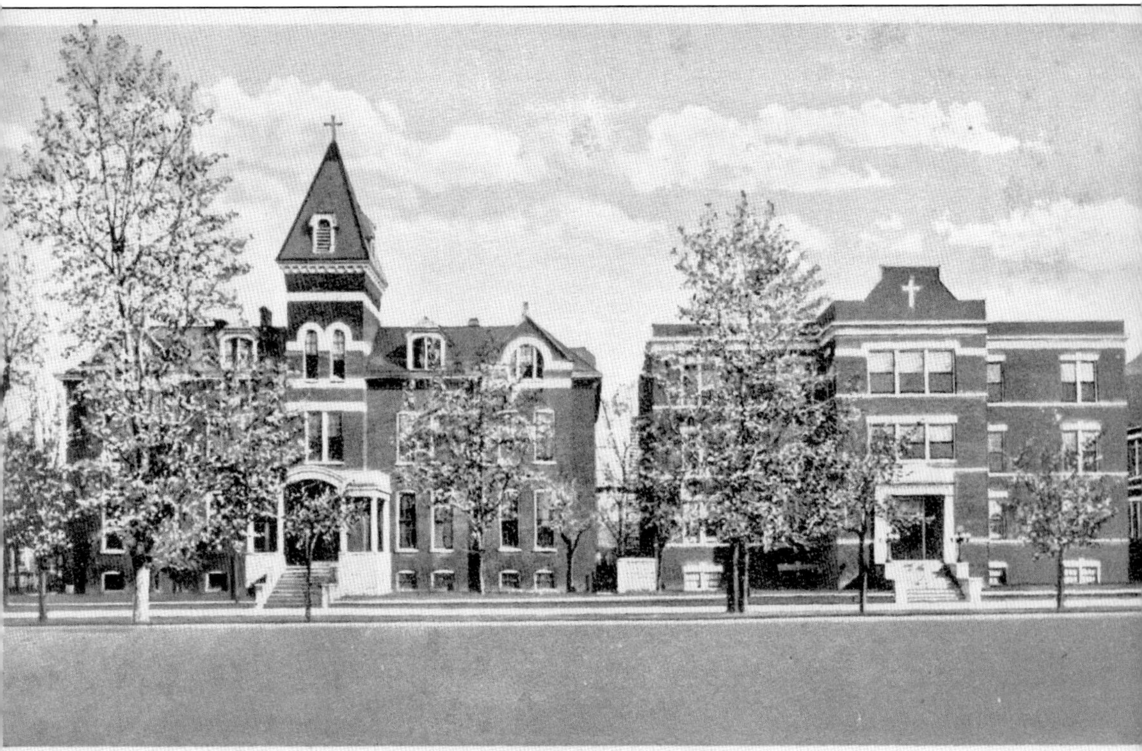

ST. FRANCES ACADEMY AND AUDITORIUM, OWENSBORO, KY.

St. Frances Academy was located on the southeast corner of Fifth and Allen Street. The school was first established in 1849 in an old hotel on the northeast corner of Third and Allen Streets by the Sisters of Charity of Nazareth, Kentucky. In 1889, a new main administration building, seen on the picture's left, was opened, and the auditorium on the right was added in 1921. Actress Florence Henderson graduated from the school in 1951 and went on to fame, starring in the 1970s television program *The Brady Bunch*. St. Frances Academy closed in 1963. Third Baptist Church, seen slightly on the far left of the postcard, purchased the property for a parking lot.

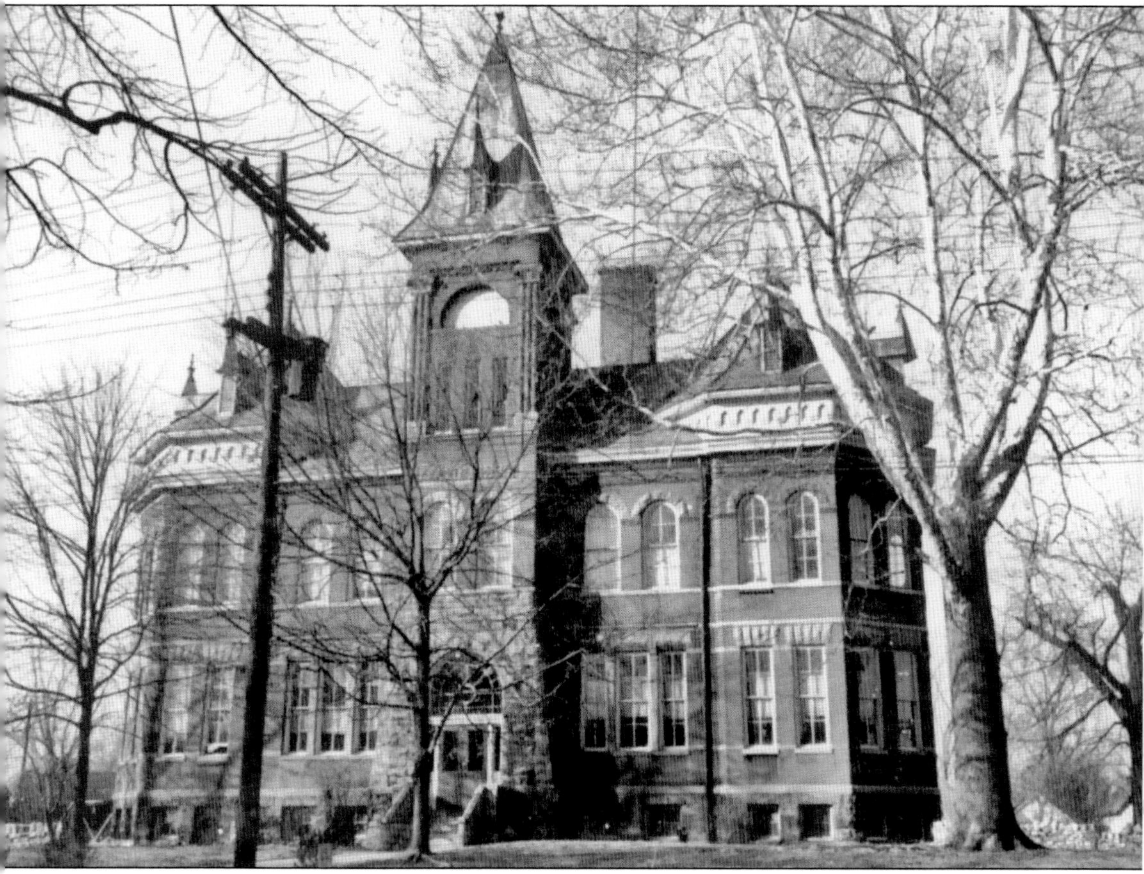

The Woodrow Wilson Elementary School is pictured above. In 1871, the Owensboro Public School System ordered that a school be built in each of the city's two wards. This site on the northwest corner of Seventh and Walnut Streets was purchased, and contractor George Brown built a $7,820 four-room structure first known as the Lower Ward School, then as the Walnut Street School for many years. In 1893, contractor J. J. Williams constructed four additional rooms in front of the school's original four 1871 rooms at a cost of $8,668. The building was later renamed for the 28th U.S. president. Eventually the city school system converted the building to administrative offices. After a century of service, the building was razed and the 1.21-acre property was sold to the City of Owensboro in 1976 to become the Max Rhoads Park.

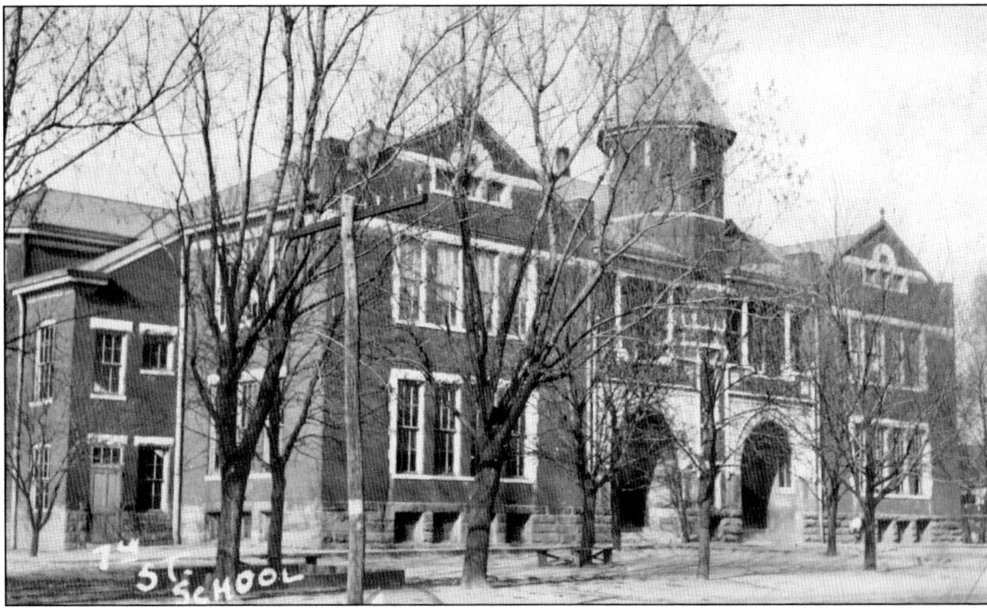

The Seventh Street School was located on the northwest corner of Seventh and Center Streets. The board of education purchased the property known as the Bowlware lot on February 1, 1895, for $2,700 and opened a new $13,332 school designed by Drach, Thomas, and Bohne of Louisville, Kentucky, on February 27, 1896. The school quickly overflowed, and a new $9,021 mirrored addition opened on the school's west side on October 21, 1905. The name was later changed to the Benjamin Franklin School. In 1947, architect Walter Scott Roberts designed the International-style building addition shown below. The school has since been razed, and currently the site serves as a part of the Wendell Foster Campus for Developmental Disabilities.

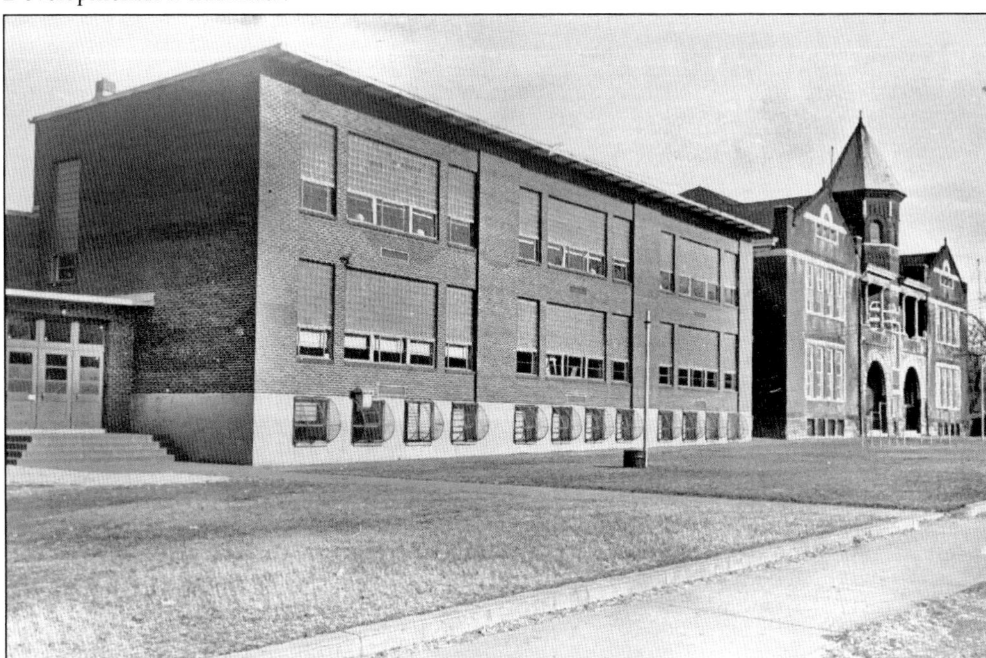

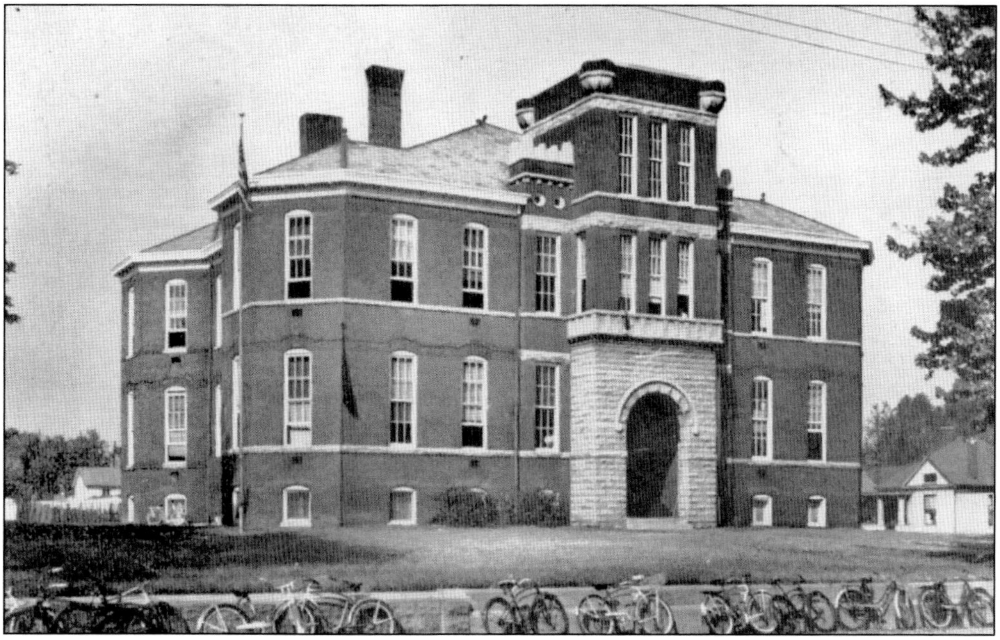

Thomas Jefferson Junior High School is pictured above as it looked in the 1940s. The original 1892 four-room structure was built near the southwest corner of Ninth and Frederica Streets to serve as Owensboro High School. In 1899, a $6,850 four-room addition was constructed by J. F. Jarboe, and a $35,826 auditorium and classroom annex was added in 1910. When the high school was moved to the new Eighteenth and Frederica Street building in 1924, this school served as a junior high until the 1950s. The building is now known as the Midtown Office Building. Abraham Lincoln Elementary School, pictured below, was located on Breckinridge Street just north of the Seventeenth Street railroad tracks. Built in 1917 by the Seven Hills Independent School System, the school was annexed by the city system in 1920.

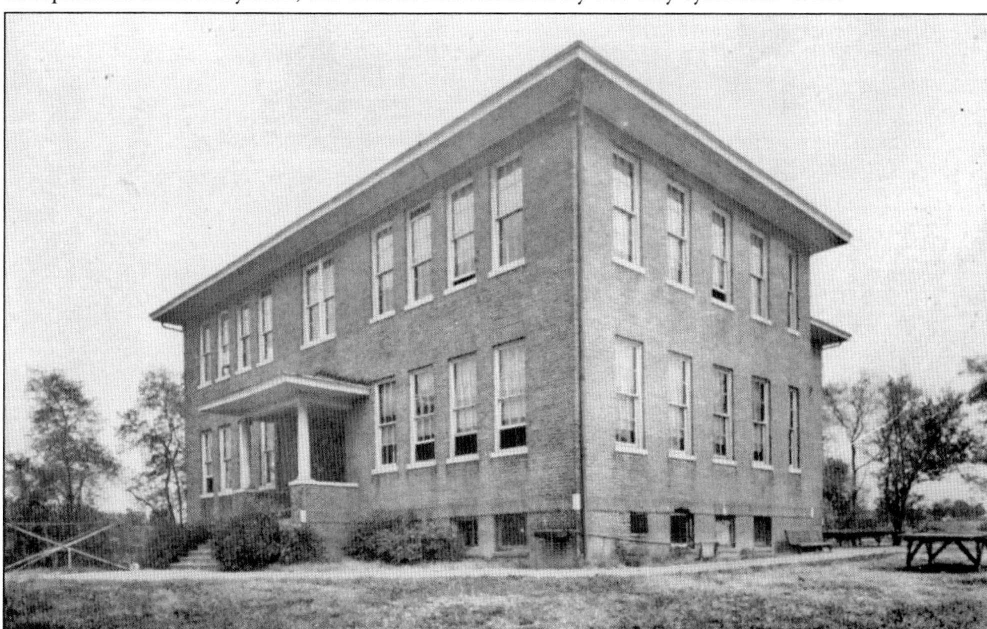

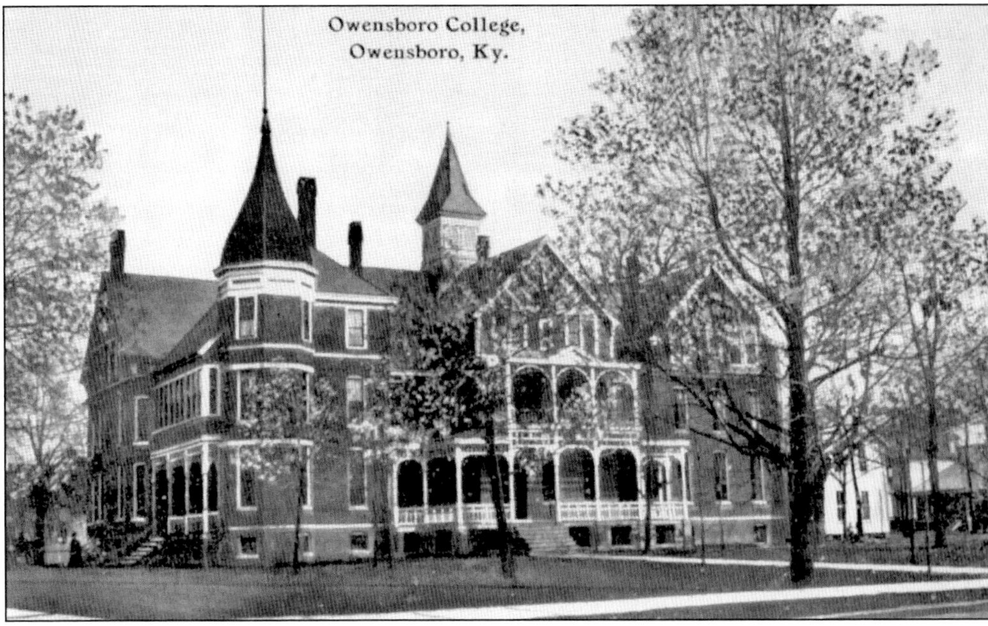


The Owensboro Female College, pictured above, was completed in 1890 on the southeast corner of Fifteenth and Frederica Streets. The building's architecture was a combination of the Victorian and Stick styles. The private school later became known simply as the Owensboro College after it became coeducational. On May 15, 1915, the Owensboro Board of Education bought the property to become an elementary school. It was christened Longfellow School but was poorly designed for this purpose. After the new Longfellow School was completed in 1932 next to the high school, the old college building became home to the Owensboro Trade High School. In 1940, this structure was razed to make room for the construction of the new Technical High School, pictured below.

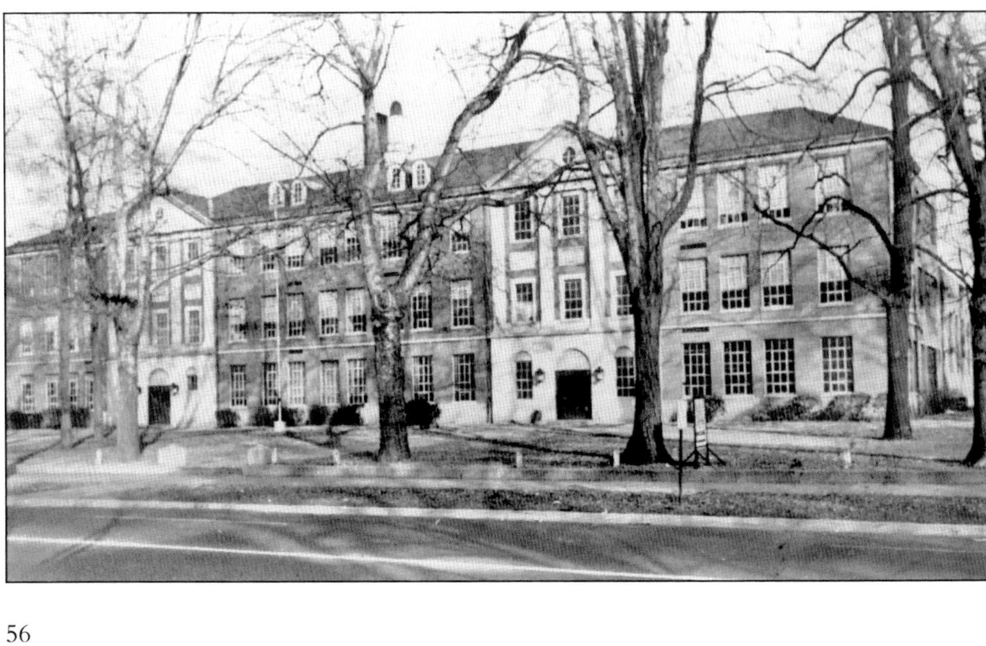

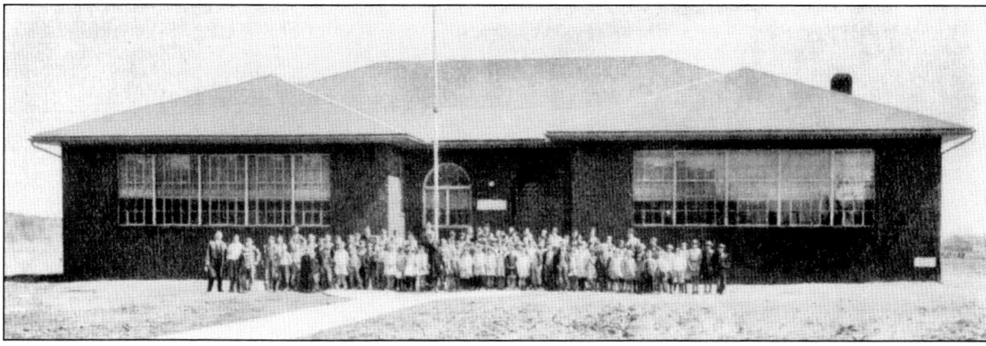

The Snyder School, pictured above, was built in 1927. It was the first modern consolidated school built by the Daviess County School System. Prior to this, the county offered more than 100 one-room schools throughout the rural areas. Completion of the Snyder School was the first step in the school system's consolidation plan. Over the next 10 years, some 40 smaller schools were abandoned and sold by the school board. This building, located on State Highway 81, was closed and sold in 1972. The consolidated school movement continued with the building of Thruston School in 1928, the Sutherland School (pictured below) in 1930, the Maceo and Stanley Schools in 1934, West Louisville School in 1936, and the Sorgho and Philpot Schools in 1937.

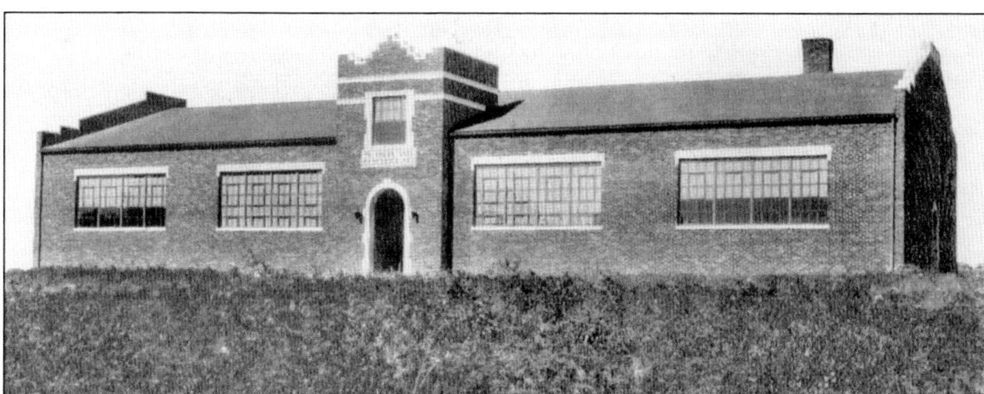

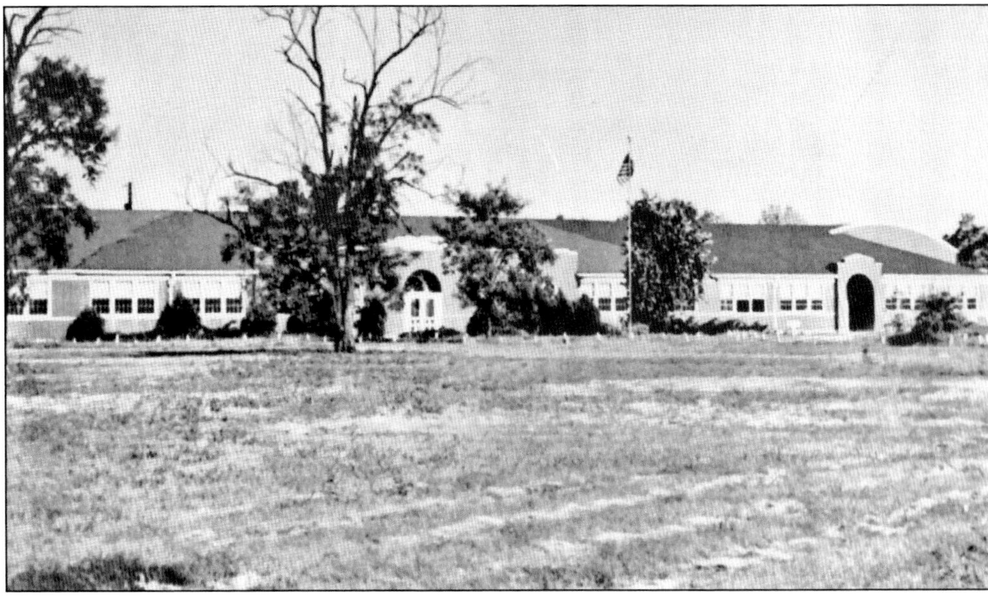

Pictured above is the Stanley Elementary School, built in 1934 on Highway 60 West in the community of Stanley, Kentucky. This building is no longer used as a public school.

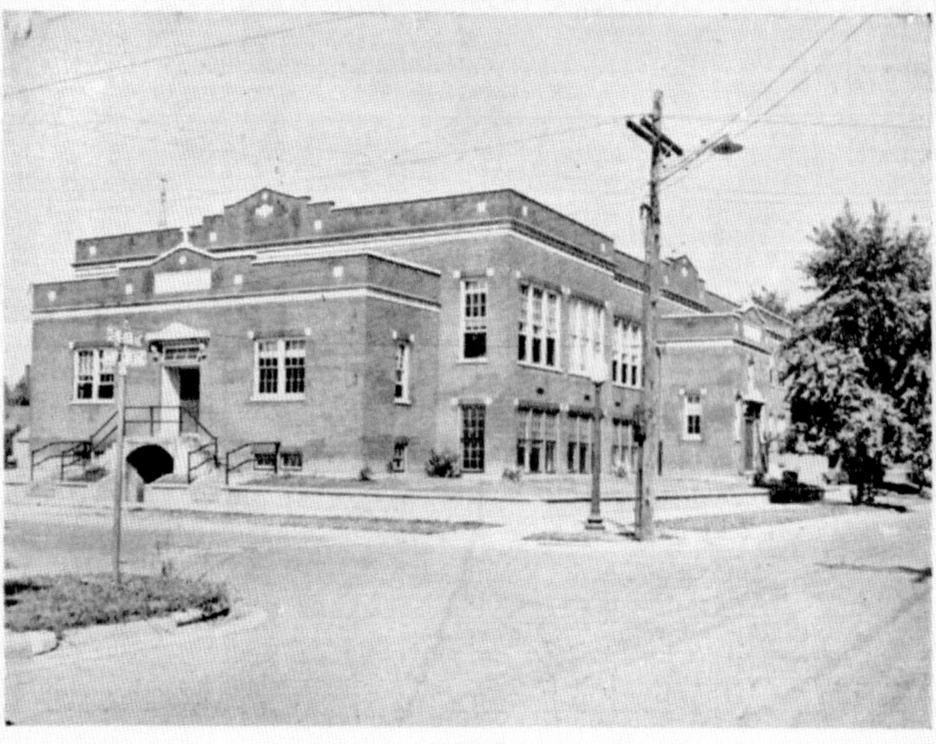

**St. Joseph's Academy, Owensboro**

St. Joseph's Academy, built in 1924, was located on the northeast corner of Fifth and Clay Streets. Under the direction of the Mount St. Joseph Ursuline Sisters, the school sat just behind St. Joseph Catholic Church.

# *Five*

# PARKS

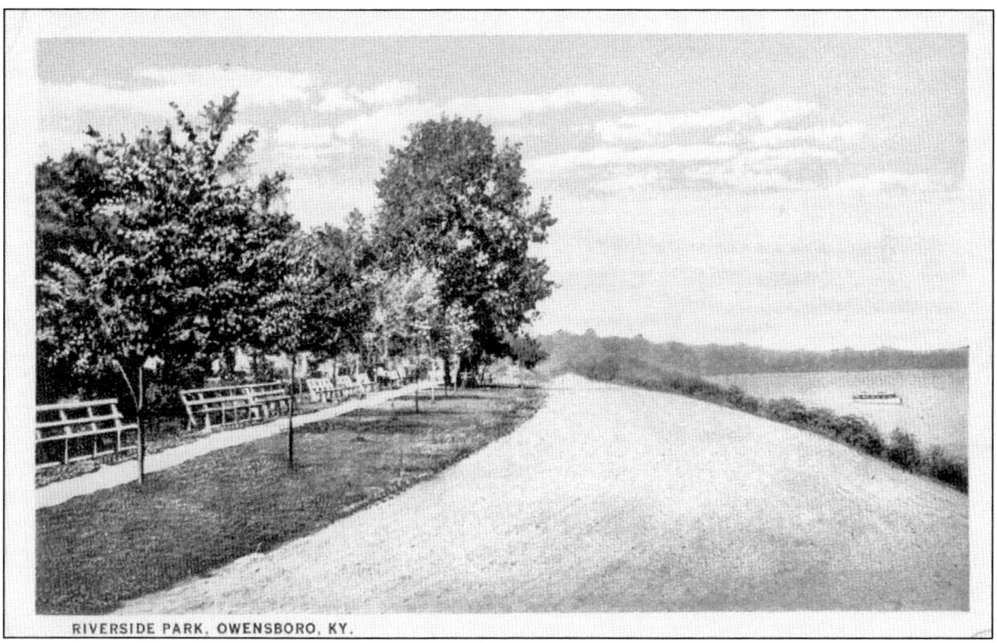


Riverside Park was established in the original 1815 city plot. This view looks westward and shows an early path wide enough for carriage rides along the Ohio River. The postcard photograph was taken by author Lee May and published by druggist W. E. Danhauer. The name of the park was changed in 1963 to Bill Smothers Pioneer Park.

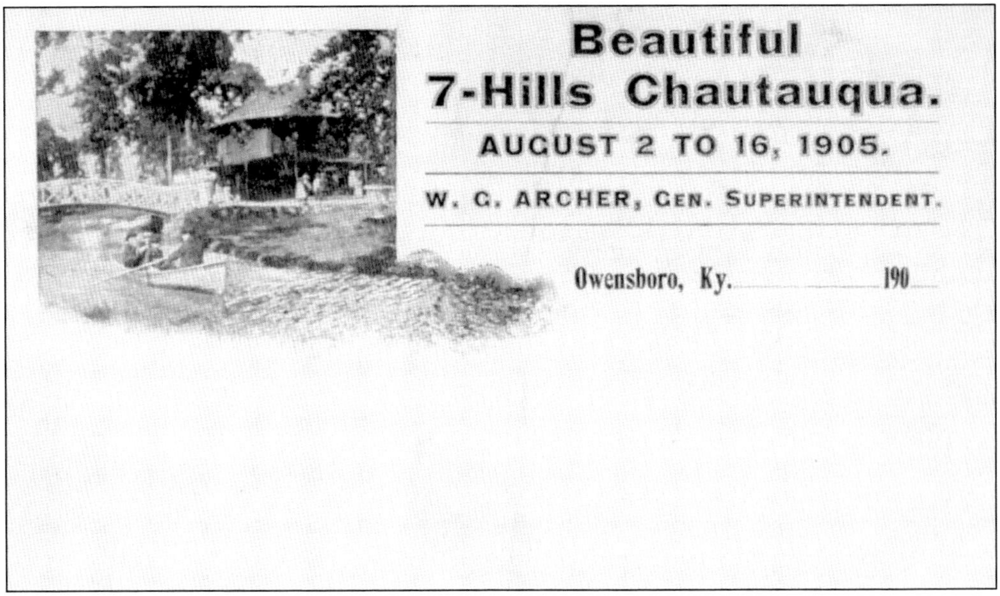


The top postcard shows a relaxing canoe ride promoting a unique place and movement. Chautauqua was a social and cultural phenomenon that began in 1874 and expanded and permeated rural America until the mid-1920s. Going to Chautauqua meant music, laughter, relaxation, and stimulation for millions of rural Americans. When Chautauqua came to the Seven Hills area near Owensboro in about 1900, there was entertainment for the whole family and the entire community. People came from all around to hear nationally renowned speakers, bands, and open discussion on relevant topics of the era. The postcard below shows picnickers enjoying an afternoon outside the 6,000-seat Seven Hills Chautauqua amphitheater.

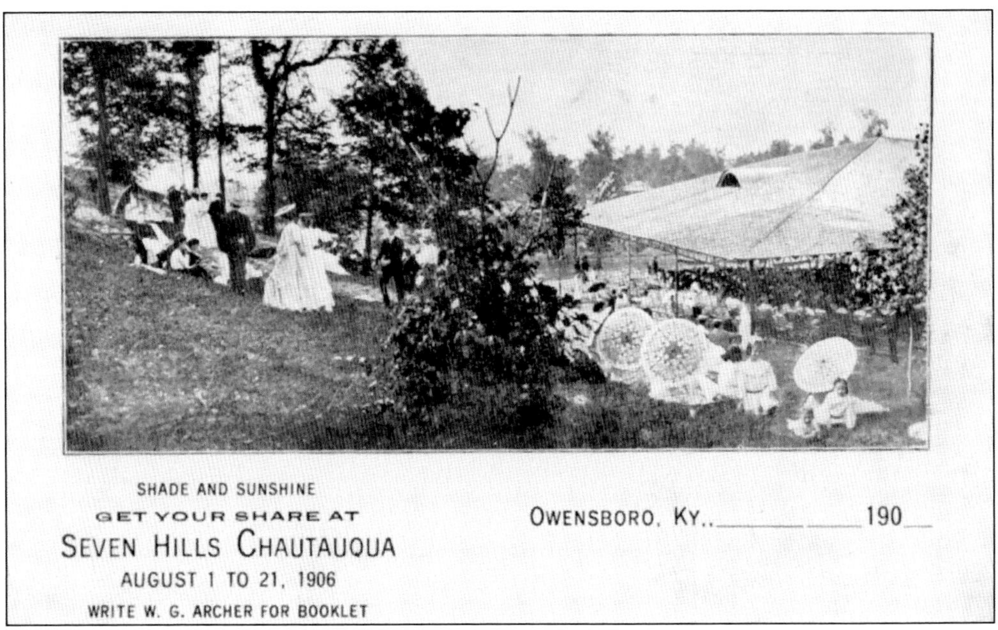

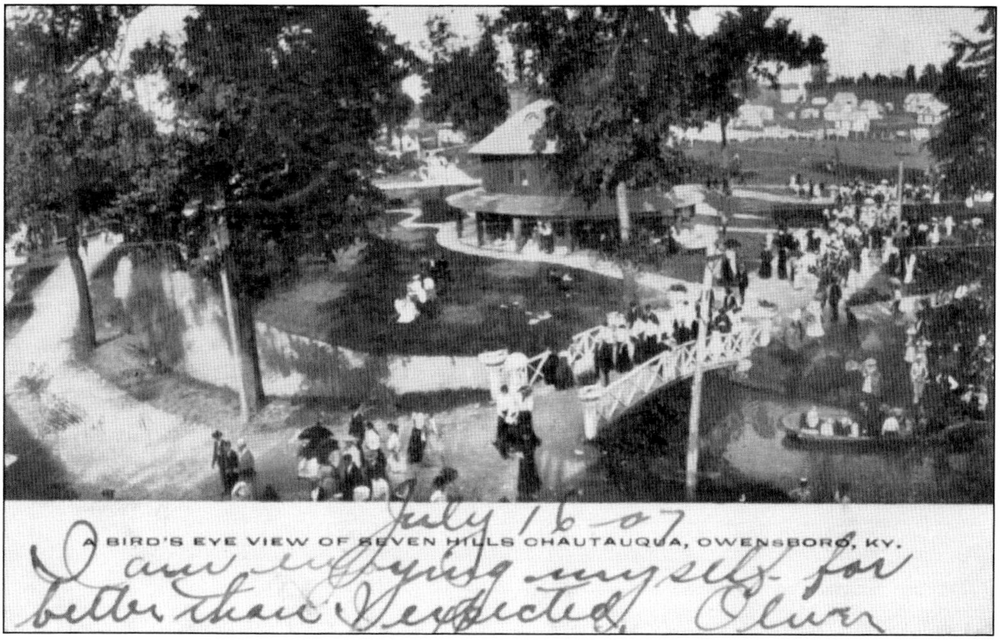


Created as a private development in 1901, Seven Hills Chautauqua Company offered patrons extensive facilities and programming. In the book *History of Owensboro Parks and Recreation 1815–1990,* author Ray Russell suggests the park may have been overdeveloped, burdening the investors with extensive capital investment and maintenance costs. When the company experienced financial difficulties in 1916, the City of Owensboro purchased the 31-acre park for $12,750.

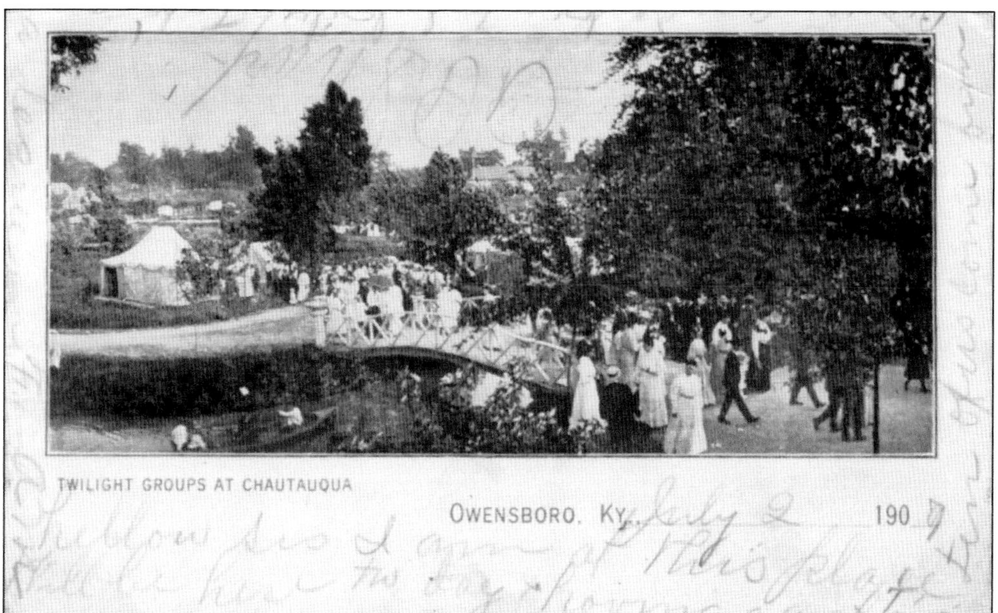

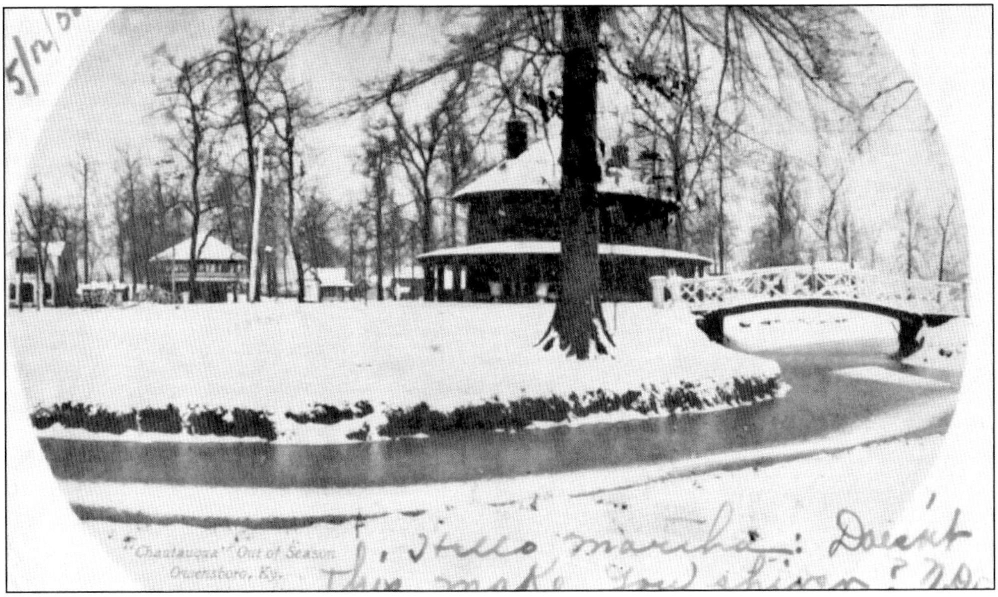


These postcards depict winter and summer scenes of Seven Hills Chautauqua Park in the early 1900s. Wooden bridges linked the park areas separated by lagoons. The top photograph centers on the superintendent's office and quarters, while the bottom shows the concessions building. The park's look changed drastically when the shallow lagoons were filled in the 1950s.

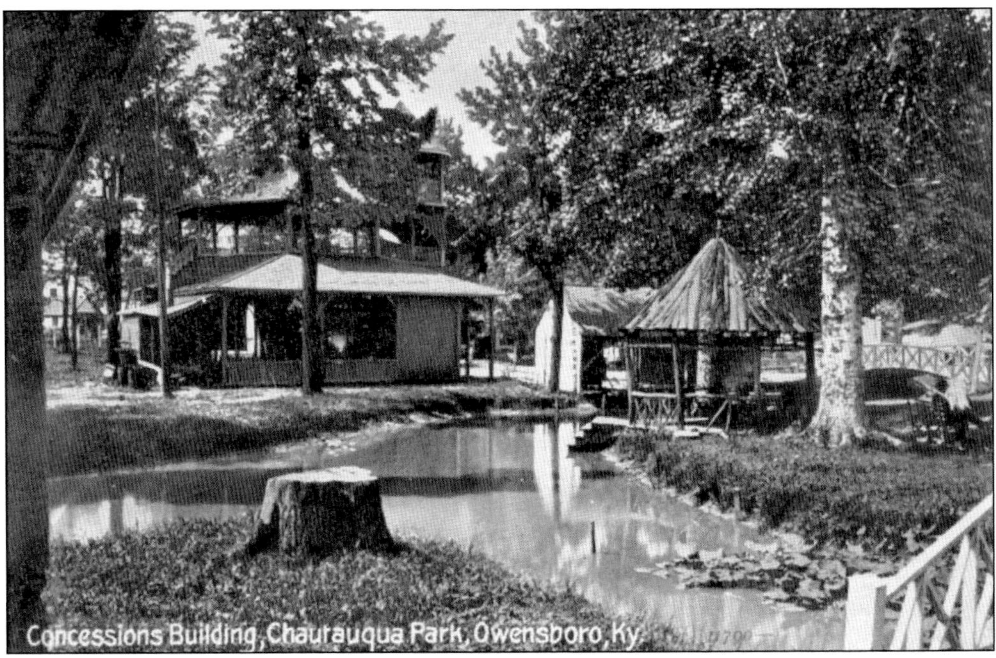

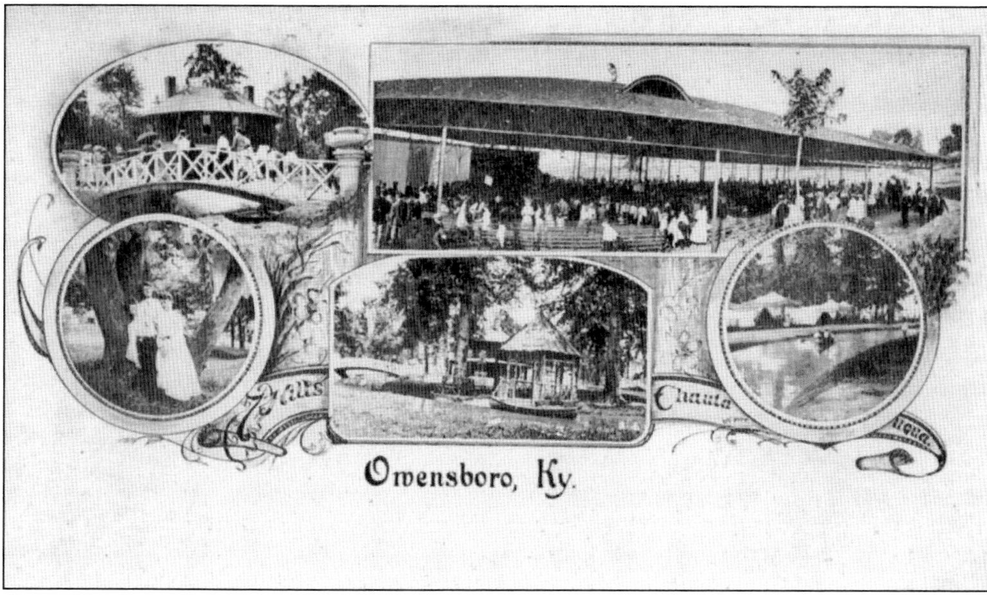


Seven Hills Chautauqua offered a one-third-mile lagoon complete with boats, merry-go-round, bowling alley, landscaped walks and drives, statuary, a 6,000-seat auditorium, a dining hall, bungalows, cottages, a miniature train, a library, a hotel, and a park office. Streetcar tracks were extended to the park linking it to downtown, where guests were arriving by train and steamboat for extended park visits.

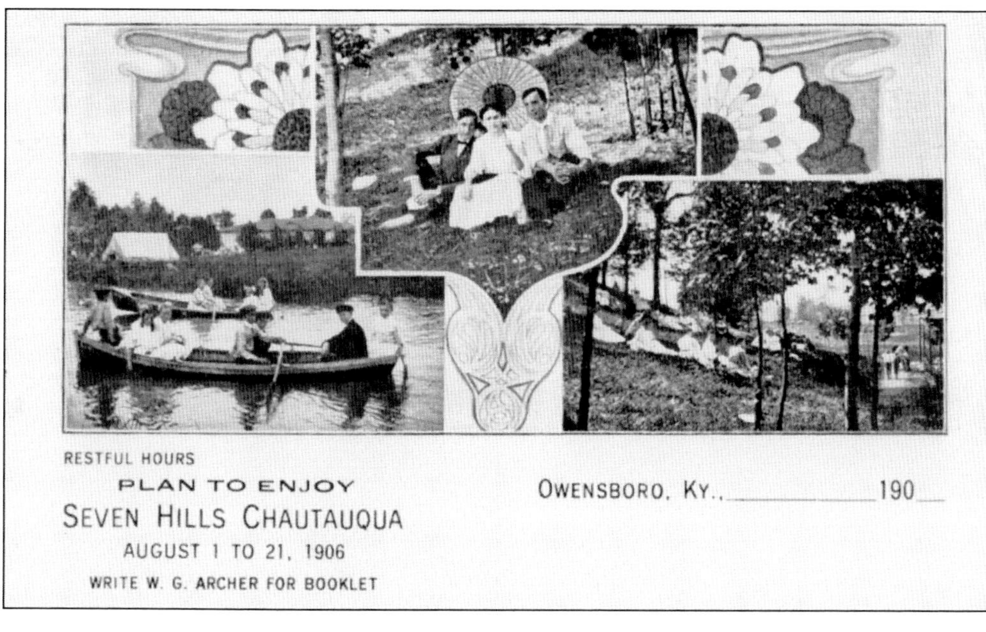

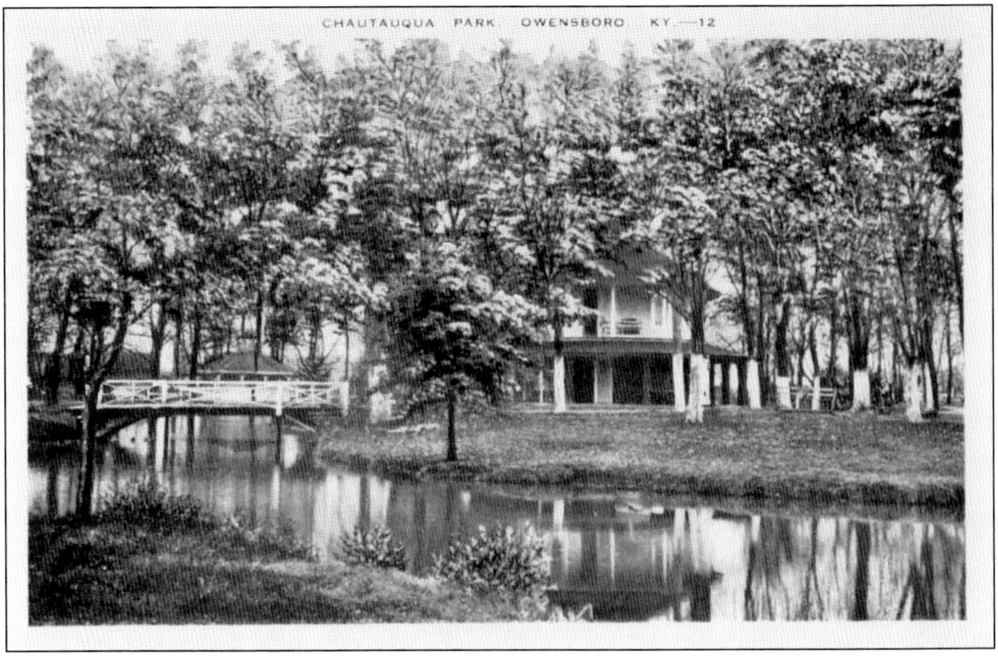


The postcard above shows an early spring view of the Chautauqua Park lagoon and the round yellow brick superintendent's quarters. The bottom postcard shows the silt and debris infill problems encountered with the park's lagoon. These issues eventually required the lagoon to be filled, but not without much flack from local residents.

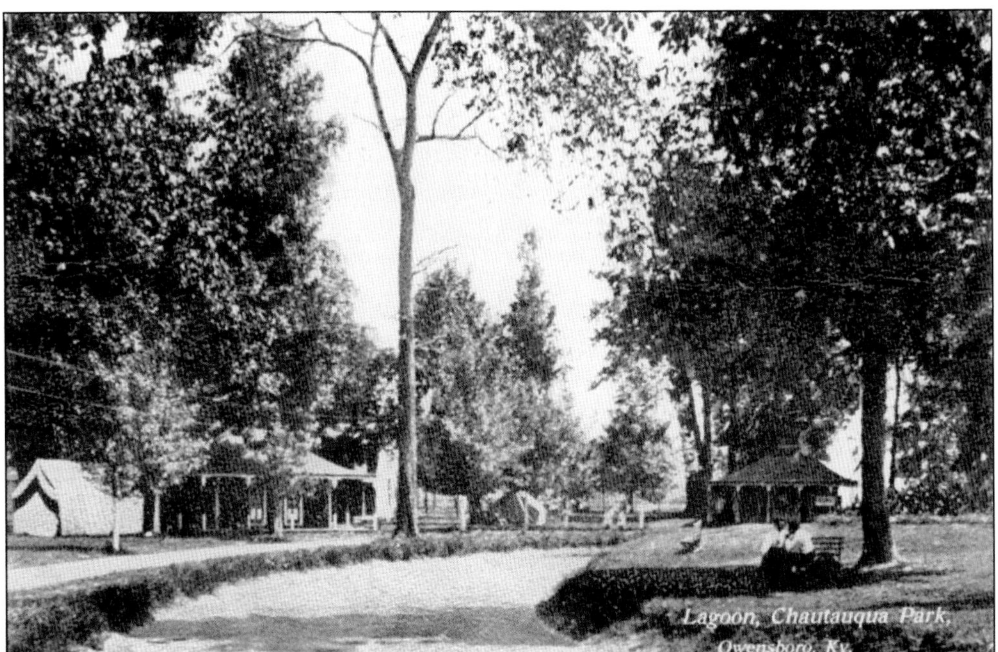

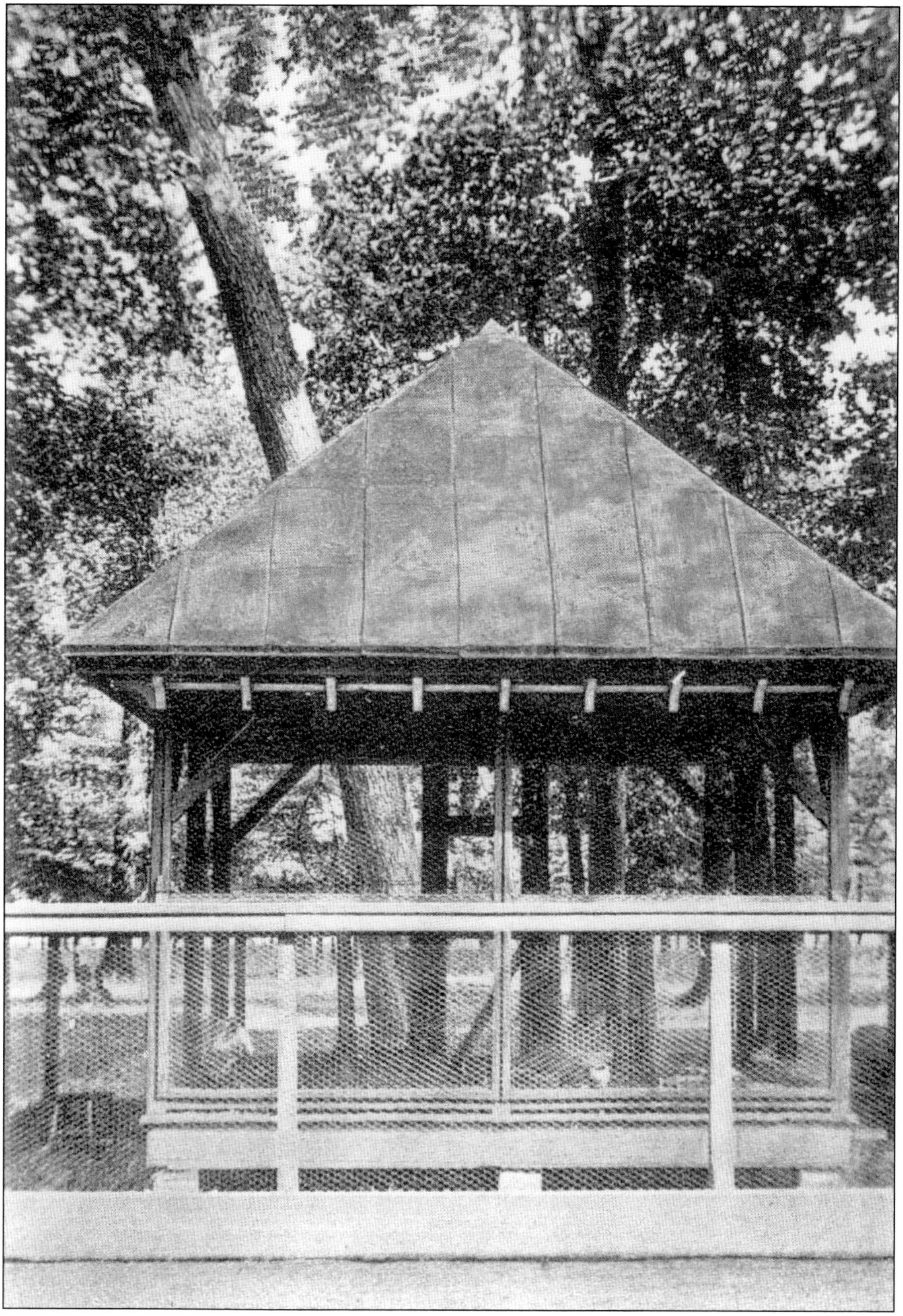

Legion Park was first called Hickman Park. The 23.75 acres of land were acquired in 1894. One of the early attractions was a monkey inside a large cage as shown in the postcard above, dated 1908.

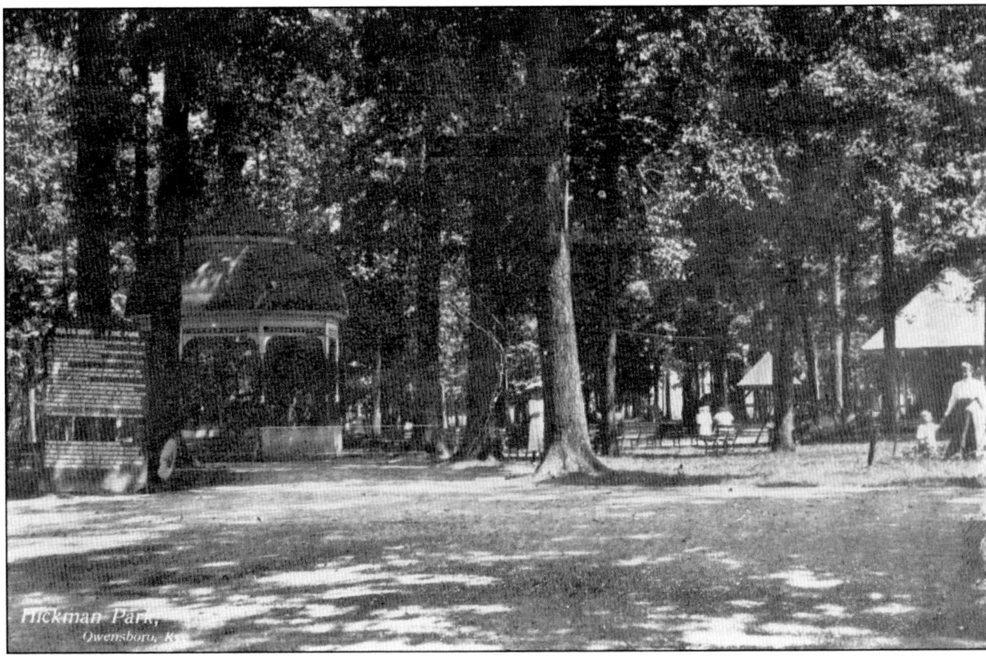


Hickman Park, known today as Legion Park, had a bandstand and concessions facilities in the early 1900s. The tree height and density seems to project more of an image of a forest rather than a park. The postcard of the deer pound allowed children and adults to catch a glimpse of what nature and the "happy hunting grounds" of Kentucky must have really been like for the Native Americans of just a few decades before.

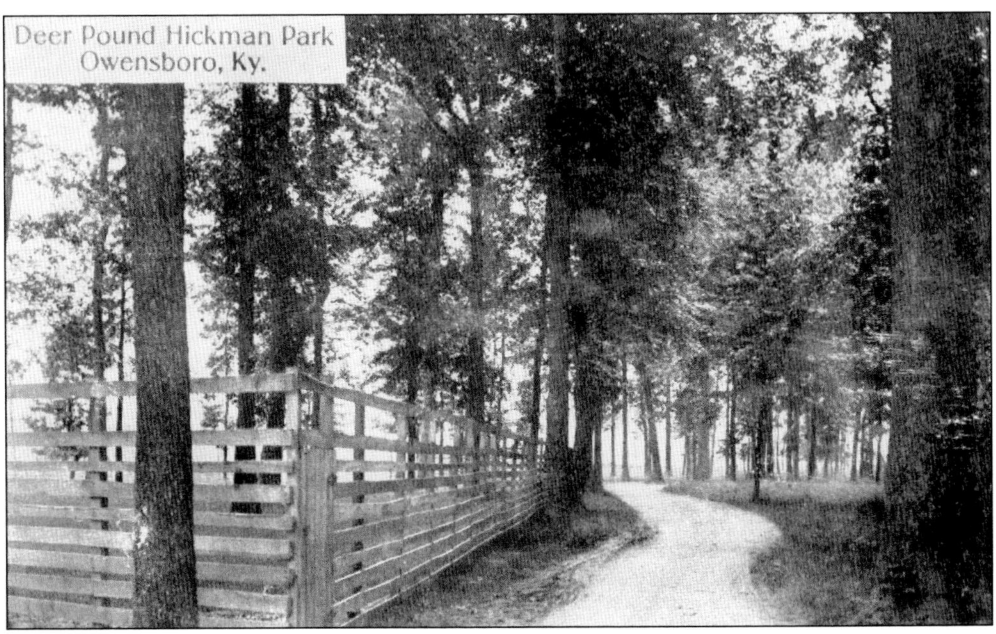

# *Six*

# Hotels and Motels

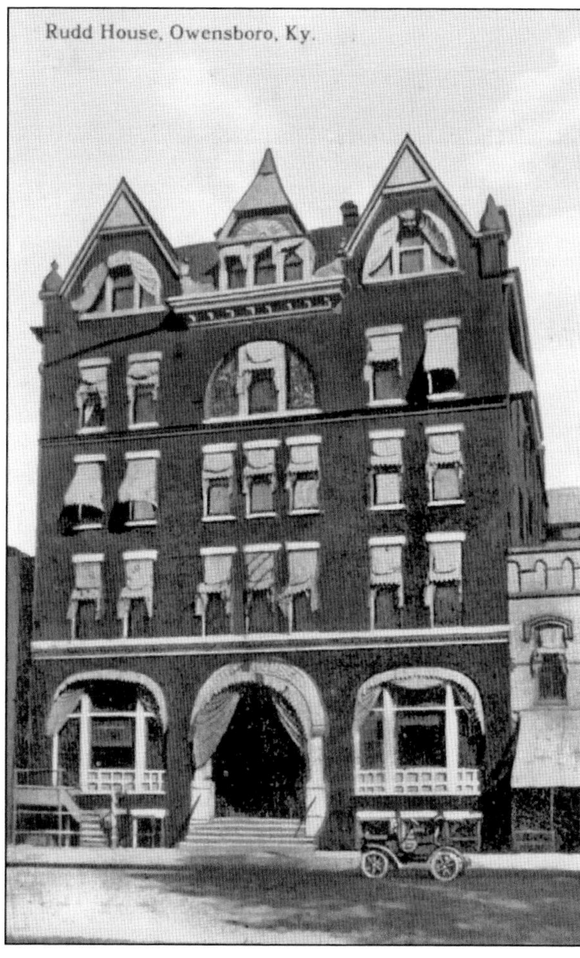


The Rudd Hotel was constructed in the 1890s by J. C. Rudd. The building is not shown on the 1885 Sanborn map. The building was renovated in 1924, with a grand ballroom added on the fourth floor. From that room's bay window was said to be quite a picturesque view of Owensboro's east side. Following the renovation, room rates for one of the 125 available guest rooms ranged from $1.50 to $3.50 per night. The five-story hotel was also renowned for its fine food. The building was razed in 1973 after it was gutted by fire. J. C. Rudd, Son and Company, an insurance agency, was Owensboro's oldest business in the 1970s, having been established in 1854.

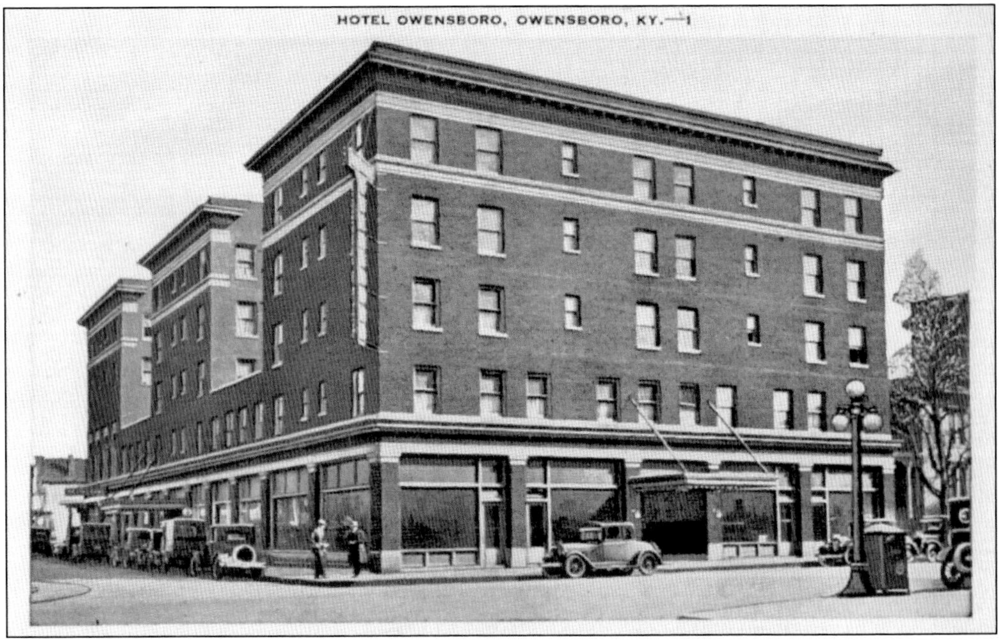


The Hotel Owensboro, pictured above and below, was built in 1926 on the southeast corner of Fourth and Frederica Streets. Owensboro architect Clarence W. Kimberlin designed the hotel, constructed by Evansville's Hoffman Construction Company. The project cost $390,000 for the land and five-story building construction. This modern hotel design was similar to the McCurdy Hotel in Evansville, Indiana, but would also have features equal to the Lafayette in Lexington, Kentucky. Room rates in 1931 were $2, $2.50, and $3. All 150 guest rooms contained private baths, uncommon at the time.

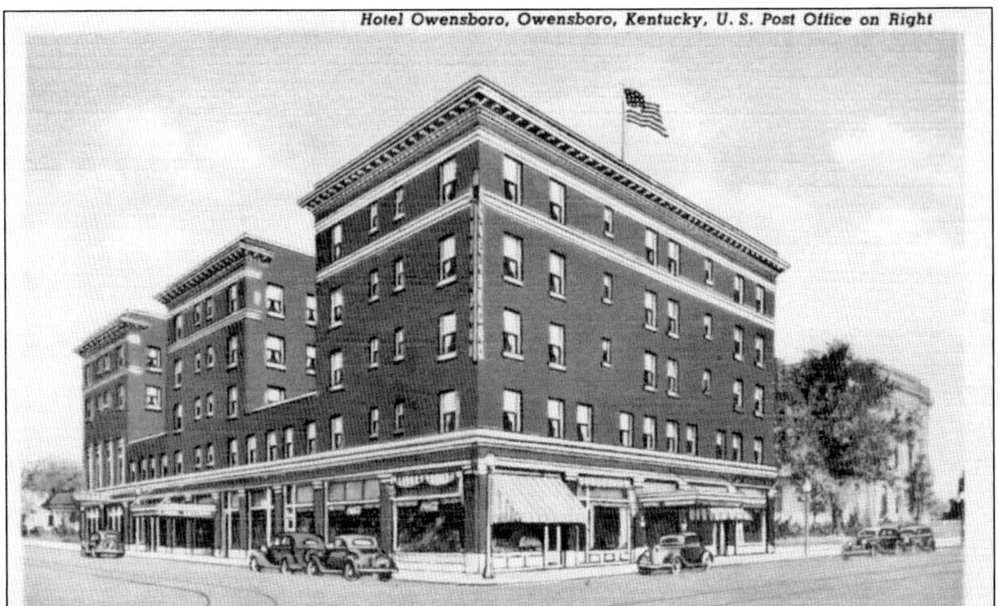

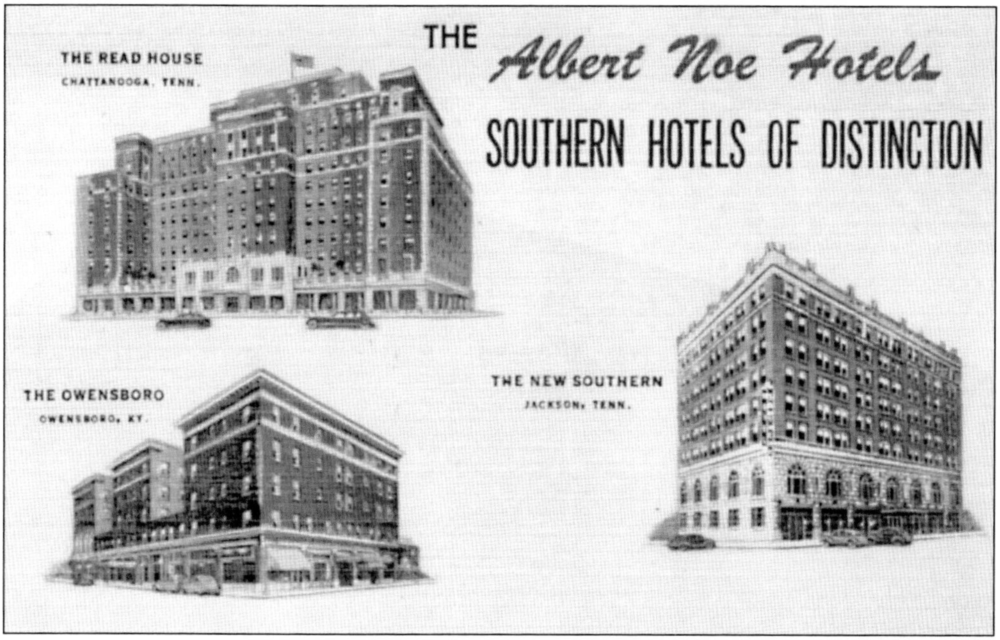


The Hotel Owensboro was one of several hotels of distinction. Other Albert Noe hotels featured in the top postcard are the Read House in Chattanooga, Tennessee, and the New Southern hotel in Jackson, Tennessee. There were many Albert Pick hotels featured in the bottom card. In addition to the Owensboro and the New Southern was the Hotel Anderson in Anderson, Indiana; the Raleigh Hotel in Waco, Texas; the Hotel Fountain Square in Cincinnati, Ohio; the Hotel Fort Haynes in Columbus, Ohio; the Hotel Chittender in Columbus, Ohio; the Hotel Miami in Dayton, Ohio; the Mark Twain Hotel in St. Louis, Missouri; the Fort Meigs Hotel in Toledo, Ohio; the Ventura Hotel in Ashland, Kentucky; the Terre Haute House in Terre Haute, Indiana; and the Hotel Antlers in Indianapolis, Indiana.

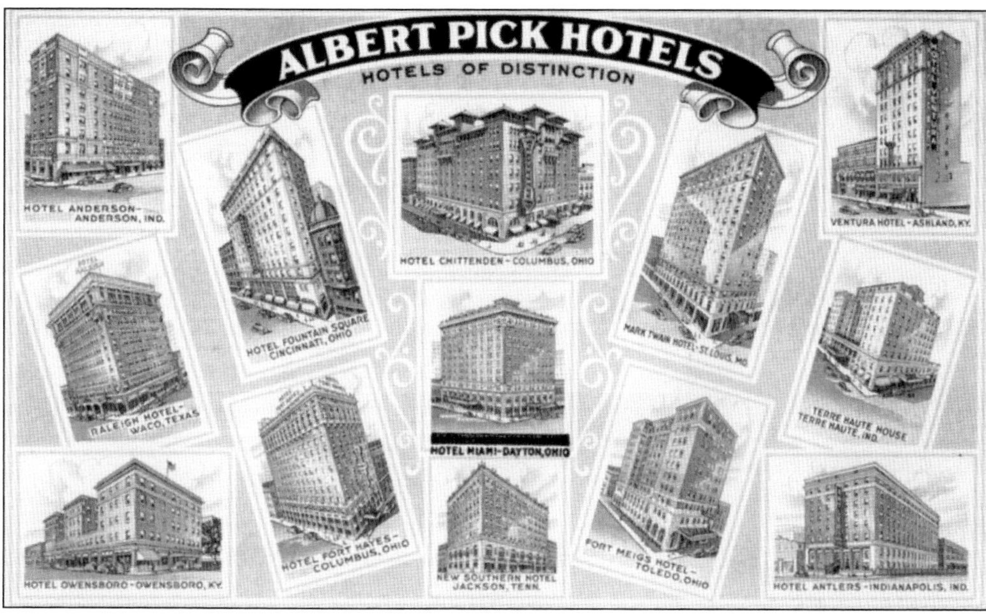

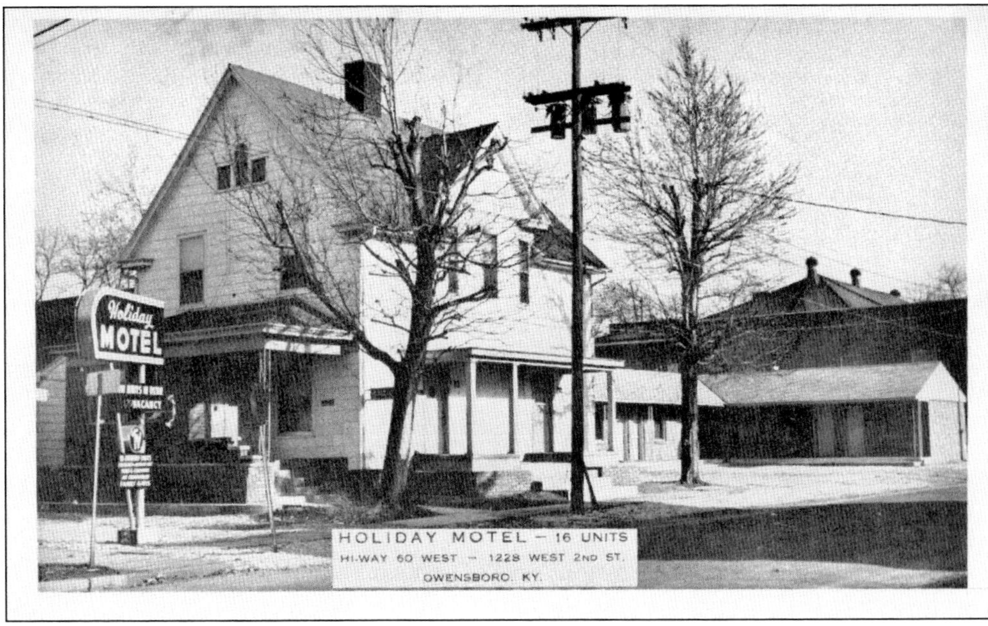


Holiday Motel was located at 1228 West Second Street in the 1950s. The 16 guest rooms featured "tubs with showers, telephones, automatic heat and air conditioning." The large main residence in the above postcard has since been torn down, but the smaller units still stand. Note the Holiday Motel sign's design similarity to the famous Holiday Inn sign. The Cadillac Motel and Restaurant were built in 1954 on the northwest side of Second and Orchard Streets. The postcard below shows the property in the 1960s. This motel continues in business today, offering 40 guest rooms.

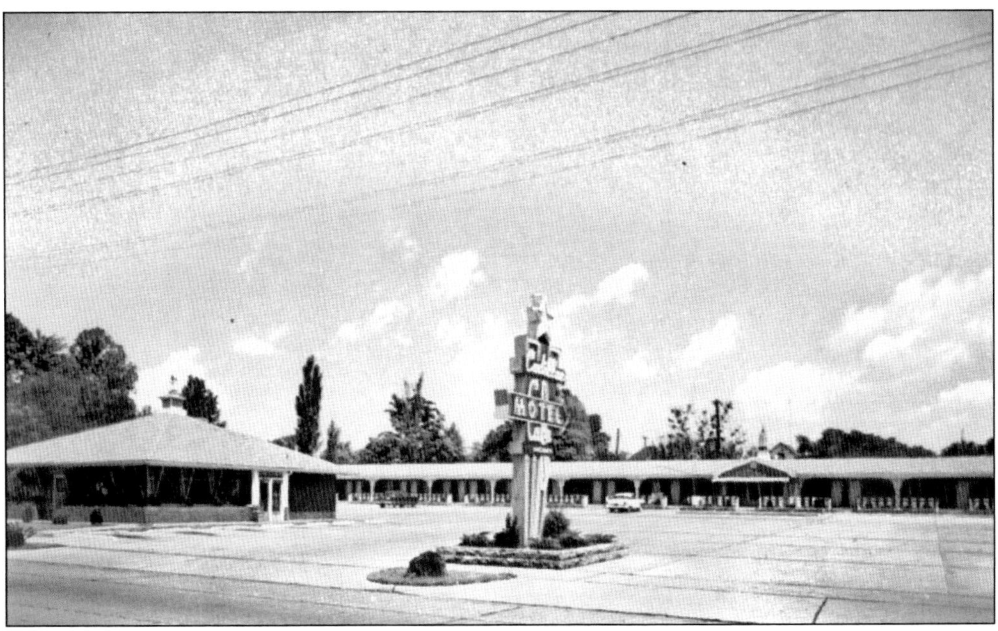

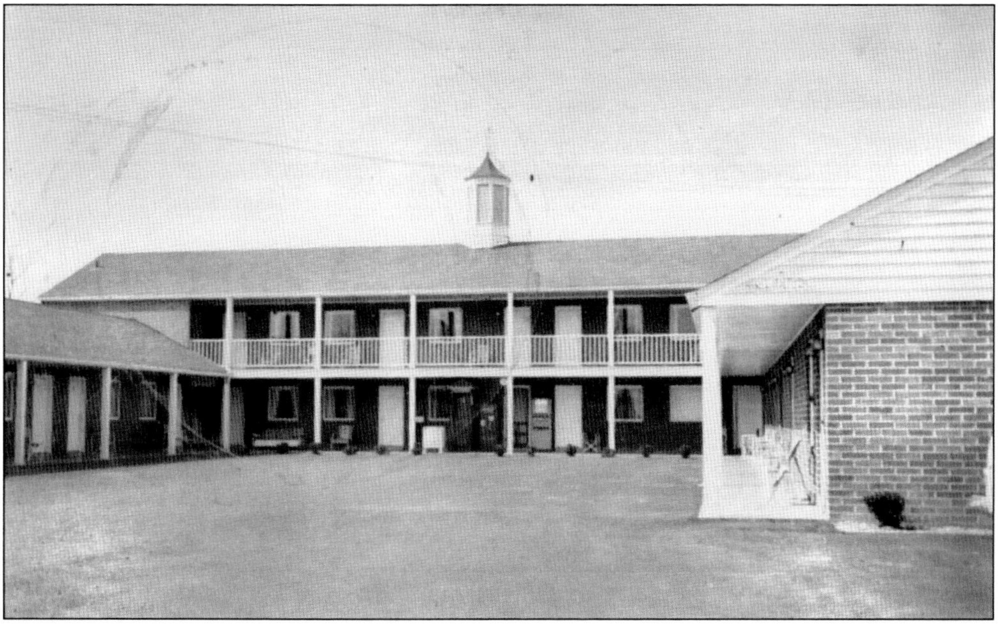

Built in 1951, the Owensboro Motel is the oldest local hotel still in operation. Advertised in this 1964 postcard as a 24-unit establishment with Beautyrest mattresses and ceramic tile baths, the facility located at 1420 Triplett Street was owned by Mr. and Mrs. Dewey A. Stubblefield and managed by Mr. and Mrs. Kelly Newton. The 1953 postcard below presents a view of the art deco interior spaces.

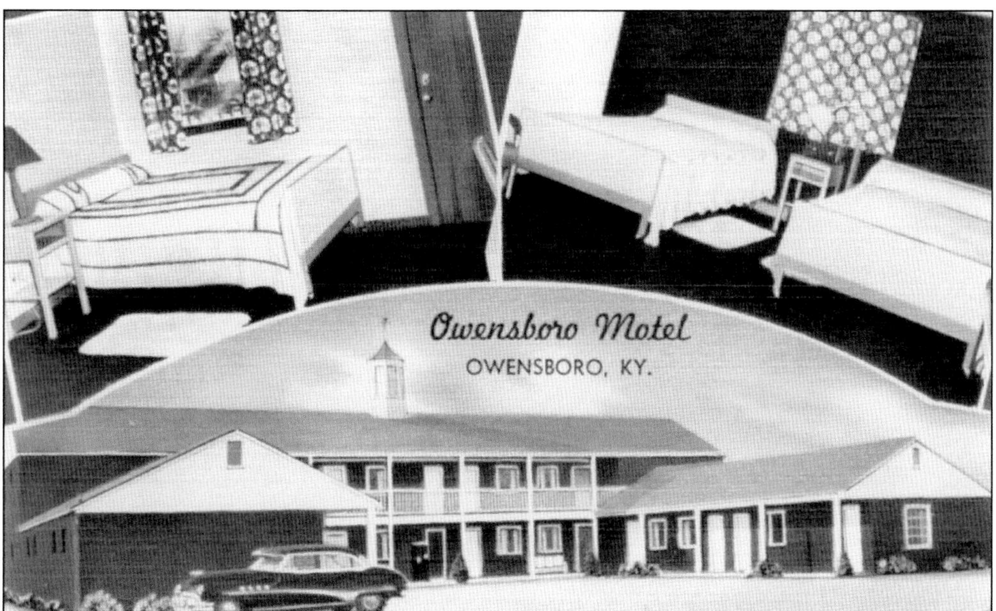

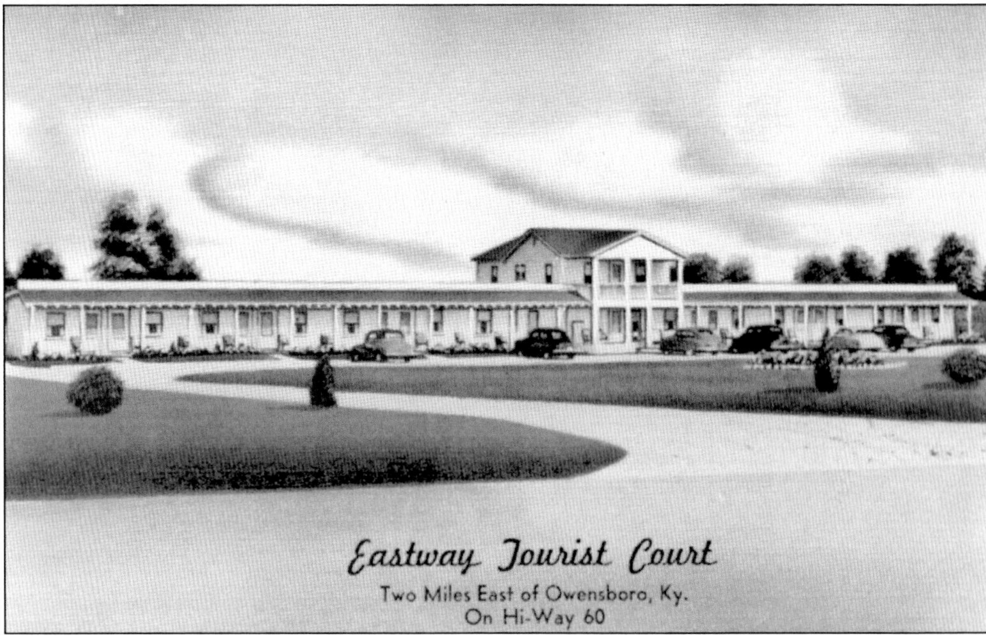


The Eastway Tourist Court was located on Highway 60 East near the Owensboro Municpal Utilities Elmer Smith Plant. This 14-unit facility was owned and operated by Mr. and Mrs. Harry L. Short. The building was demolished in 1993. Motels like this were especially designed for overnight guests stopping along the highway. The ease of cross-country travel created by the U.S. highway system development of the 1930s popularized these motorist-hotels, or motels. Rather than providing room access from hallways connected to a common entrance lobby, motel guest rooms opened directly into the parking lot close to the traveler's vehicle. The Towne Motel was built in 1953 on the southwest corner of Third and Crittenden Streets. The photo postcard below was taken by photographer Frank D. Sweeney of Owensboro around 1958. The hotel continues to operate today as the Budget Inn with 40 rooms.

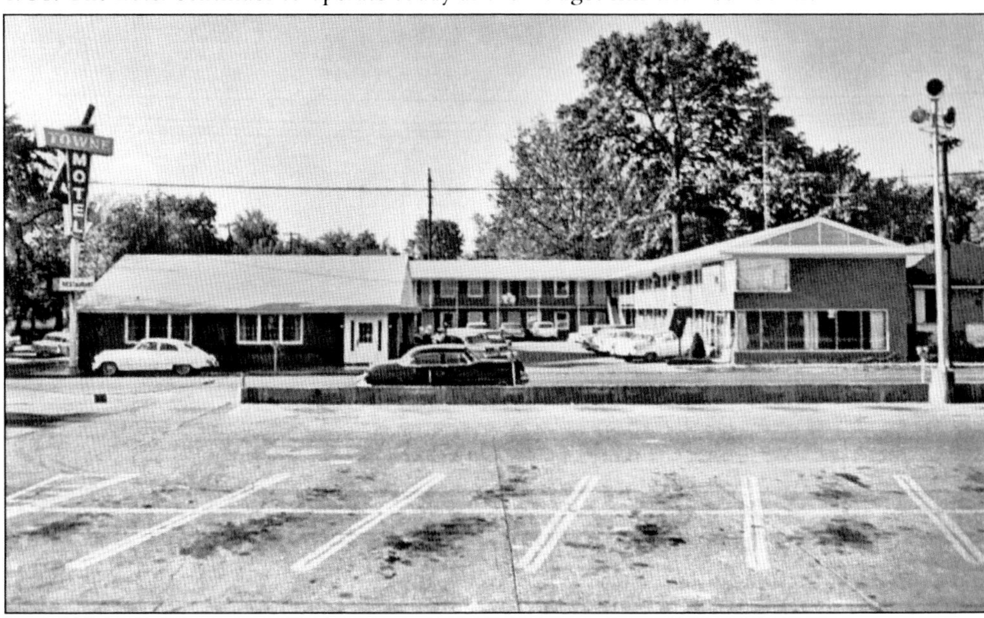

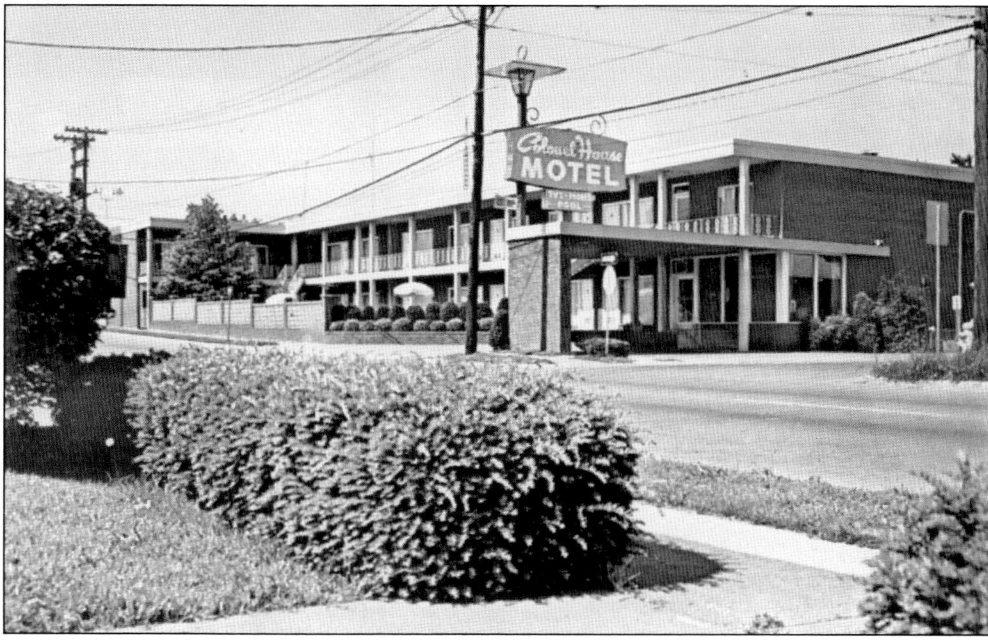


Colonel House Motel opened in 1959 on the northeast corner of Nineteenth and Triplett Streets. The 49-room hotel was designed to attract families, offering a fine swimming pool and televisions and telephones in every room. Triplett Street was a growing commercial strip in the late 1950s and early 1960s, attracting hotels, restaurants, bowling alleys, and numerous retail shops. Like Gabe's famous restaurant located across the street, the Colonel House's roof awning, shown below, overhung the hotel entrance to protect guests dropped off at the door from inclement weather.

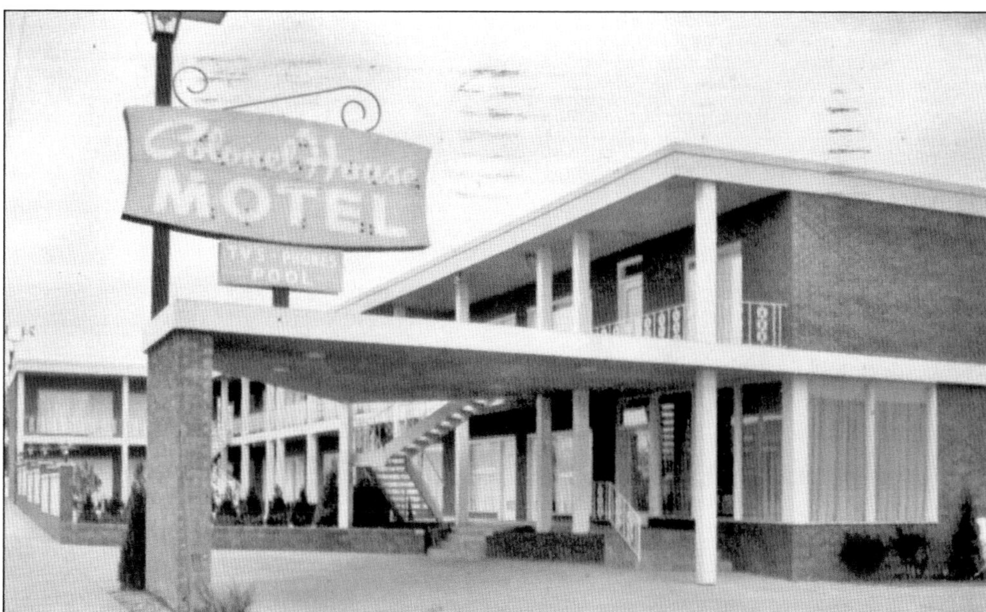

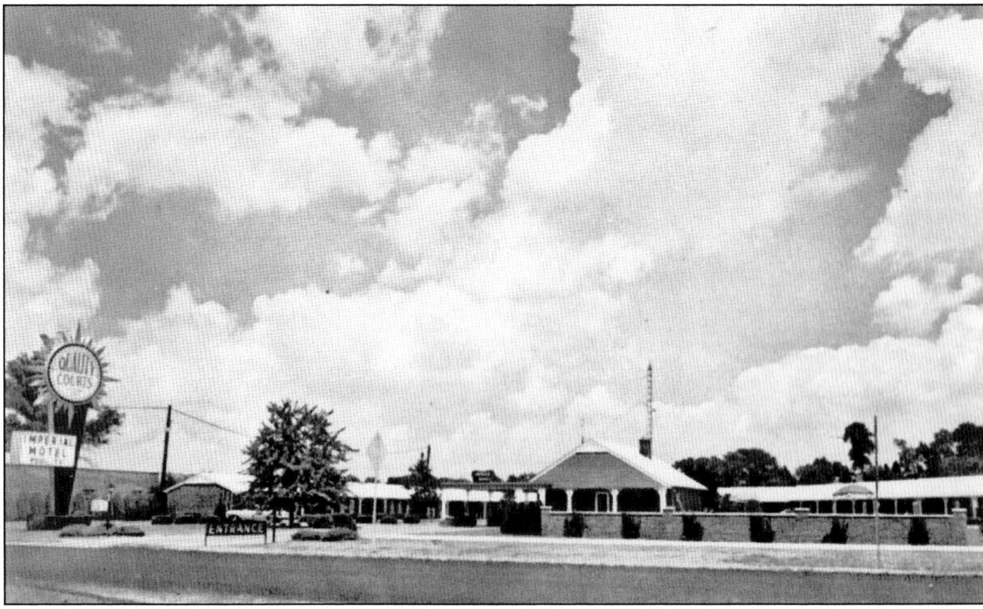


Quality Courts, also known as the Imperial Motel, was located at 2609 New Hartford Road. U.S. Highway 231 divides as it enters Owensboro, with the northbound lane becoming Breckinridge Street and the southbound lane becoming Triplett Street. These were very commercial streets, and several hotels were built on Triplett Street in the 1950s and 1960s. Mr. and Mrs. A. M. Cornell owned Cornell's Restaurant, a popular restaurant on Owensboro's south side. The Cornells built this hotel adjacent to their restaurant. It was razed in the mid-1990s and is now the site of a BB&T bank branch. The postcard below is of Chapman's Cabins, also located on Highway 231, five miles outside Owensboro in the community of Masonville.

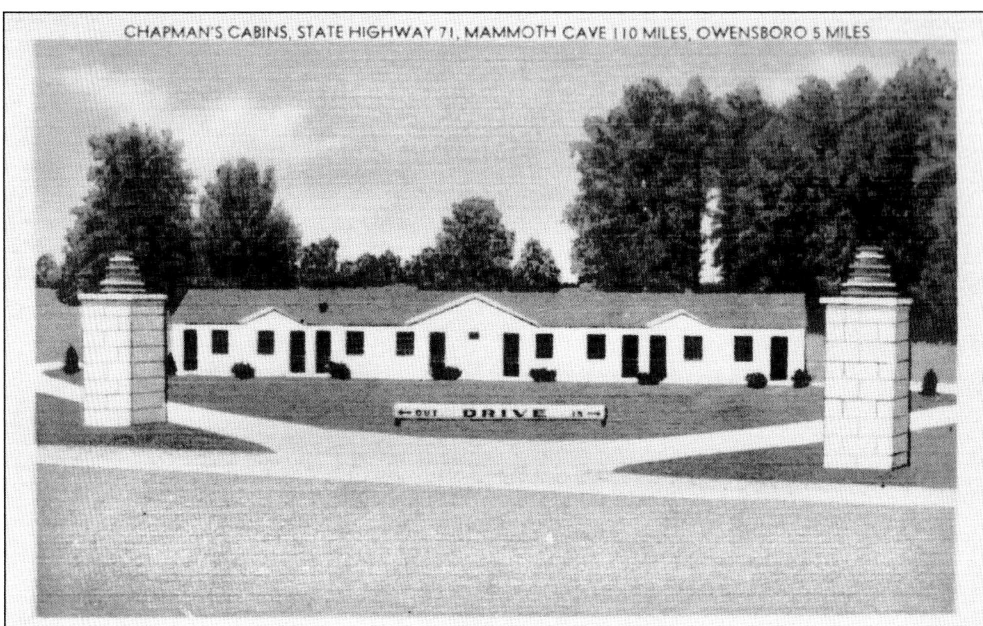

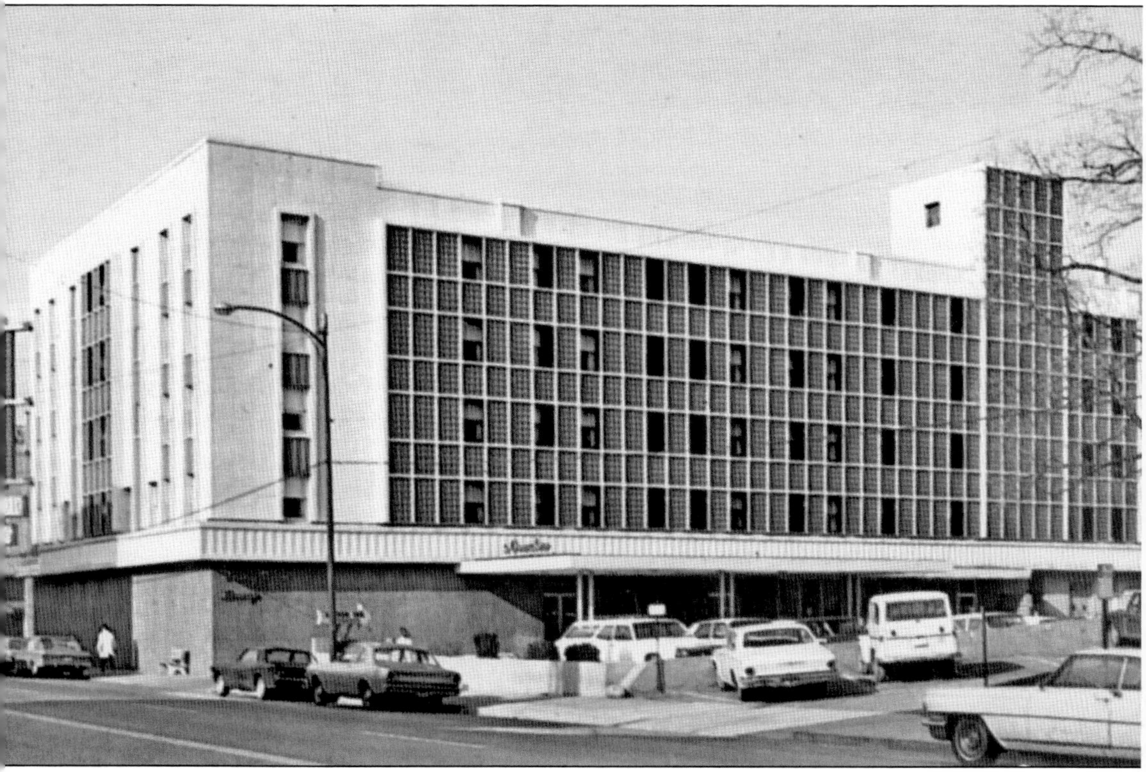

The Hotel Owensboro was built in 1926 with 150 guest rooms on the southeast corner of Fourth and Frederica Streets. In the 1960s, the hotel was remodeled and renamed the Owensboro Motor Inn. The property then housed 119 hotel rooms, a dining room, lounge, and free guest parking. It was razed in 1990 to make room for construction of the Corporate Centre office complex, built in 1991.

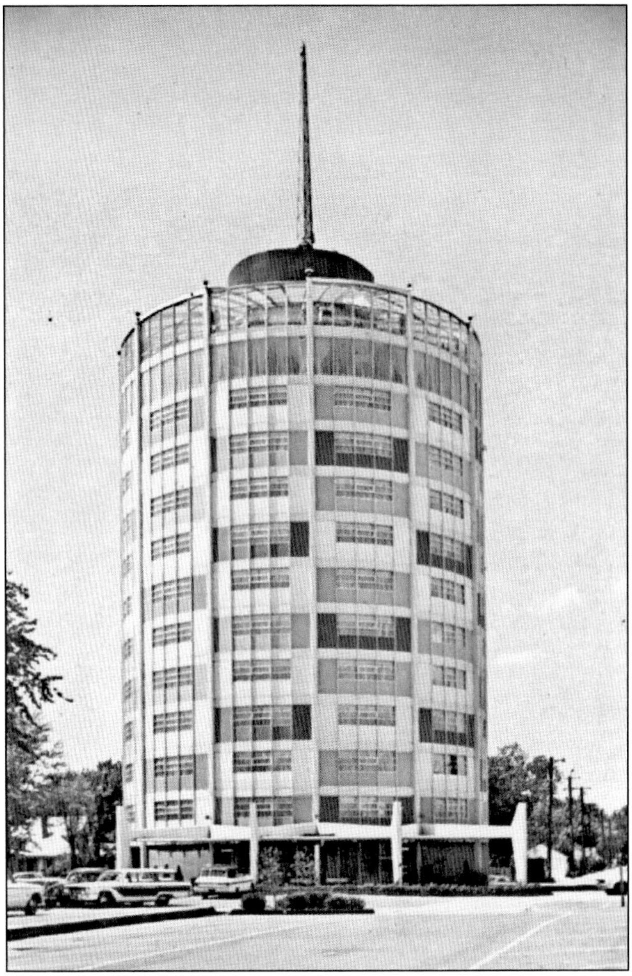

Gabe's Motor Inn was built in 1963 in Gabe's Shopping Center near the northwest corner of Twentieth and Triplett Streets. The 13-story building employs a circular design, providing a premium view from each guest room. The building's stairways and elevators are located in its center, with 12 rooms per floor lining the perimeter. There are 10 housing floors, giving the hotel 120 total guest rooms. The top floor has an enclosed, heated roof garden with a retractable sky roof and pool, as shown in the photograph below. The 12th floor houses a restaurant and lounge with a view overlooking the city. Owensboro architect R. Ben Johnson designed the structure, and it was built by Clark Construction.

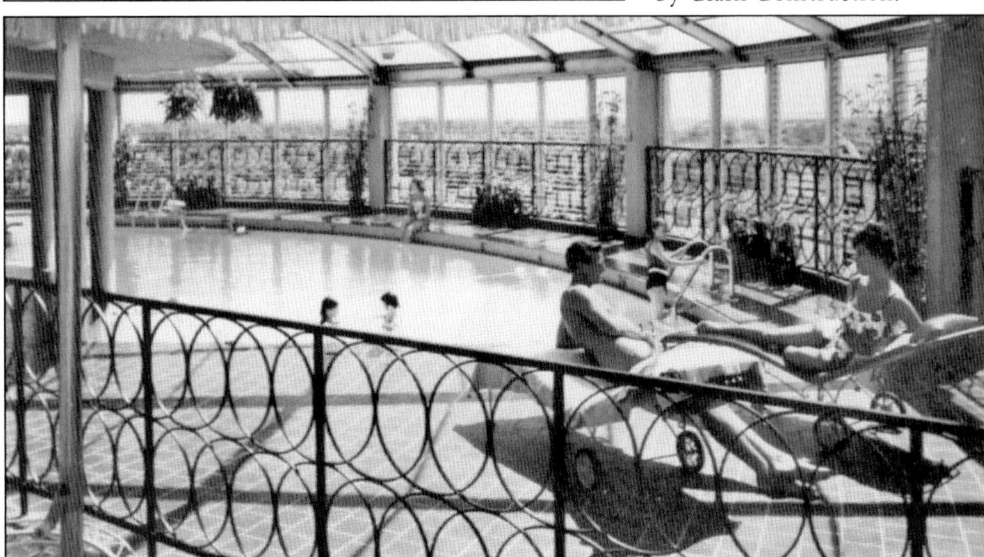

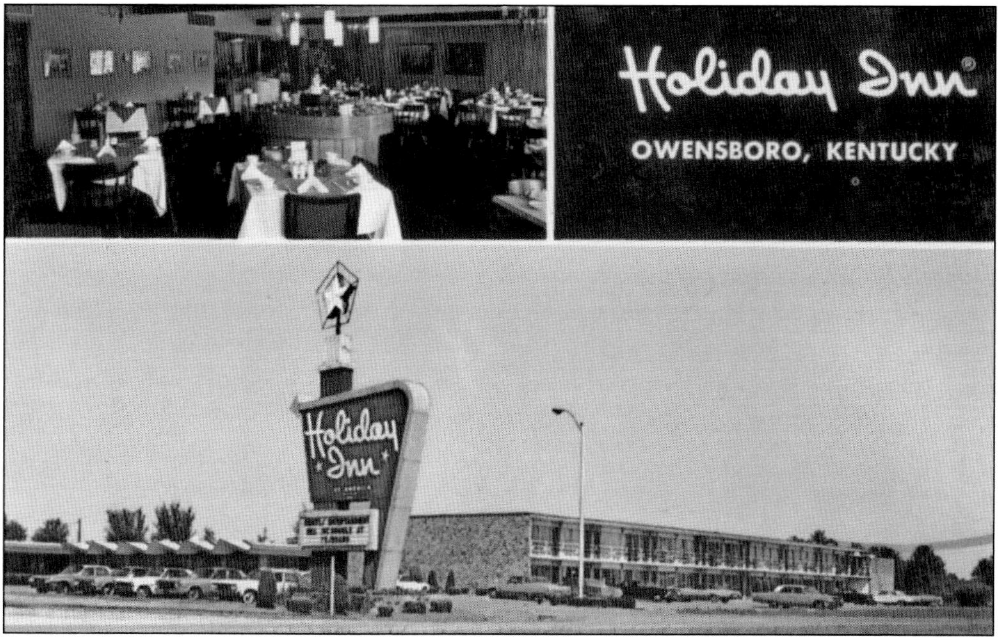


The Holiday Inn hotel opened in 1962 on Highway 60 West near the Carter Road intersection. The postcard above shows views of the hotel's original exterior and restaurant area. Ten years before, the hotel chain was founded in Memphis, Tennessee, to provide consistently high-quality, inexpensive family accommodations for travelers within the United States. Roadside motels of that era offered inconsistent quality standards. The generic postcard below was produced to promote the rapidly growing Holiday Inn hotel chain, which had reached nearly 500 properties nationwide by the time Owensboro added the famous sign to the city's west side. Architect Bob Hitchcock designed a hotel update and building addition in the late 1970s or early 1980s. The hotel with 151 rooms now operates as the Ramada Inn.

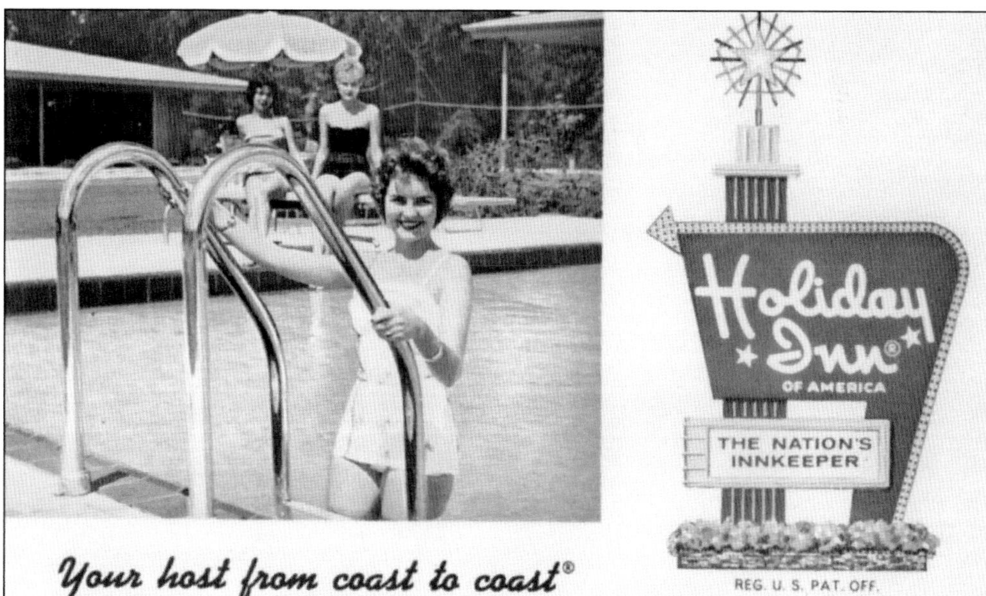

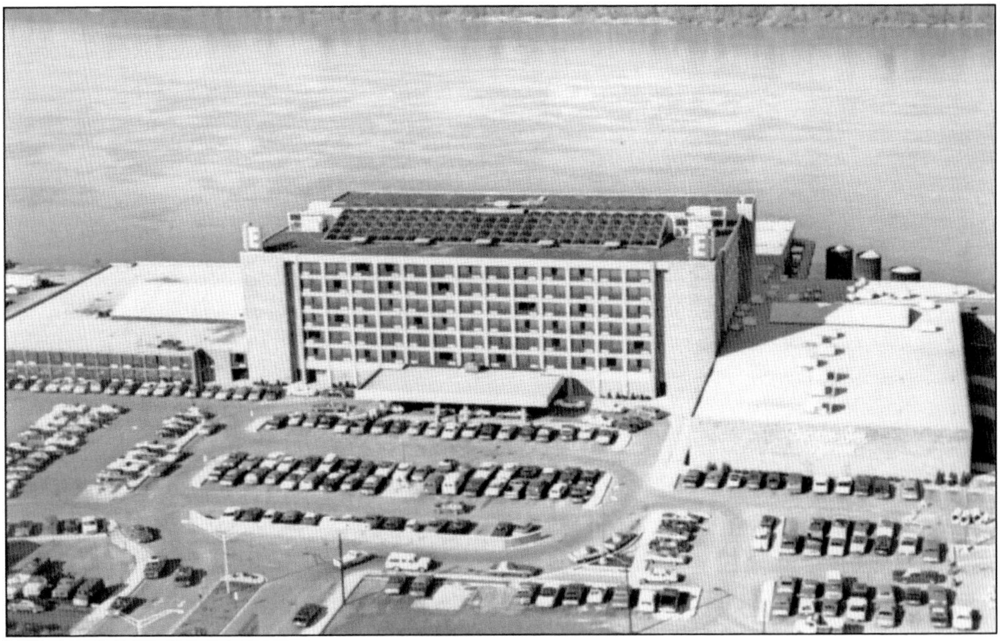

The Owensboro Executive Inn Rivermont opened in October 1977. Indiana Coal Company owner Bob Green originally developed the property as seen in the above photograph with a center seven-story guest tower flanked to the east by a convention center, to the west by the indoor pool and guest room area (pictured below), and to the south by an outdoor pool and Las Vegas–style Showroom Lounge built out over the Ohio River. Originally designed with approximately 350 rooms, the hotel later added wings, growing to eventually offer more than 600 rooms. Boasting the top names in entertainment and more than 100,000 square feet of convention space, this property took the city's tourism to a higher level, attracting millions of guests to Owensboro for over 30 years.

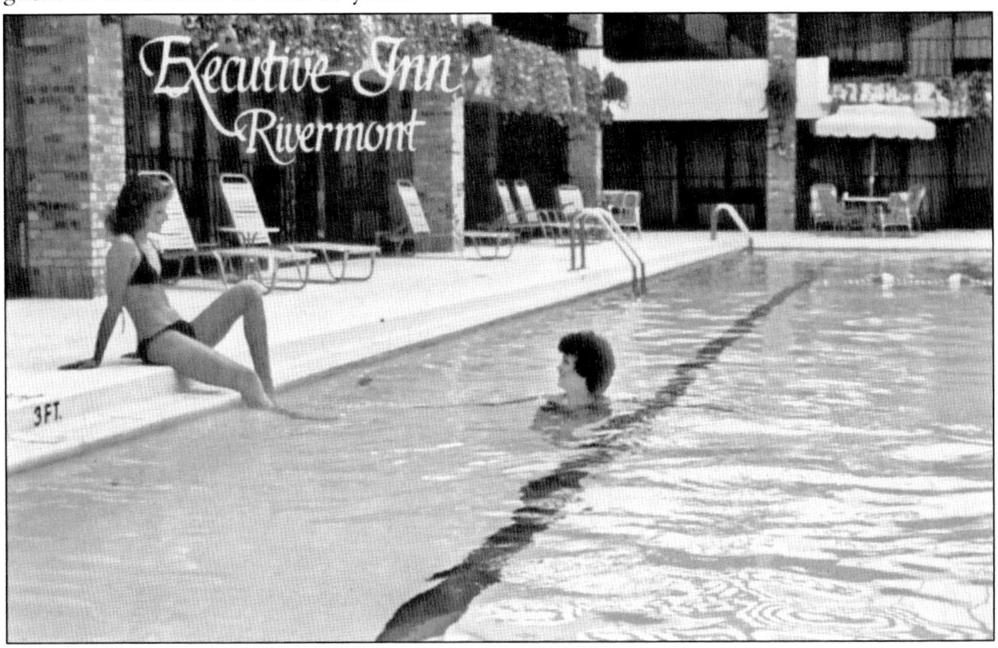

# *Seven*

# PUBLIC PLACES

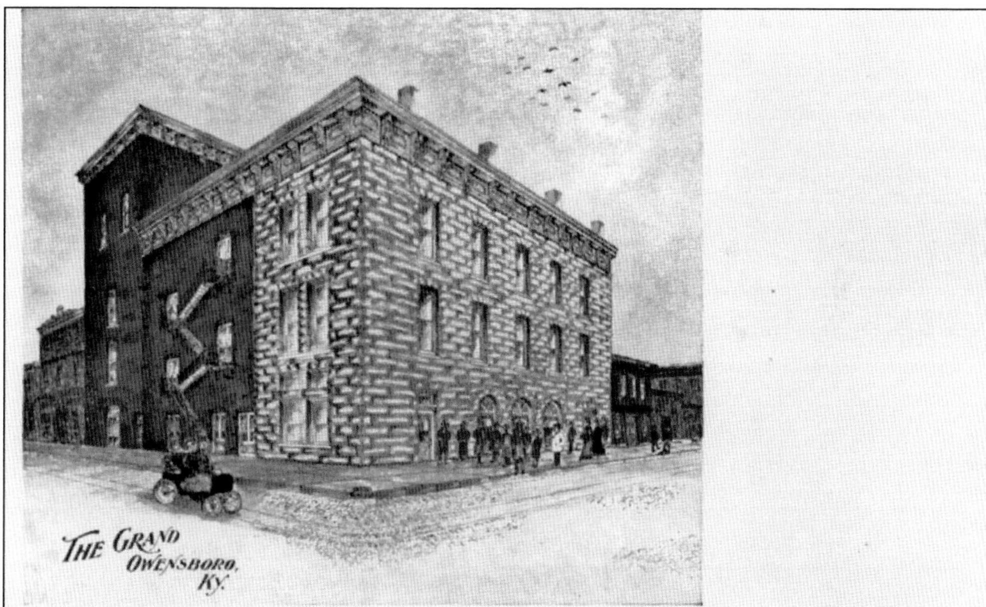


The Grand Theater was located on the southeast corner of First and St. Ann Streets. The 19th-century building shown on the right side of the above postcard faced west toward St. Ann Street. The Grand was actually larger than its current successor, RiverPark Center, offering seating for 1,800 patrons. This showcase theater offered such productions in 1919 as *Fifty Miles from Boston* and *Parsifal*. The building was torn down in 1934 to make way for the construction of the American Legion Building.

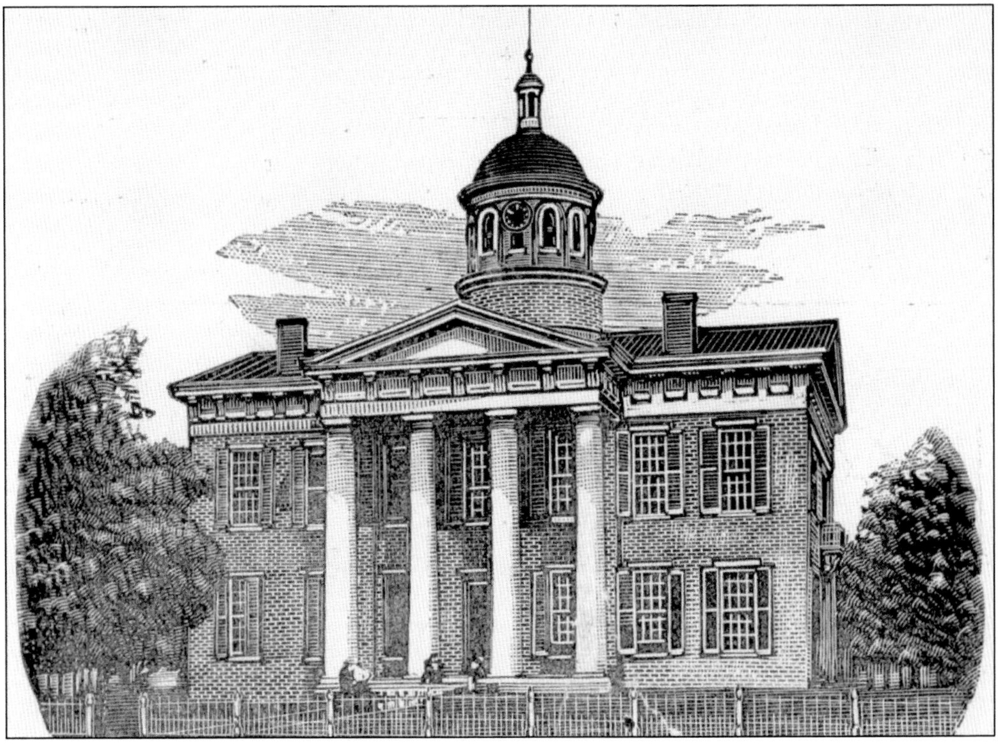

The illustration above is of Daviess County's third courthouse building as it appeared from 1858 to 1865. It was burned toward the end of the Civil War on January 4, 1865, by guerrillas, or Confederate soldiers, because it had been used to quarter Union soldiers. Captain Davidson allowed most records to be moved before the fire was set. It is somewhat ironic, but the footprint of the building remains on the 1885 Sanborn map and scales out at 78 feet by 56 feet. The postcard below shows the fourth Daviess County Courthouse, completed July 6, 1868, and razed in April 1964 after the completion of the present-day building.

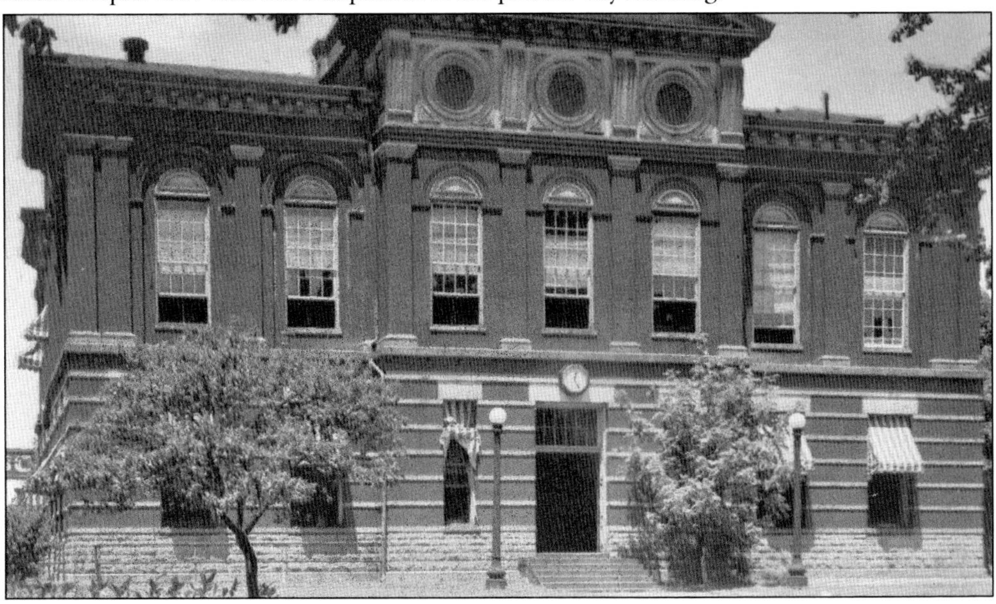

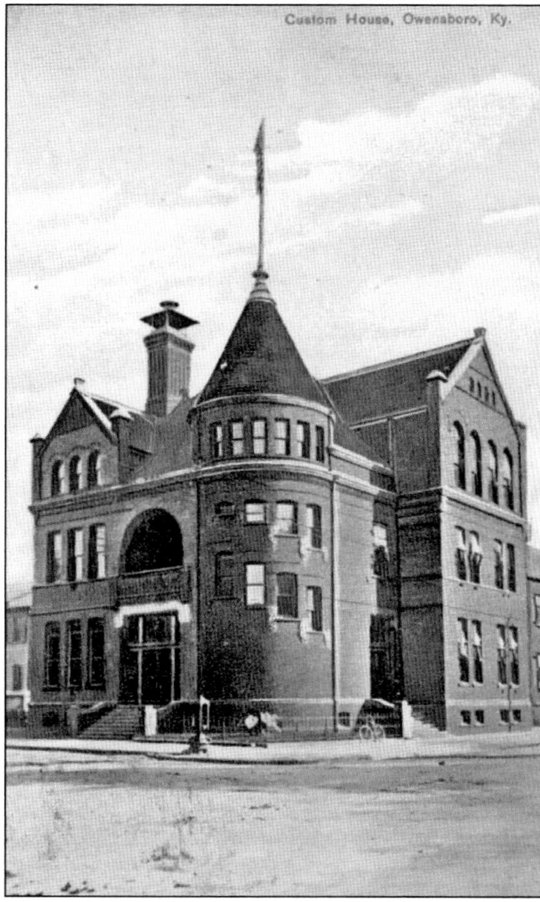


The U.S. Custom House and Post Office facility seen above was built in 1890 on the southeast corner of Third and Allen Streets. The customhouse was the place where duties and other charges were paid and accounted for by the federal government. Until the introduction of the federal income tax, the government relied on the duty taxes collected by the customs service. Later this building served as the home for the *Messenger-Inquirer.* In 1914, Daviess County High School began offering its first classes on the building's third floor. The newspaper moved to its new location in 1968, and this building was razed in February 1969 to create a parking lot for Anderson's Department Store. The customhouse postcard below also shows the Elks Club just south down Allen Street.

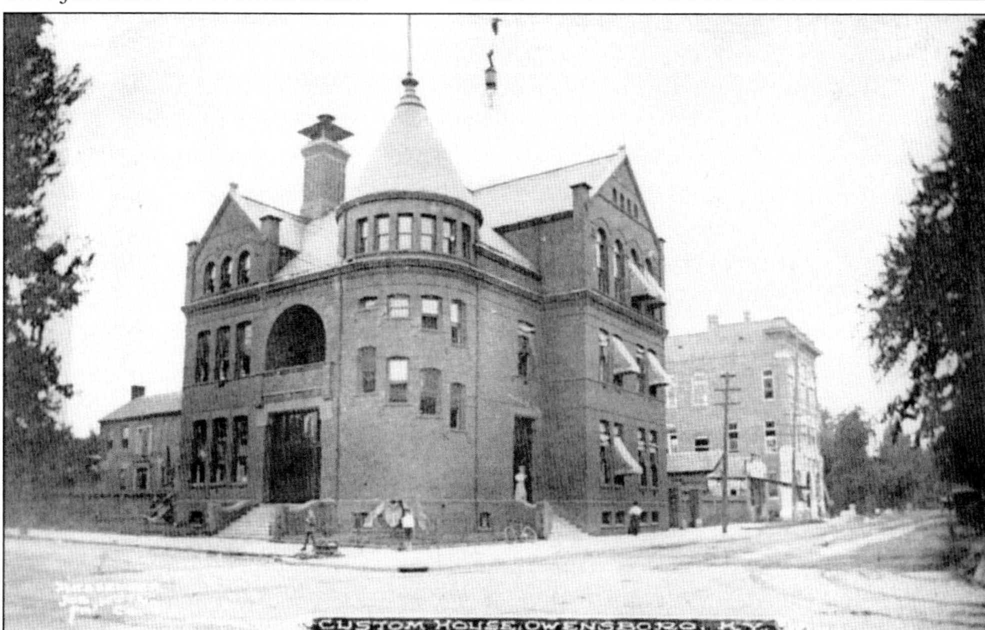

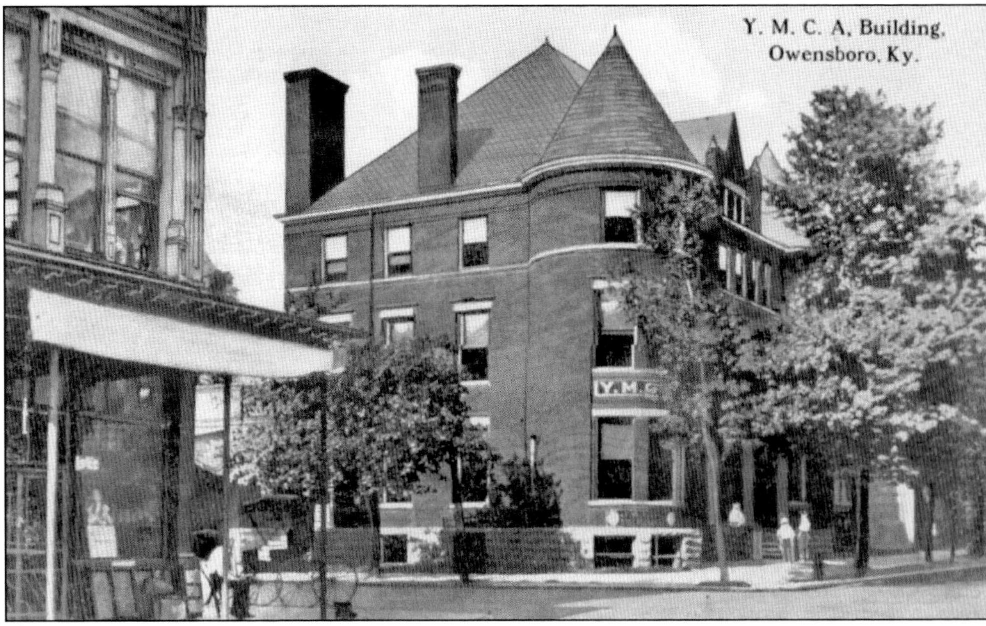


The Young Men's Christian Association, or YMCA, first organized in Owensboro in 1877. After a decline, the group formally reorganized in 1893. The postcard above shows this building constructed for the YMCA in 1898 on the northeast corner of Third and Allen Streets. It featured the only swimming pool in town. The site is now the home of RiverPark Eye Care. The postcard below was published by the Messenger Job Printing Company of Owensboro and provided a message space for handwritten notes on the side. Nothing but the address was to be placed on the back side of this 1¢ postcard.

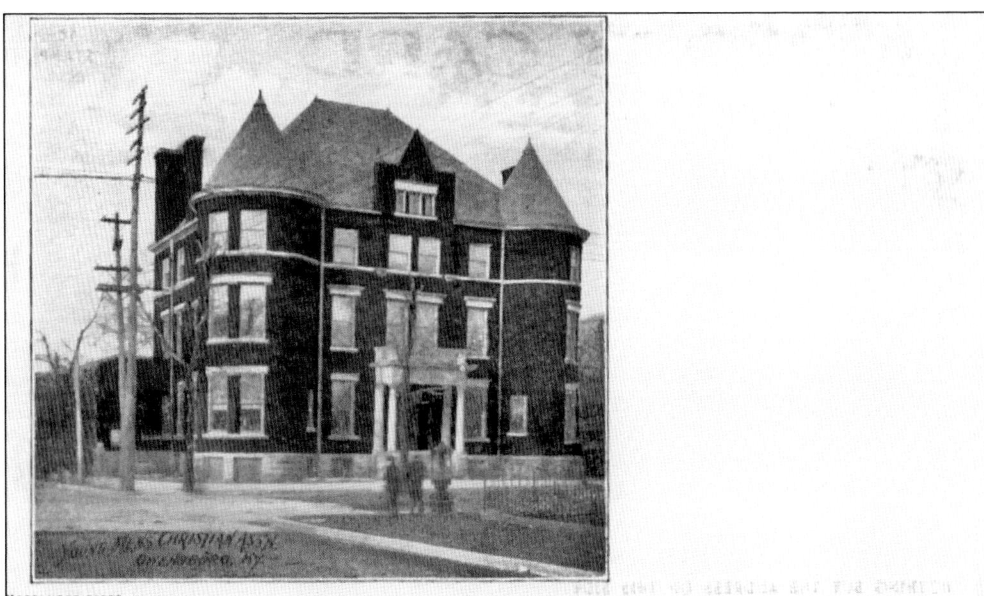

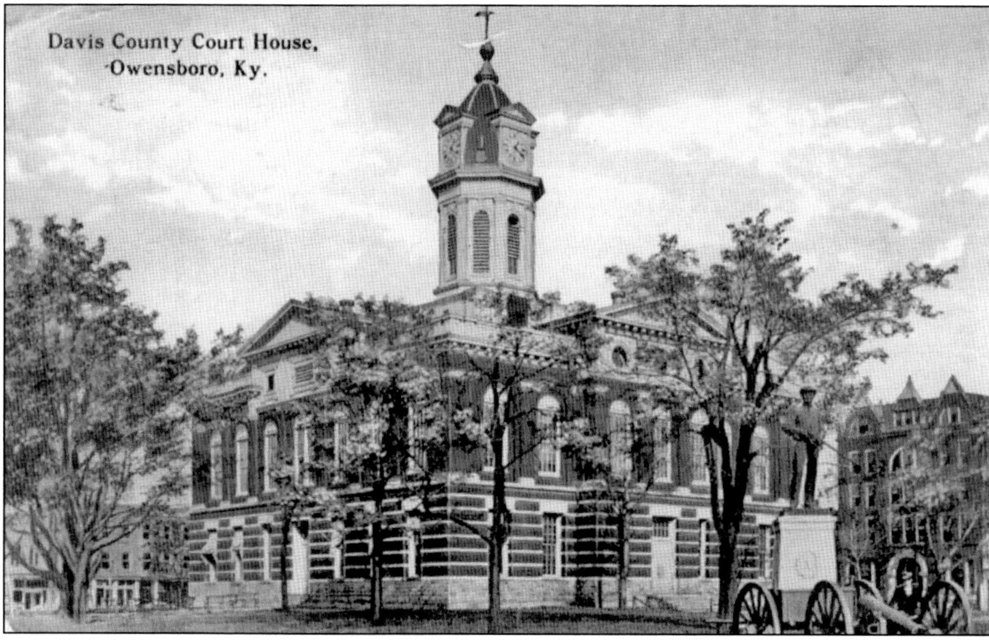


Daviess County's fourth courthouse was completed on July 6, 1868. Although the postcard above misspells the county's name, it compensates by showing the full beauty of this building with its projecting clock tower, large expanse of green space, Confederate memorial statue, and cannon. The county added the clock tower at an additional expense of $200. Its 1,200-pound bell could be heard for miles and served as the only timepiece for many city and county residents. Records indicate the City of Owensboro paid to have the clock repaired in the 1880s. The large bell tower was removed sometime after World War I, and the community donated the cannon to the World War II scrap metal drive. The postcard below shows a later view of the building with the domed roof structure.

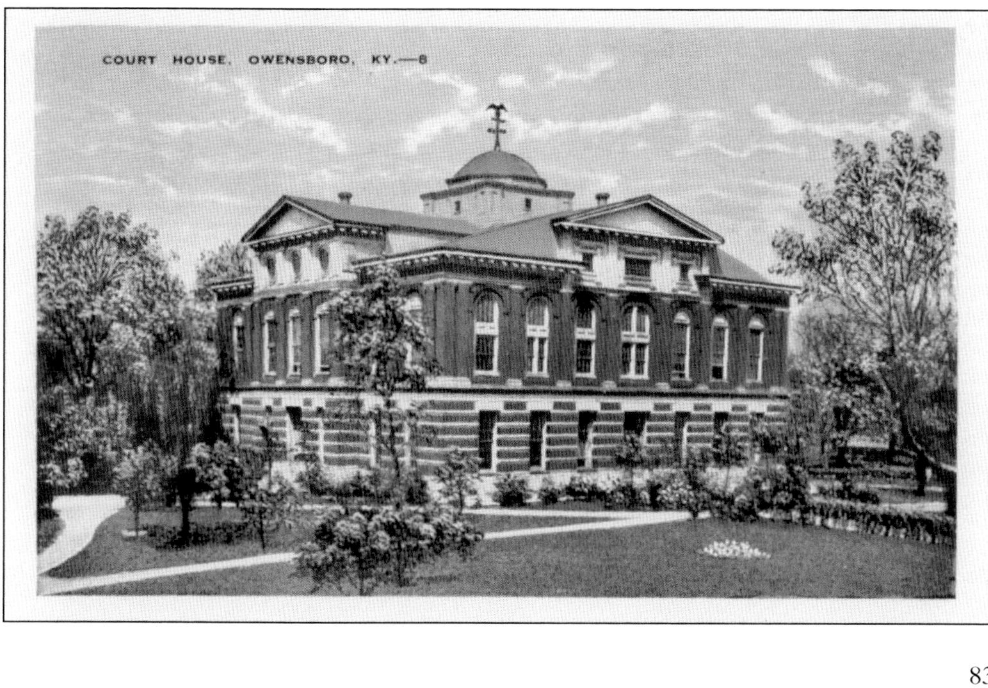

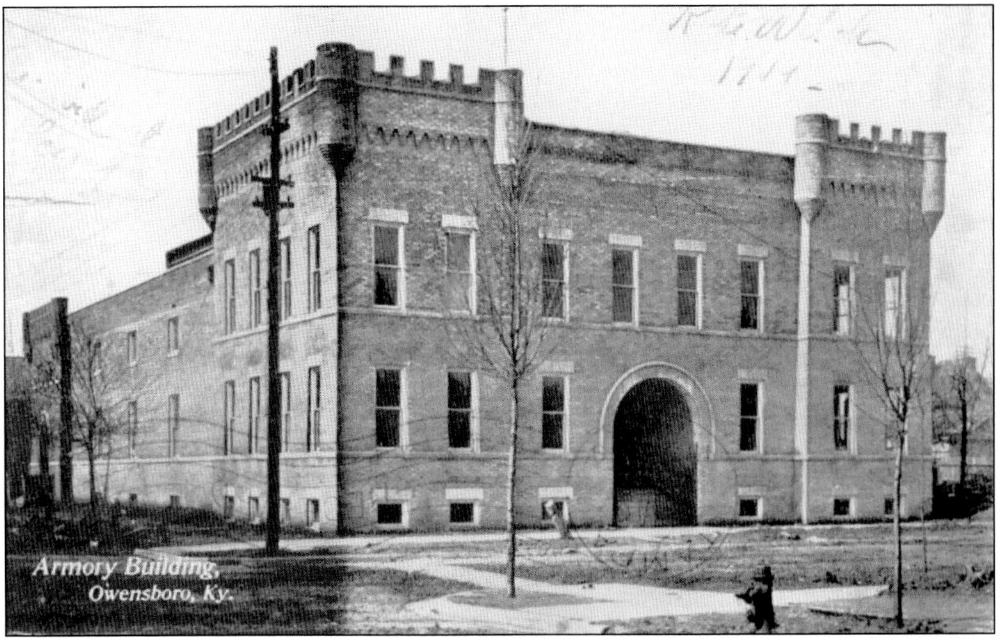


The earliest postcard of the Owensboro Armory is postmarked 1909. The building was located on the northwest corner of Third and Cedar Streets, now known as Executive Boulevard. In the 1920s, this building was the home of Daviess County High School and later Owensboro Ice Cream and Dairy Products. Velvet Milk Company later occupied this building in the 1950s.

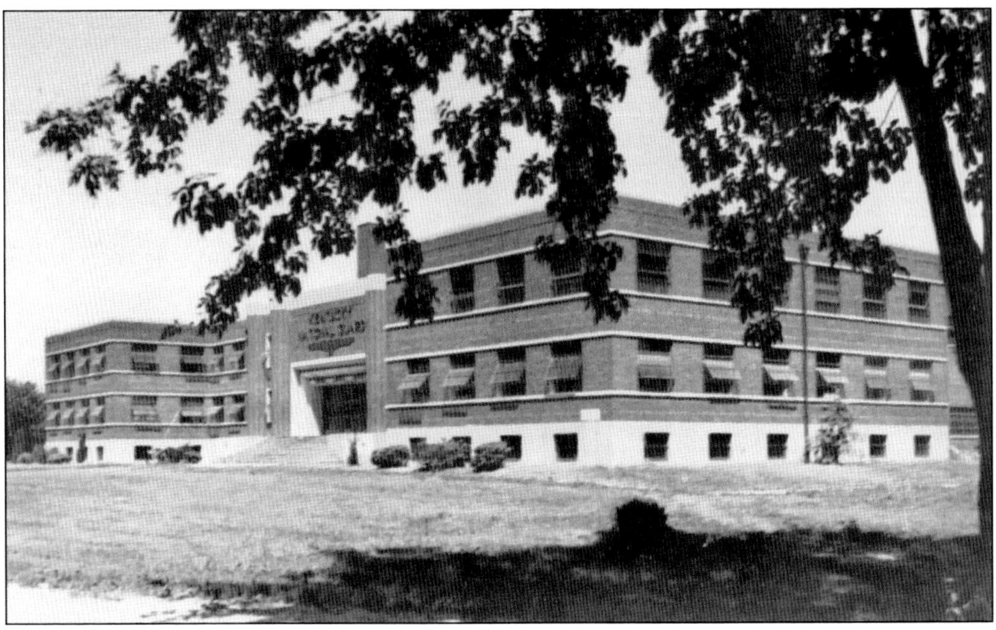

The Kentucky State Armory was later located at 1501 Parrish Avenue in 1947. The building may best be classified as an International design. The corbelled main entry is recessed at the symmetrically designed facade. Twin brick engaged columns rising from a stairway and crowned by a symbolic thunderbird medallion flank the entry.

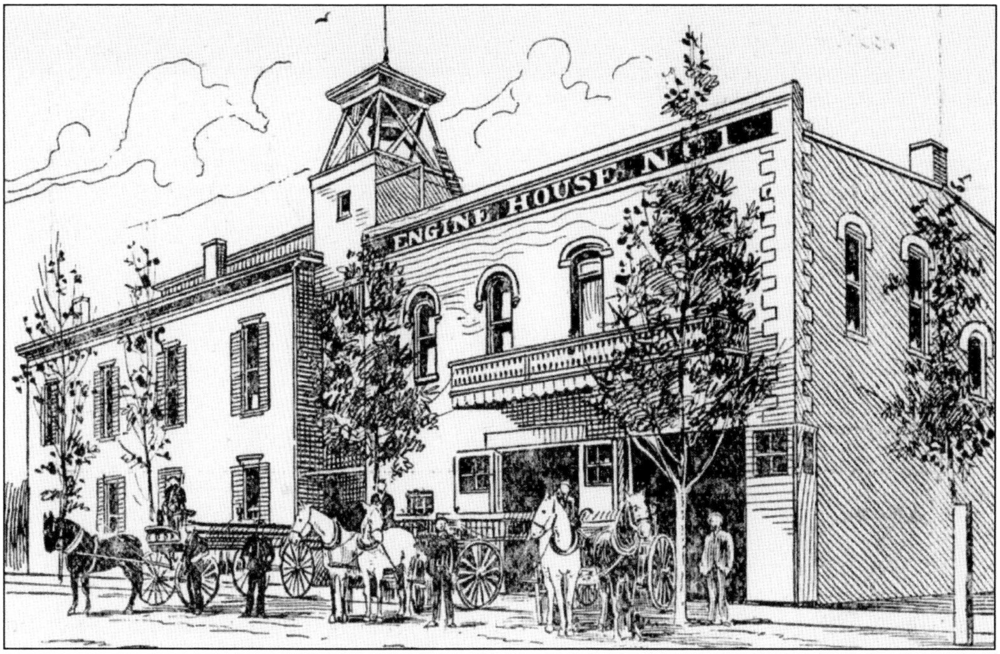


This 1892 illustration depicts one of the earliest images of Owensboro's city hall and the Fire House No. 1 located on the northwest corner of Fourth and St. Ann Streets. Built in 1862 as an all-girls private school known as Bransford's Institute, the building was later purchased by the city for $10,000 after public schools were established. Chartered in 1866, the Owensboro Fire Department was manned by volunteers until 1901.

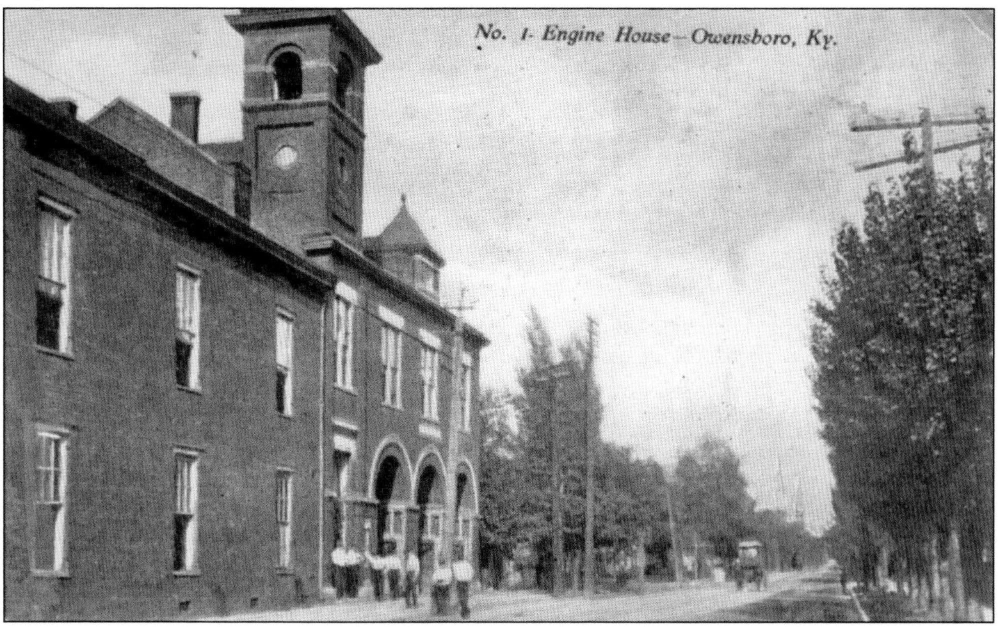


This real-photo postcard looks eastward up Fourth Street showing the same building, but by 1898, the facade of Engine House No. 1 had been changed and the hose tower extended upward. The building served two terms as city hall until a new city hall building was completed in 1973 and this structure was demolished. It is currently the site of Old National Bank's parking lot.

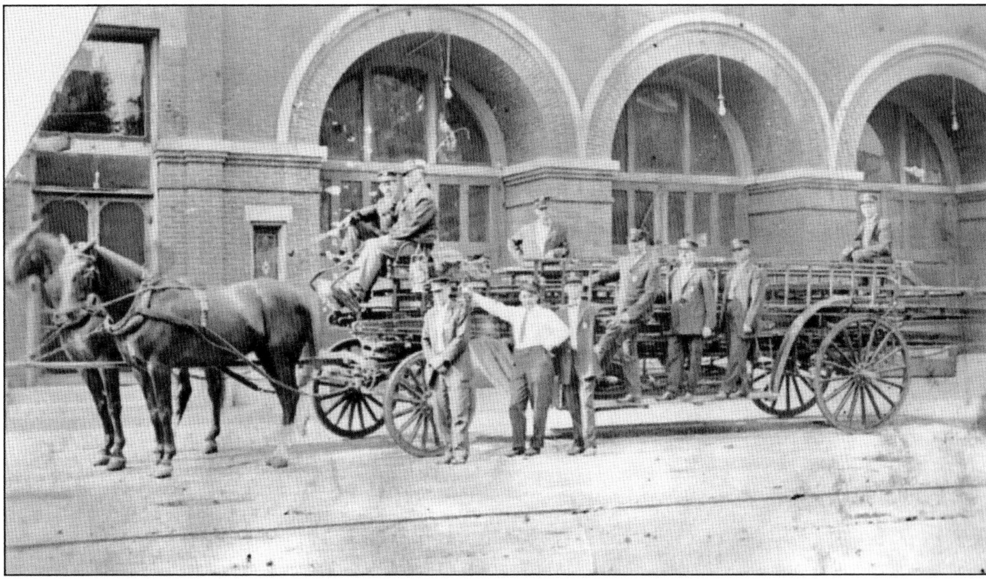

The real-photo postcard above shows a close-up view of the early horse-drawn firefighting equipment used at Engine House No. 1 around 1910. The large arched openings in the background served as the main service-vehicle exits during emergencies. The big all-brick recessed barrel vaults within each opening served to protect the south-facing door systems (shown above) made entirely of wood and glass. The real-photo postcard below shows the early chemical engine units used in firefighting during that same era.

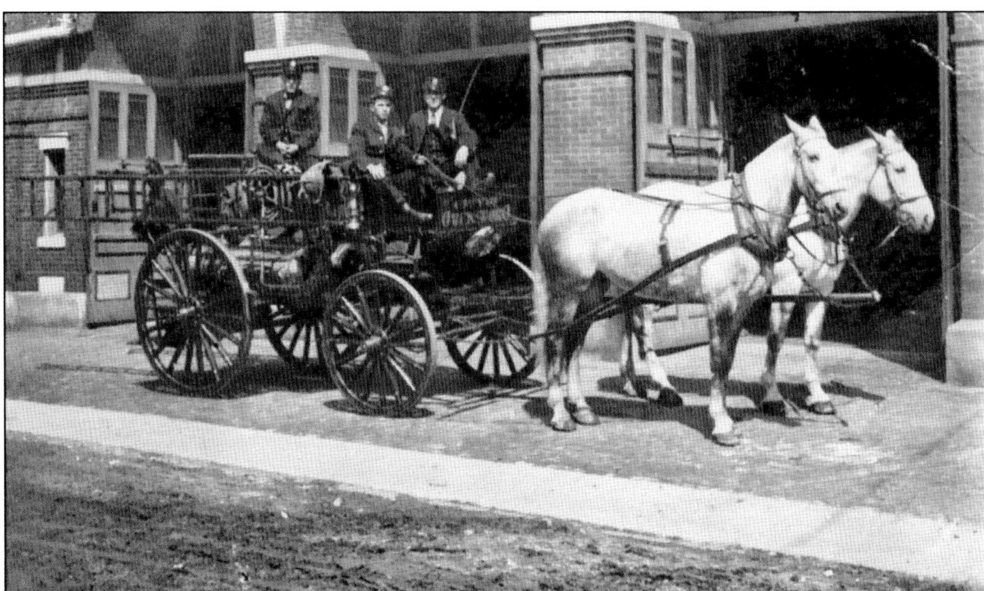

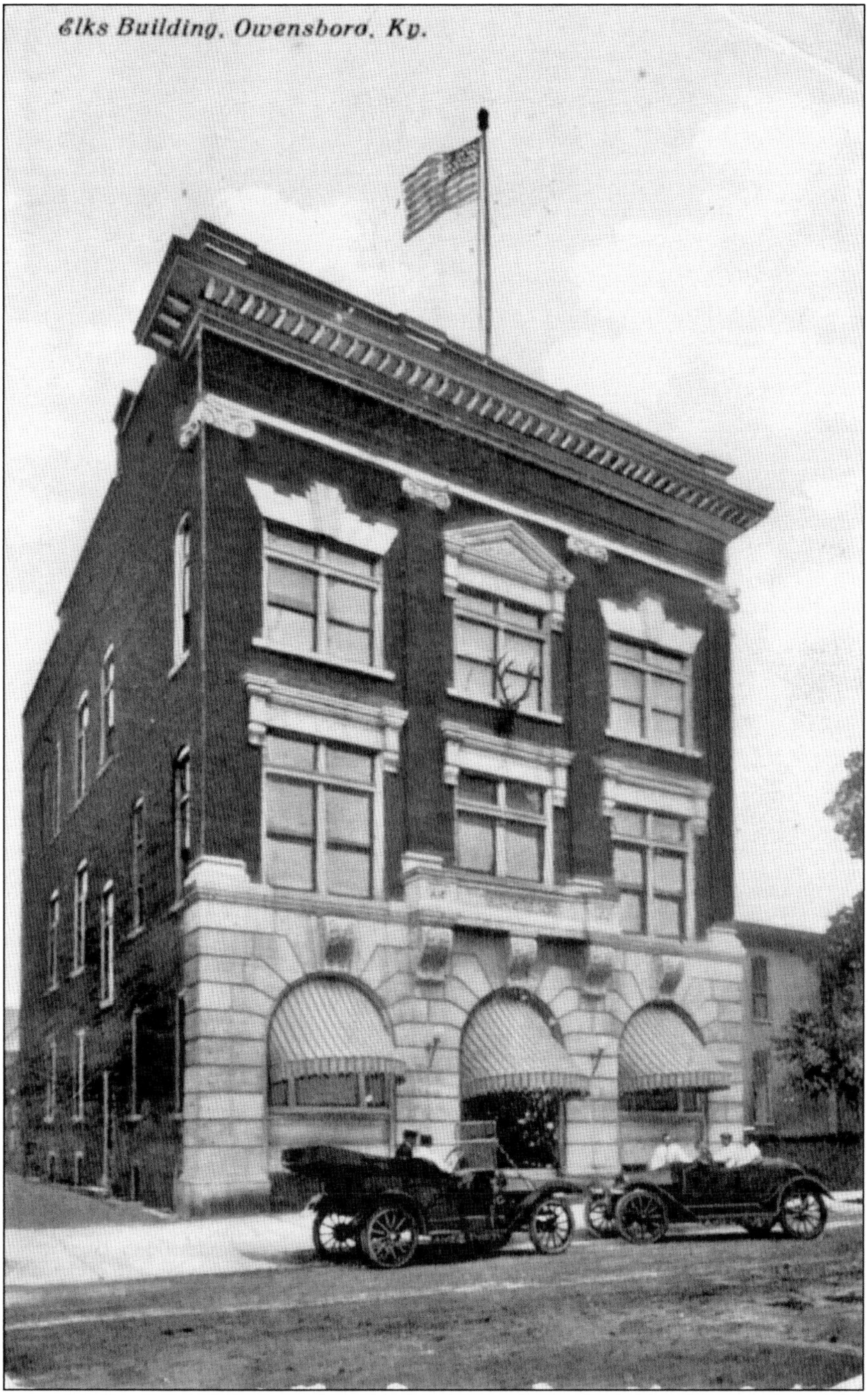


The Elks Club was located at 321 Allen Street. Constructed in 1906, the Benevolent and Protective Order of the Elks served as a local charitable lodge. The building shown in this postcard was razed in 1973 to make room for the construction of the current city hall. The alley visible on the club's left side is still in use. Note the elk's head mounted on the facade of the building.

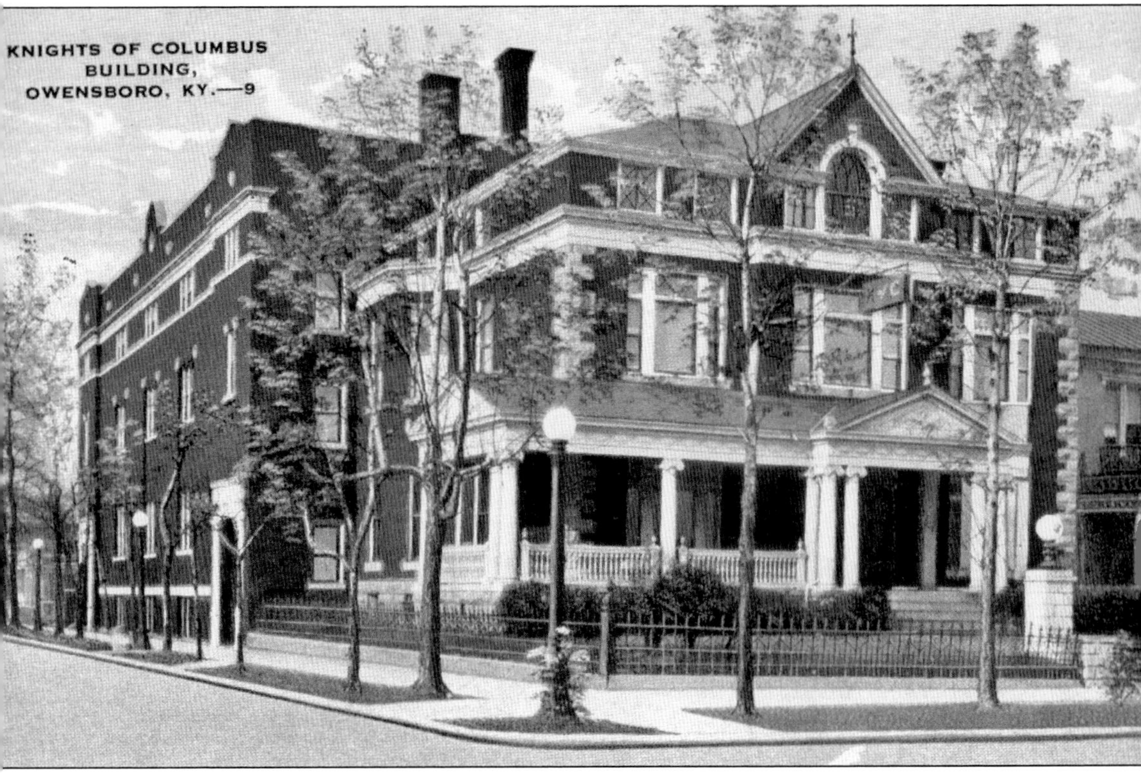


The Knights of Columbus Building was located at the northwest corner of Seventh and Frederica Streets. The Roman Catholic organization was established in 1903 and reached a membership of nearly 600 under the Owensboro Council No. 817. In 1922, the council purchased additional property, renovated the existing building, and constructed a rear addition. The property was purchased from the late C. W. Blansford. Note the streetlight and the lighted entry post leading to another beautiful residence on Frederica Street. Western Kentucky Gas later built its corporate office building on this site. That building is now part of Brescia University.

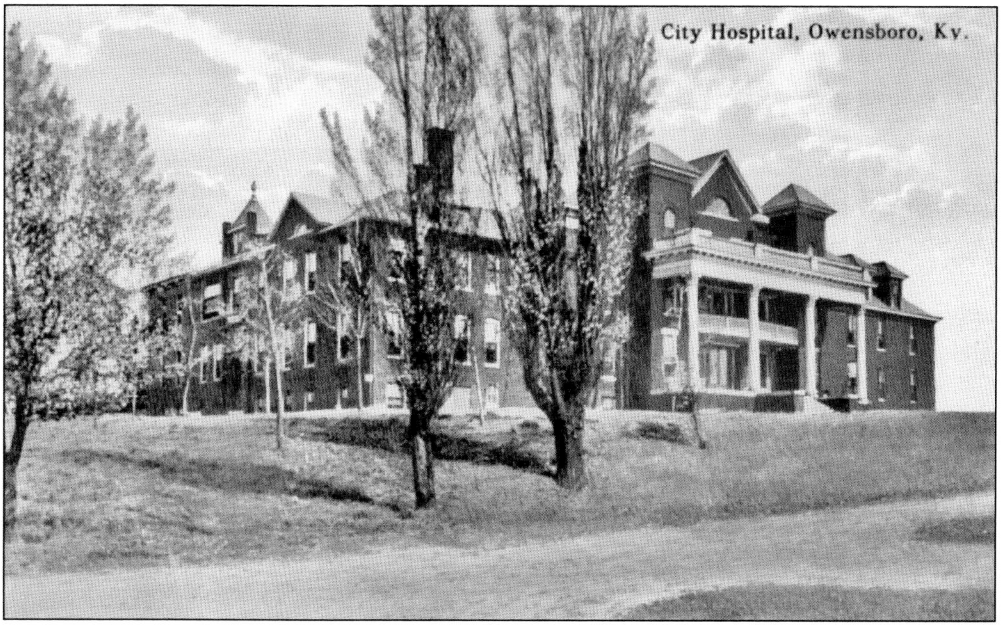


This postcard, postmarked 1916, shows one of the earliest City Hospital views. In 1898, Owensboro's first public health care organization was chartered, and construction began on a three-story, 46-room hospital facility.

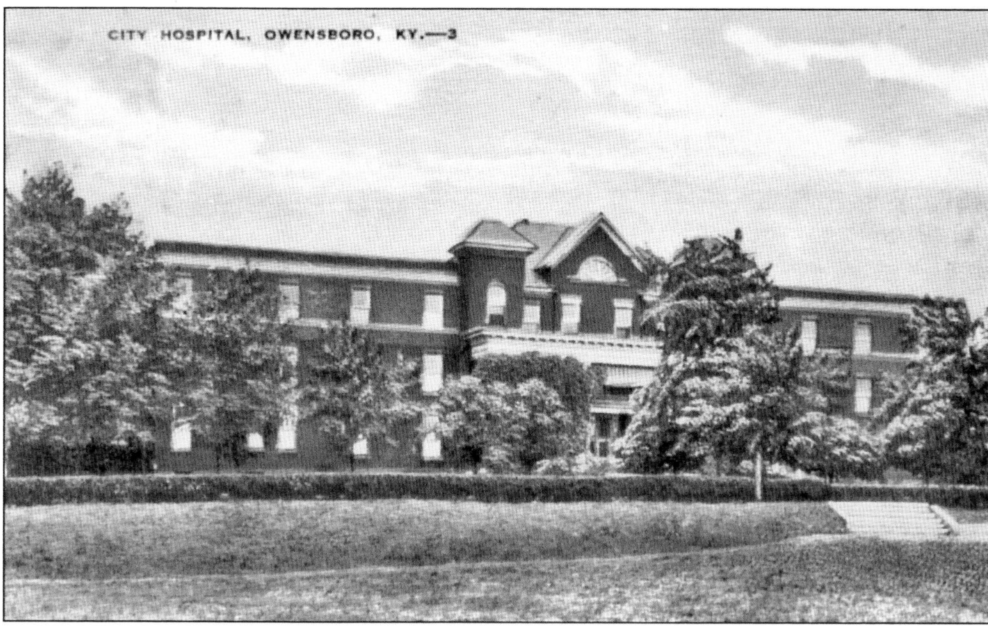


This postcard's view of the old City Hospital is slightly newer, judging by the mature landscaping. The 1898 building faced west and was located on the southeast corner of Tenth and Center Streets. Twenty-three additional rooms were added in 1908 to meet the city's growing demand.

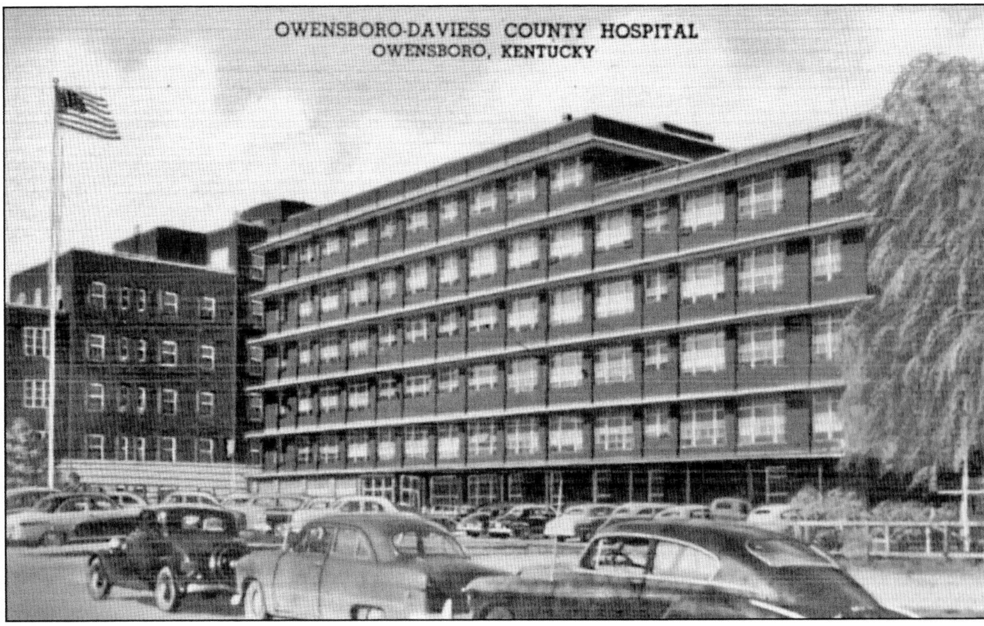


This postcard's 1941 view shows a new seven-story hospital wing addition. This project doubled the hospital's capacity to 125 beds and was made possible by a $125,498 construction grant through the federal government's Works Progress Administration. By this time, the facility had become known as the Owensboro–Daviess County Hospital.

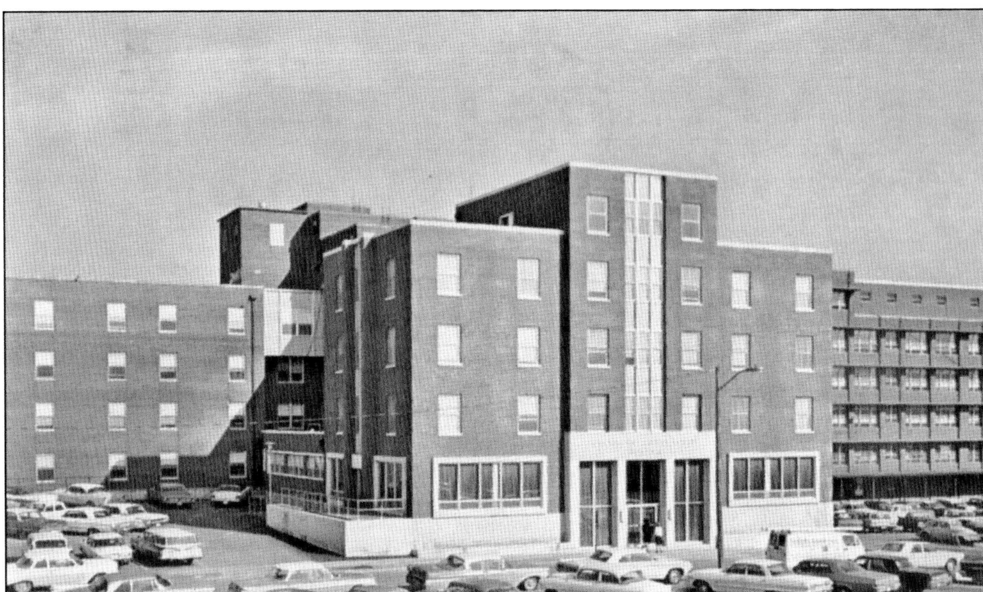

The 1960s postcard above is of the Owensboro–Daviess County Hospital's main entrance. The facility during this era offered 350 beds and faced west towards Triplett Street.

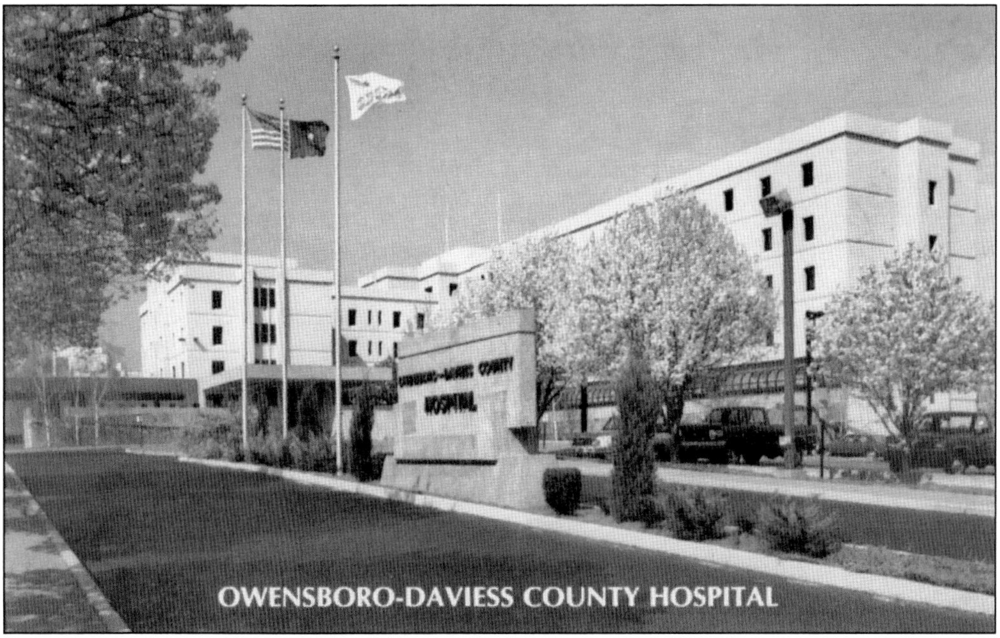


This 1980s Owensboro–Daviess County Hospital (ODCH) postcard shows a facility continuing to grow in order to meet the community's health care needs. In 1995, the publicly owned ODCH merged with the privately owned Owensboro Mercy Hospital to form Owensboro Medical Health Systems (OMHS). Primarily to address the area's aging population, OMHS announced in 2006 a 10-year plan to build a new 1-million-square-foot, $500-million hospital.

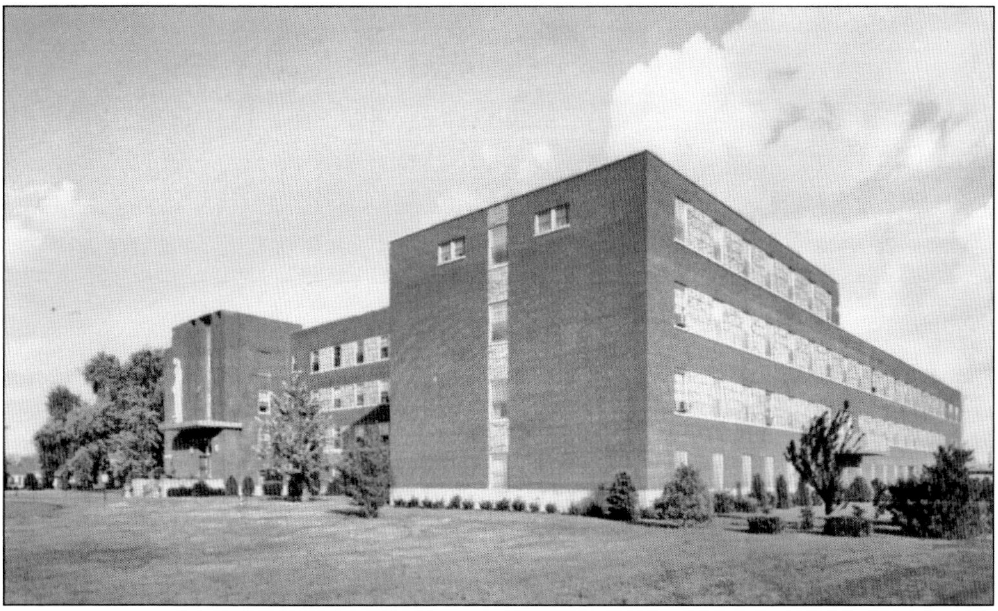

This is a postcard of Our Lady of Mercy Hospital, which was built in 1948 at 1006 Ford Avenue. The four-story, 80-bed facility was designed by Louisville architects Thomas J. Nolan and Sons and constructed by A. G. Schneider and Company for $370,000. When Owensboro's two hospitals merged in 1995, this building was abandoned and demolished to make room for construction of the Owensboro Medical Health System HealthPark.

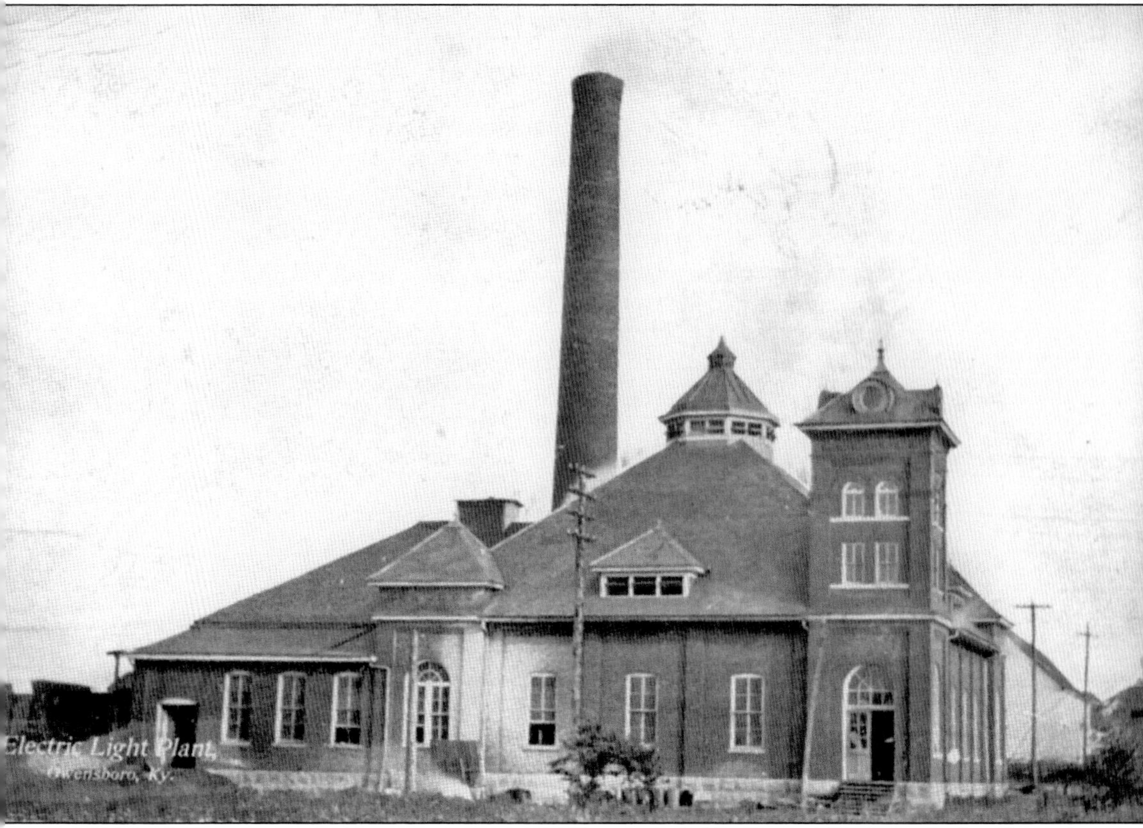


The Electric Light Plant pictured above was located on a five-acre site on the southeast corner of Daviess and Fourteenth Streets, now occupied by Thriftway Home Center. Architect Albert Killian designed the power plant, later known as Owensboro Municipal Utilities, which the City of Owensboro built for $44,500 in 1901 to meet the community's energy needs. From the very start, runaway consumer demand required constant power plant expansion, totaling some 15 building and machinery additions. In 1938, the city acquired a new site on Highway 60 East to build a new $27-million facility that could provide both power and water utility service from one location. It was named for the plant superintendent, Elmer Smith.

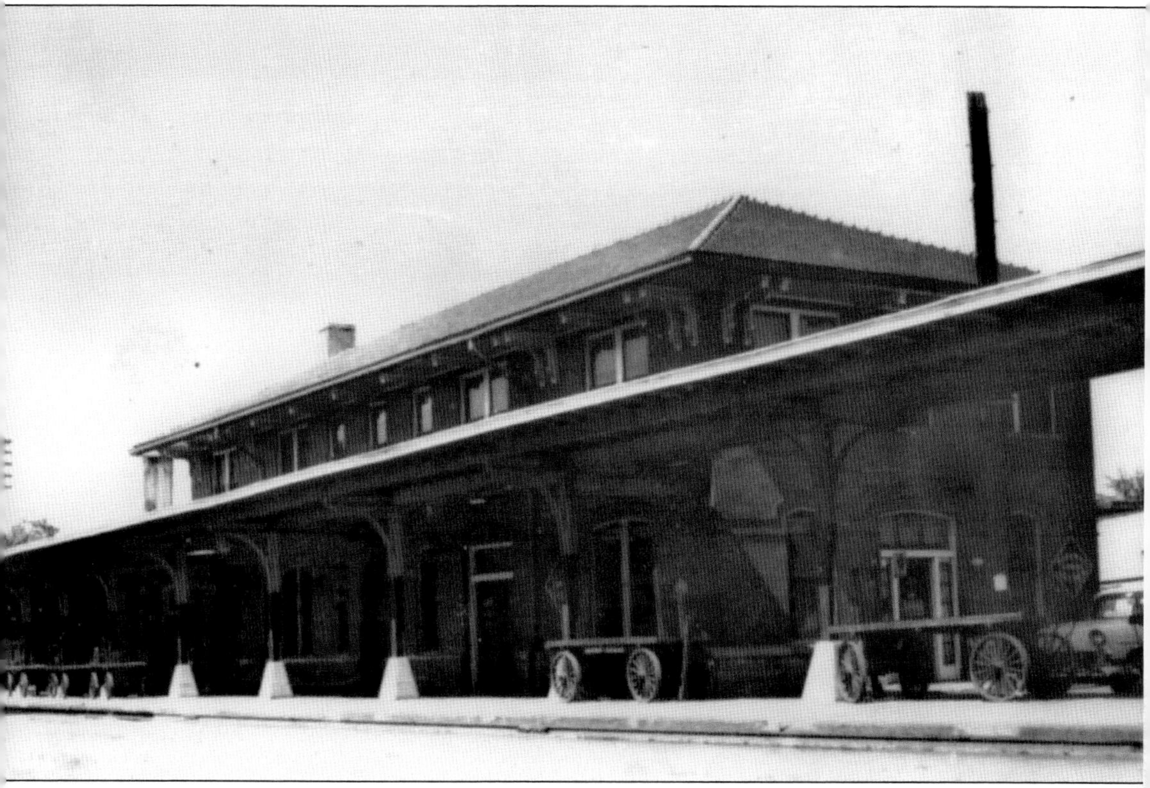

Above is a 1956 real-photo postcard of Union Station taken from the east end and showing the area where freight and baggage were received. The depot's second floor served as the administrative office and support services for the Louisville and Nashville (L&N) Railroad. For many years, Union Station has been a work in progress. In 1931, a two-story addition was constructed. The function of the building changed in 1958, when passenger service ceased at Owensboro. The building went through various hands before developer David Hocker and Associates renovated the building in 1982. More changes came in 1988, when Owensboro general contractor Lanham Brothers Contractors, Inc., built the two-story office and atrium addition on the complex's east end. The project was designed by architect James O. Bethel.

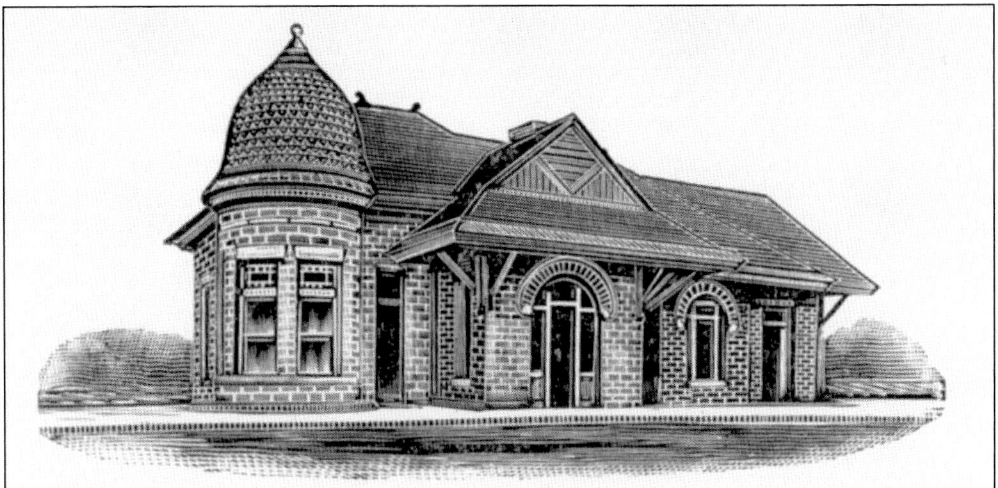

NEW O. & N. PASSENGER DEPOT.

The Owensboro and Nashville Railroad Passenger Depot, illustrated above, was located in the area of the present-day Messenger-Inquirer Building at 1401 Frederica Street. The 1903 photograph below shows a view of the depot building's back or north side. The building pictured in the background to the right is the Owensboro Female College at the present-day Owensboro Vocational Technical School at 1501 Frederica Street. The railroad opened in 1872 as the Owensboro and Russellville (O&R) and eventually evolved into the Owensboro and Nashville (O&N). Passenger service on the O&N line stopped on February 5, 1941.

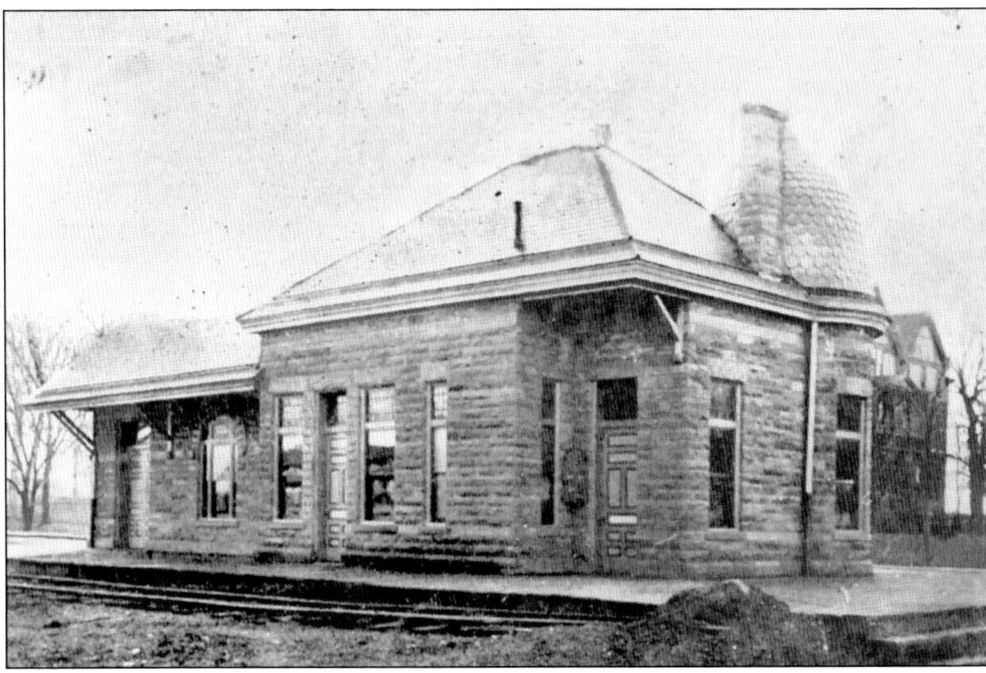

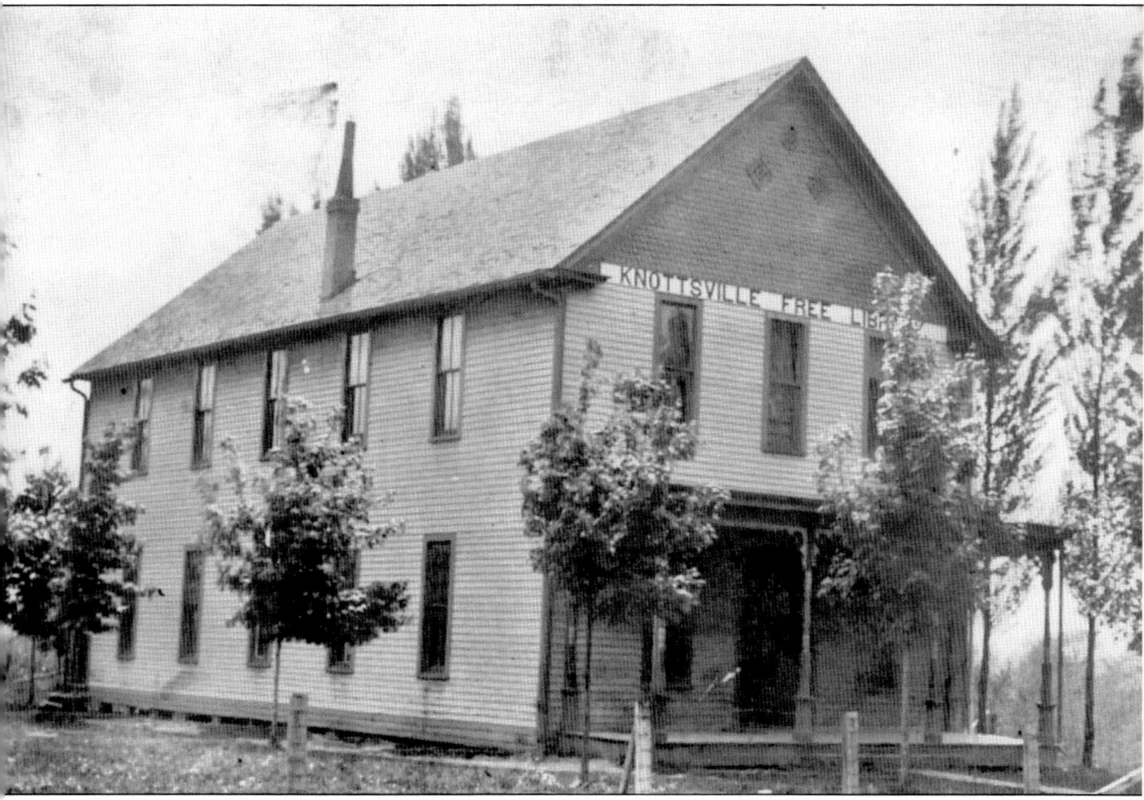


The early real-photo postcard above postmarked 1910 is of the Knottsville Free Library. St. William's Catholic Church of Knottsville established a school with the first circulating library in Daviess County. Beginning in 1895, patrons paying an annual fee of 50¢ could have access to the 1,000-volume library 20 years before the Owensboro Public Library was established. This school and library were destroyed by fire in 1926.

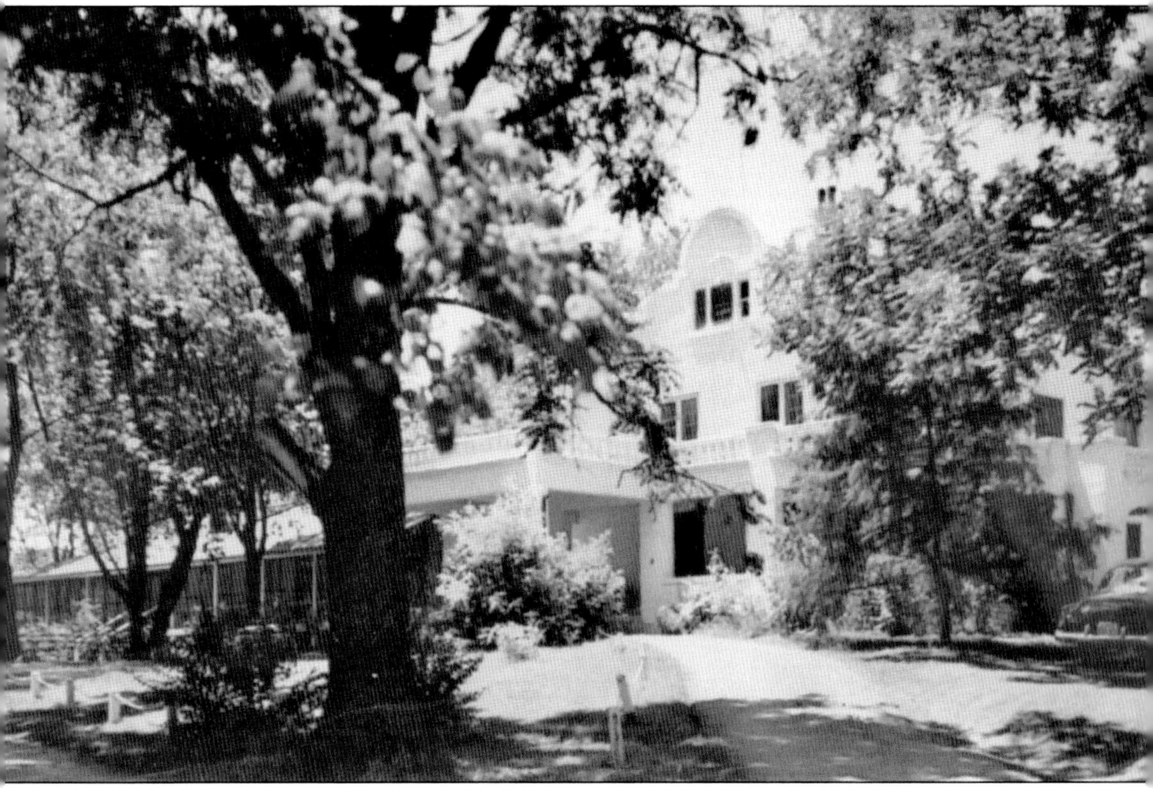

The Owensboro Country Club was incorporated in 1919. The postcard above is an early view of the previous Spanish-Revival clubhouse.

# *Eight*

# PEOPLE

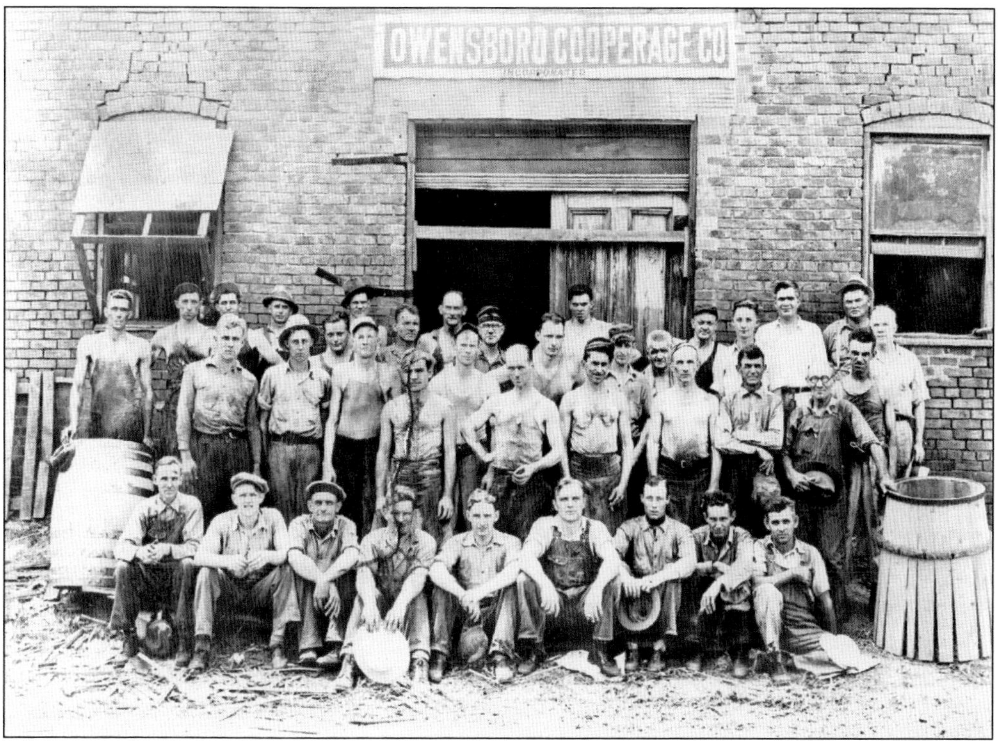


Few people today may remember Owensboro Cooperage, Inc., or be knowledgeable of its product. Fortunately, this 1936 photograph gives us a glimpse into this bygone business. These men are the coopers who created barrels for the local distilleries. On the left is an example of a finished oak barrel, while on the right is an unfinished one with open staves. Barrel slats or staves must be hand-formed from oak lumber, cut, shaved, bent, and bound by steel rings to form a proper whiskey barrel. Note the layer of wood shavings at their feet.

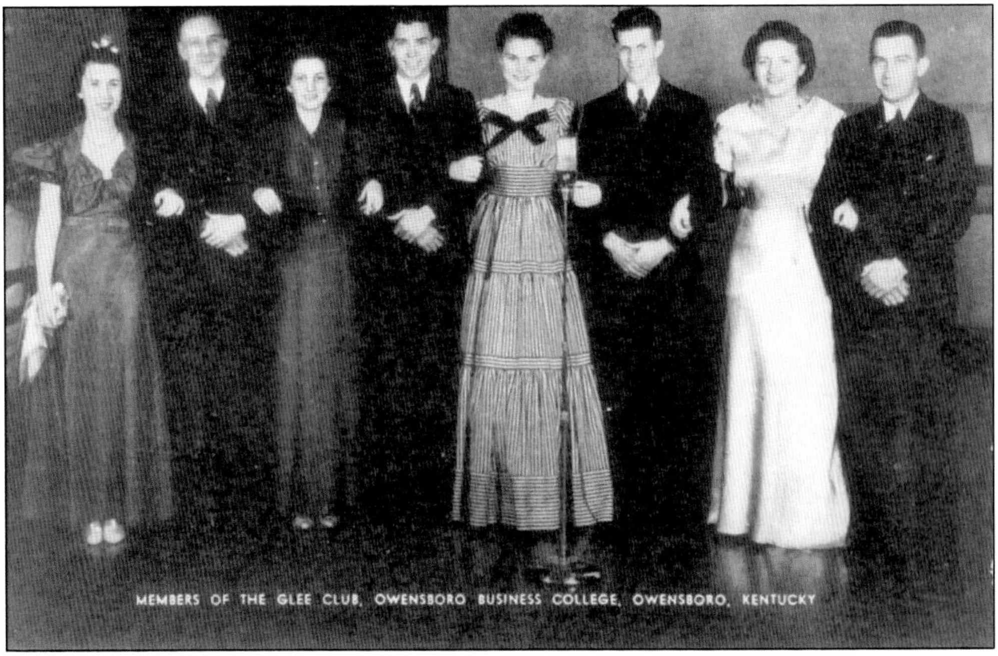


The Owensboro Business College was located at 506 Frederica Street in 1945. The college served to develop the skills necessary for students to enter into the service sectors of the businesses and industries of Owensboro and Daviess County.

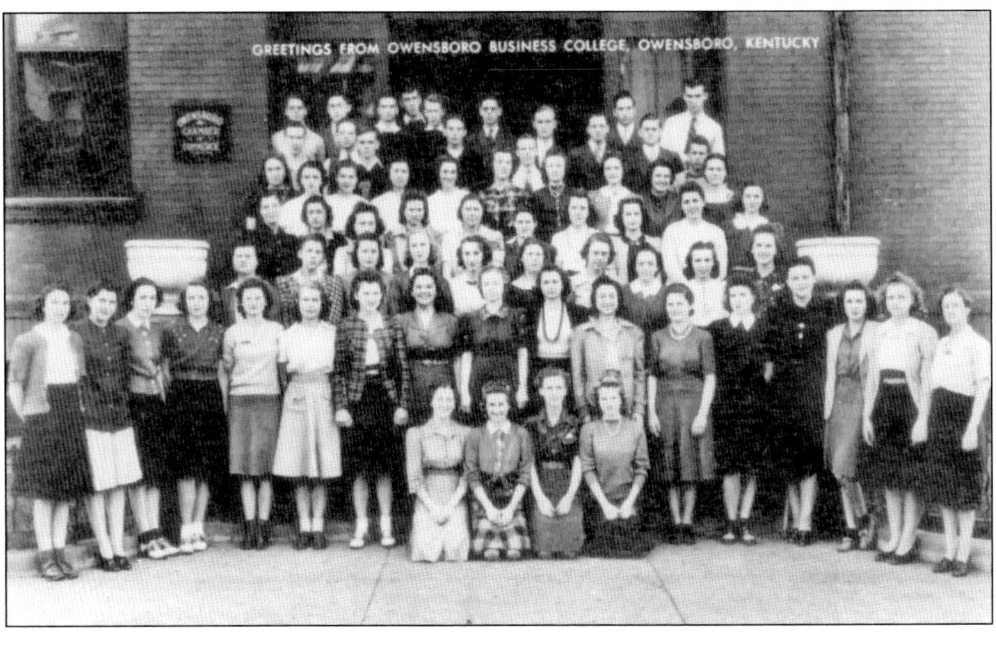

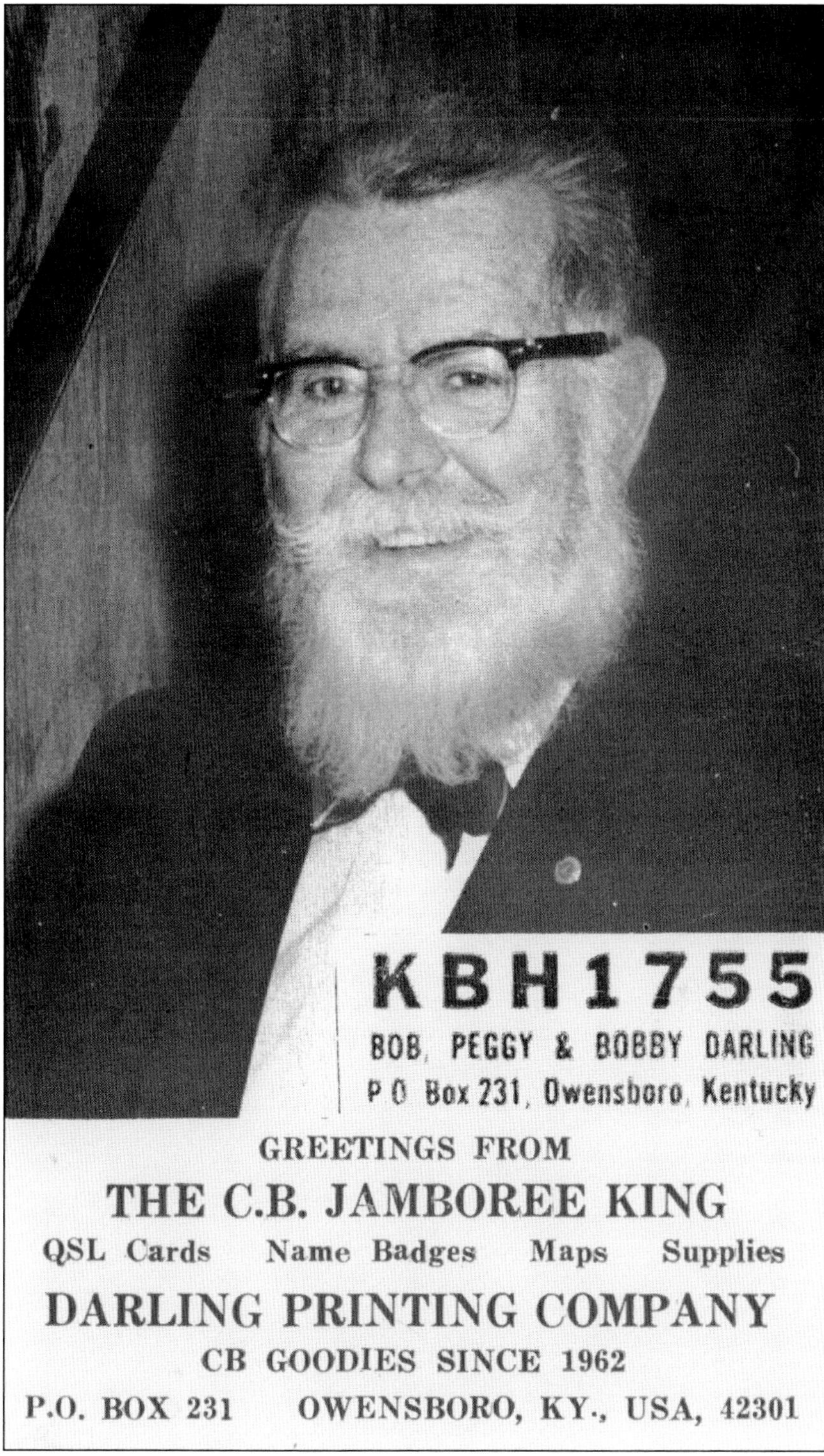


The Citizens Band (CB) radio fad peaked in the 1970s. Postcards were used as an inexpensive way of communicating upcoming events to enthusiasts outside the community. Fans exchanged promotional postcards at local meetings and CB jamborees.

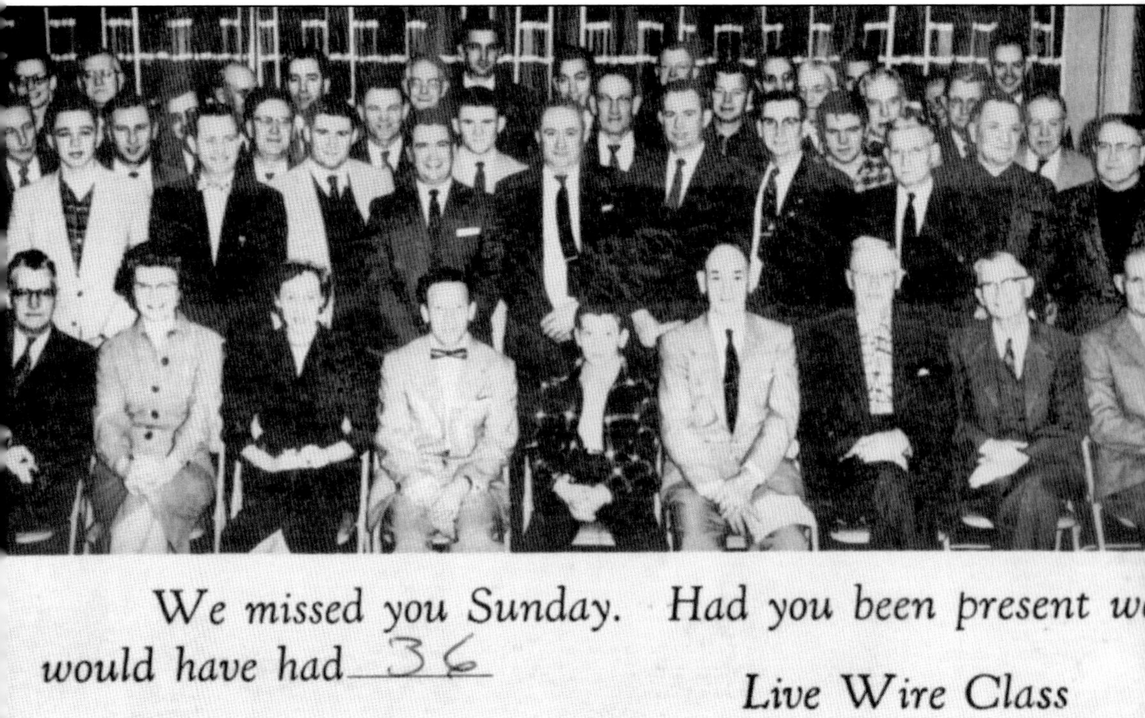


The postcard above was used by the local Sunday school class as a method of maintaining attendance. Starting in 1914, the Live Wire Class at Central Cumberland Presbyterian Church was well attended and widely known throughout the community. In 1983, the class was recognized by WOMI for its many contributions to the community.

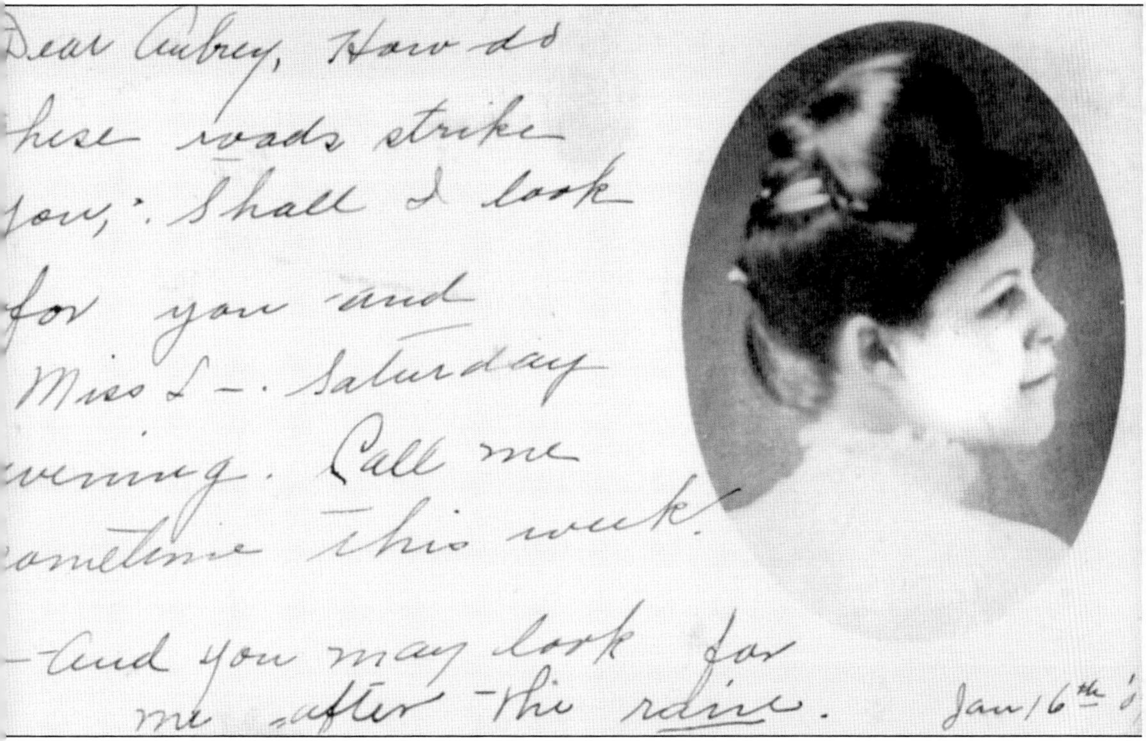

Dear Aubrey, How do
hese roads strike
you;. Shall I look
for you and
Miss L-. Saturday
evening. Call me
ometime this week.
-And you may look for
me after the rain. Jan 16th

Above is a 1907 personal postcard used to write a friend at Pleasant Ridge, Kentucky. The young lady is unidentified. A penny postcard and a penny stamp allowed friends and relatives to stay in touch. "Postal" was a term commonly used for early postcards. Friends would exchange community photographs and collect them in albums for mementos to share with guests.

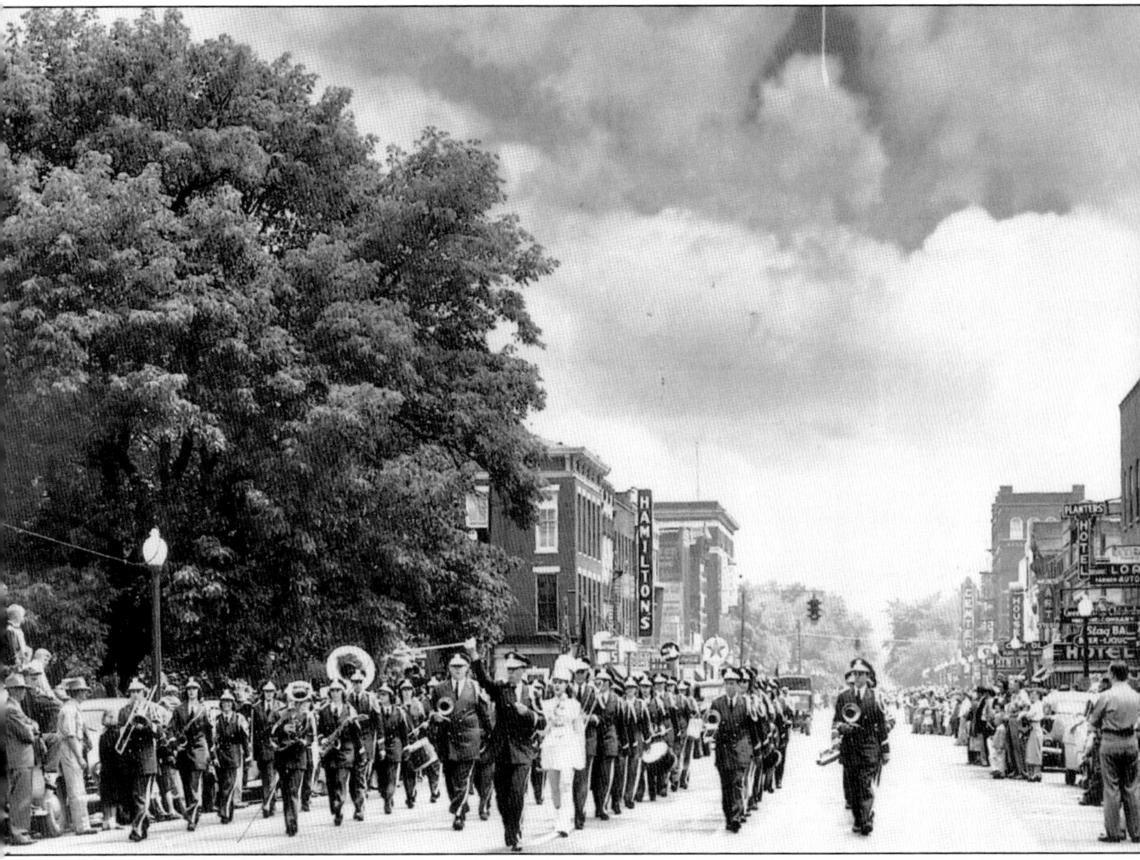


This real photograph was taken in the late 1940s or early 1950s by the local General Electric photographer. It shows citizens watching a parade move north on Frederica Street between Second and Third Streets during a warm part of the year with storm clouds threatening. This view shows a large number of trees on the courthouse lawn.

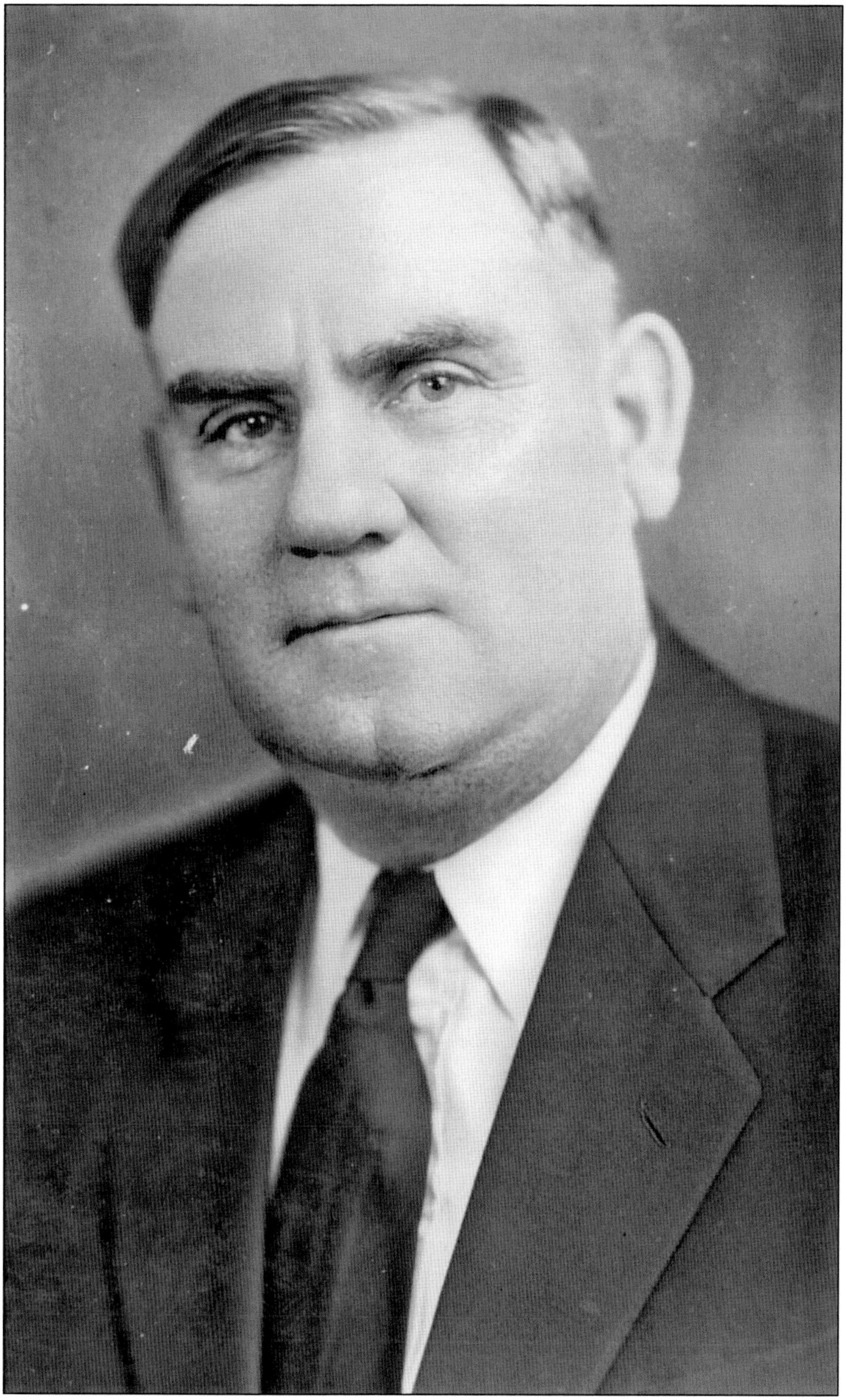

W. P. ("Pack") Morris in 1941 used the postcard as a mass media instrument in his bid for sheriff of Daviess County.

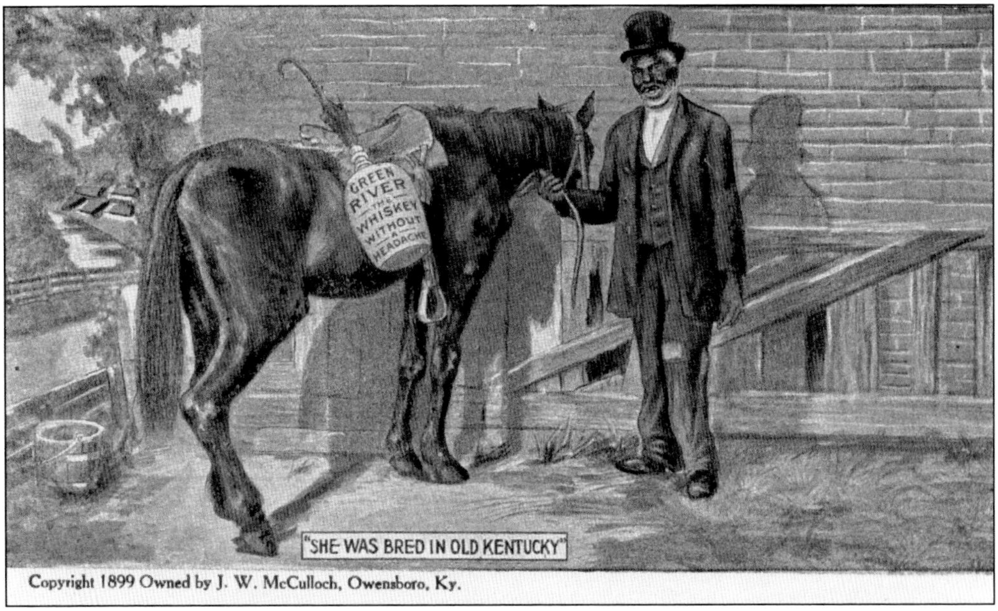


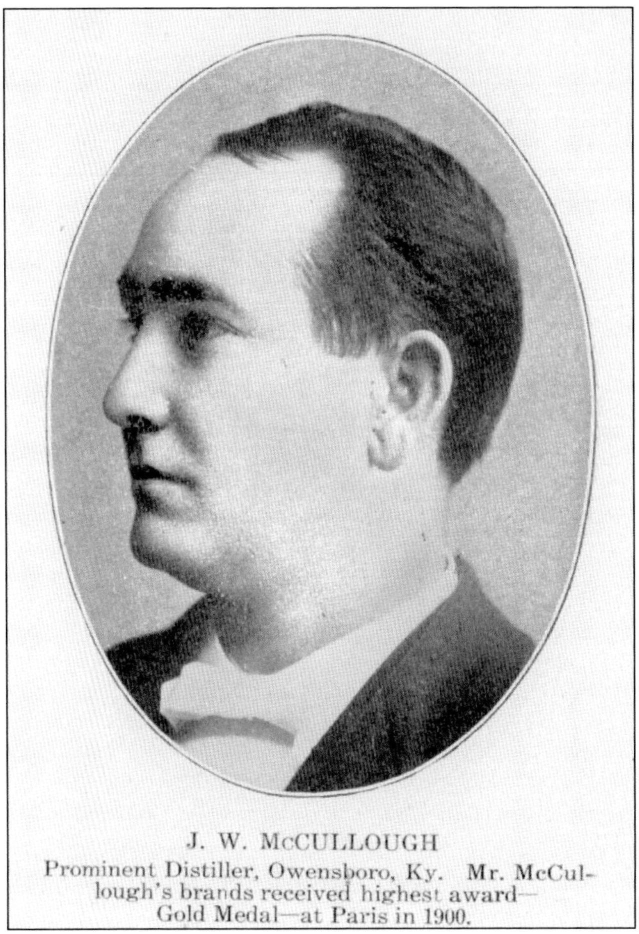


John W. McCulloch understood the value of advertising, placing this famous "She was bred in old Kentucky" image on postcards, tin lithographs, newspapers, and magazines nationwide. The gentleman in the illustration is "Luke, his faithful old man servant." Whiskey distilling began in the first cabin in Daviess County and continues to this day. In 1911, J. W. McCullough and his wife, Jessie, lived at 902 Frederica Street. He died in 1927.

# *Nine*

# Residences

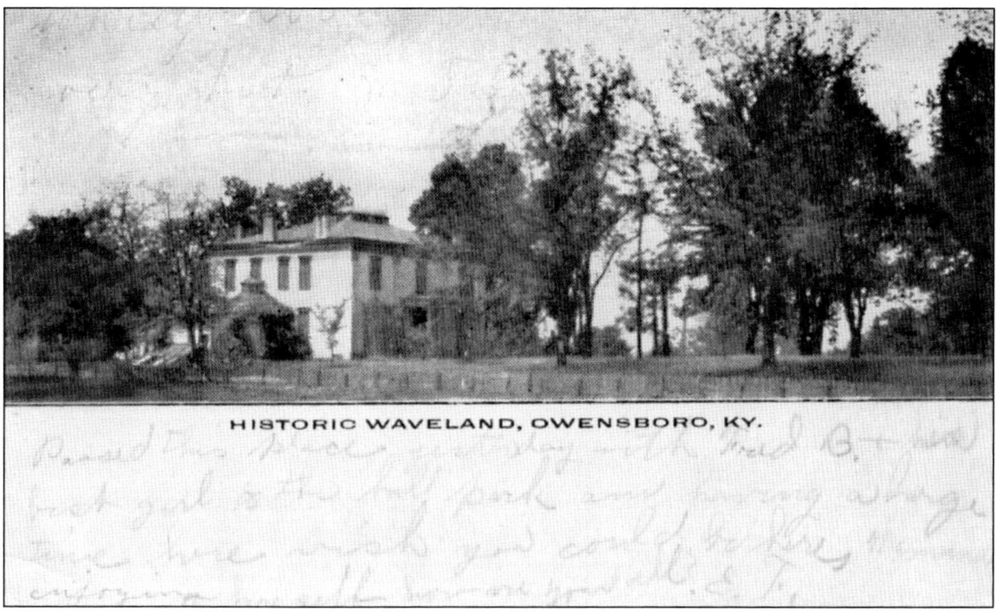


Historic Waveland was a south Frederica Street home owned by James Weir, a lawyer, businessman, and Centre College graduate who died in 1906. The origin of the title Waveland is unknown, but the book *Our Community Then and Now* says, "The broad halls and large, airy rooms were beautifully frescoed, and on the ceiling of the library was a picture of Washington crossing the Delaware." The building was demolished to make room for city growth. The handwritten portion of this card postmarked September 3, 1907, reads, "Passed this place yesterday with Fred B. and his best girl to the ball park. I'm having a large time here. Wish you could be here. Mamma enjoyed herself. How are you all? E. T."

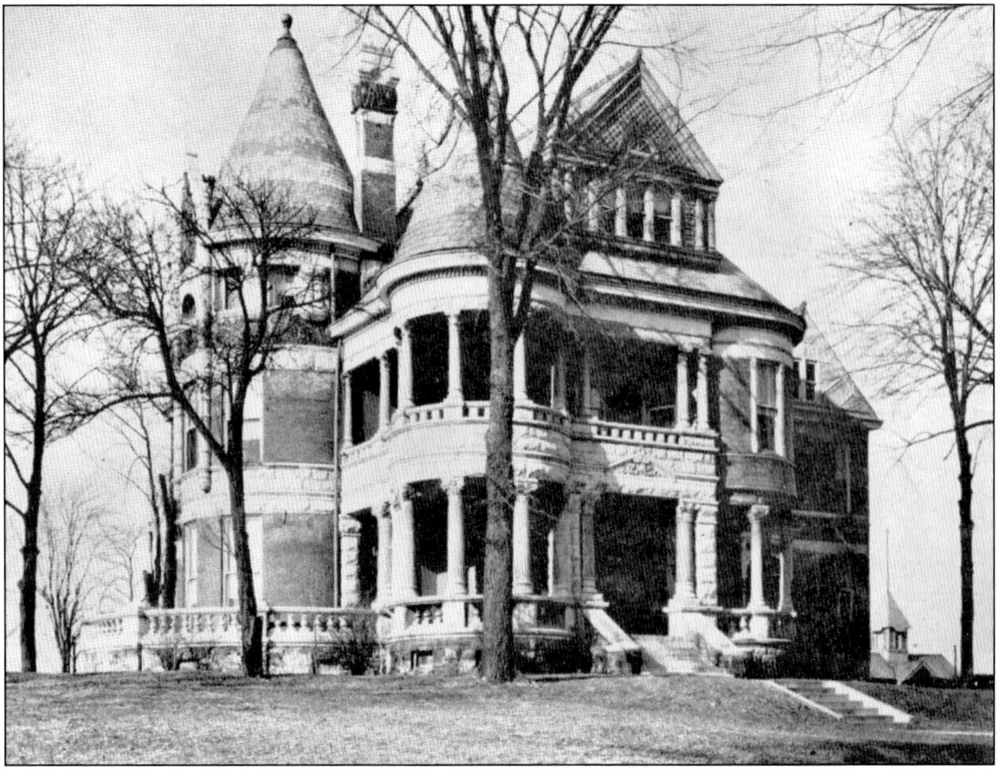

This Victorian-style home sat on East Fourth Street where Daviess County Middle School resides today. With its ornate stonework and polished marble columns, the majestic house was built by distiller Richard Monarch and his wife, Bettie England Monarch. It adorned the neighborhood known in the 19th century as Distiller's Row, which was remarkable for the grand river-view estates built by that local industry's barons. When ownership transferred to Hiram E. and Nellie B. Rose in 1903, the ornate home began to be known as Rosedale. Daviess County Public Schools purchased the property in 1927 and hired local architect Clarence W. Kimberlin to design a classroom addition and later a gymnasium. It provided a home to Daviess County High School until 1958. The home was razed in 1960 to make room for a gym for the middle school.

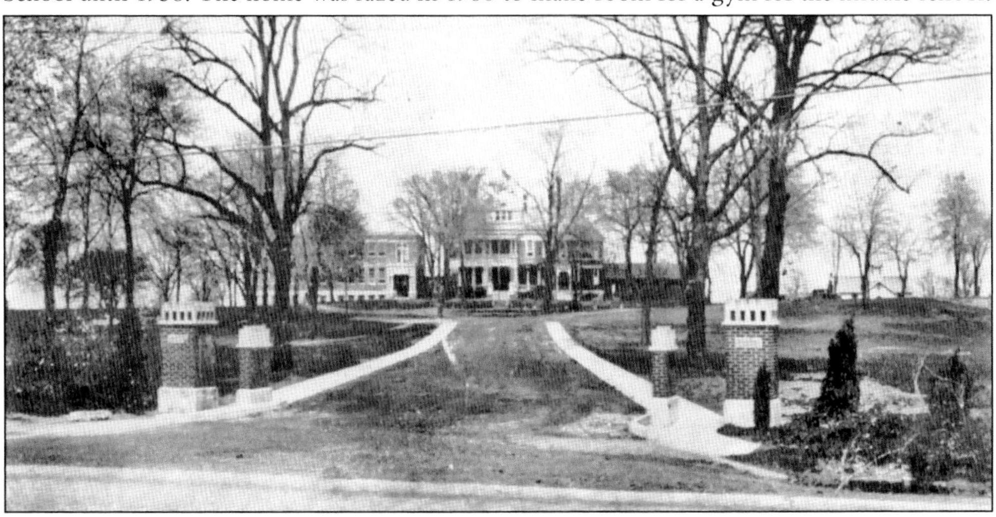

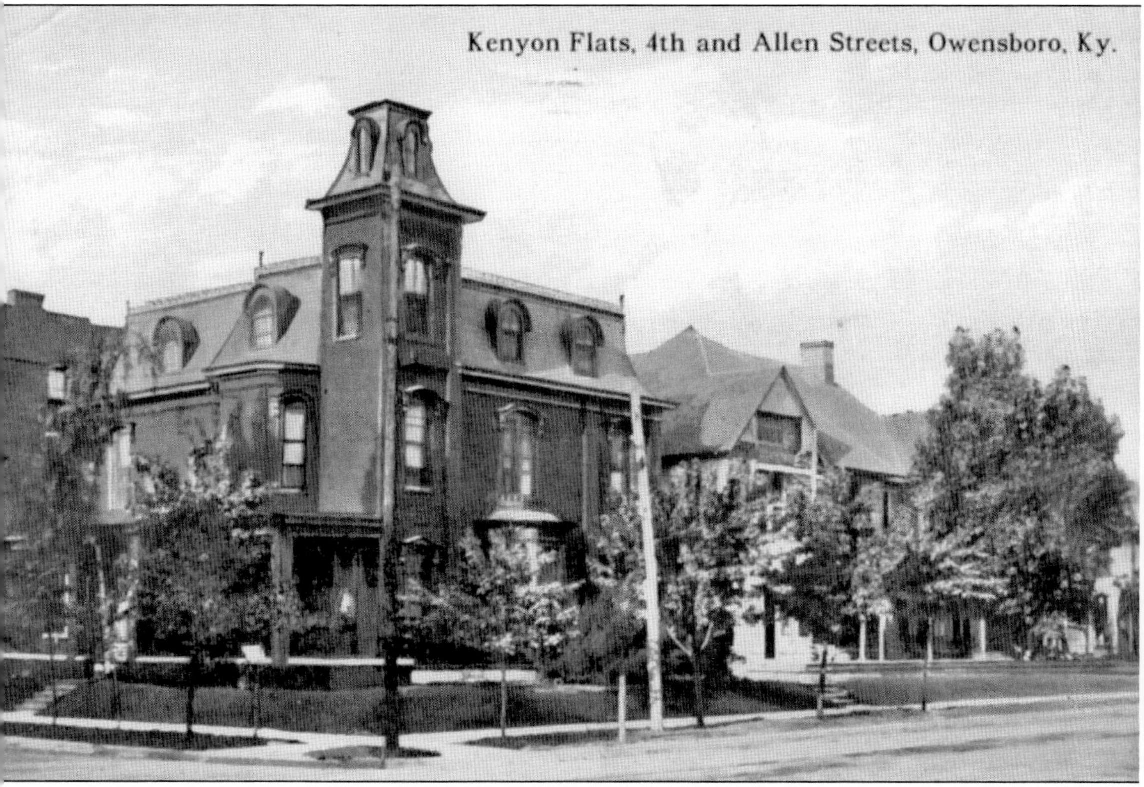


Kenyon Flats was a boardinghouse located on the southwest corner of Fourth and Allen Streets. Citizens highly valued residential locations close to Main Street prior to the proliferation of automobiles, and in the 19th century, Fourth Street was lined with large fine homes. As these houses aged, owners began renting rooms to boarders for additional income. The above postcard's perspective is from present-day city hall looking southwest. This Kenyon Flats site is now a parking lot for the downtown post office, which stands in the vicinity of the large tree on the far right.

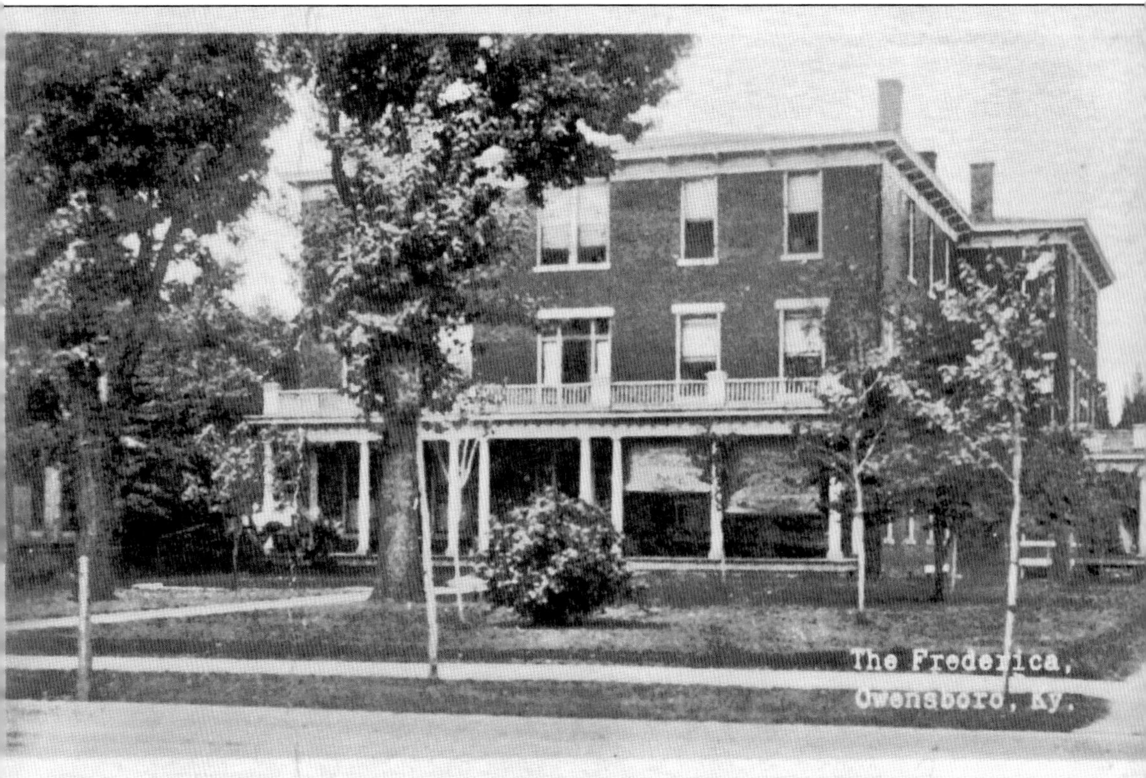


Frederica Flats was a boardinghouse located at 704 Frederica Street. In 1951, Kentucky Wesleyan College relocated to Owensboro after local citizens raised $1 million to help finance a new 70-acre campus. The first parcel of property purchased by the school was Frederica Flats to serve as the school's first women's dormitory in Owensboro. The apartment building was later razed in the early 1960s to provide the site for construction of a new bank building for Owensboro Federal Savings and Loan Association. That building is now a U.S. Bank branch.

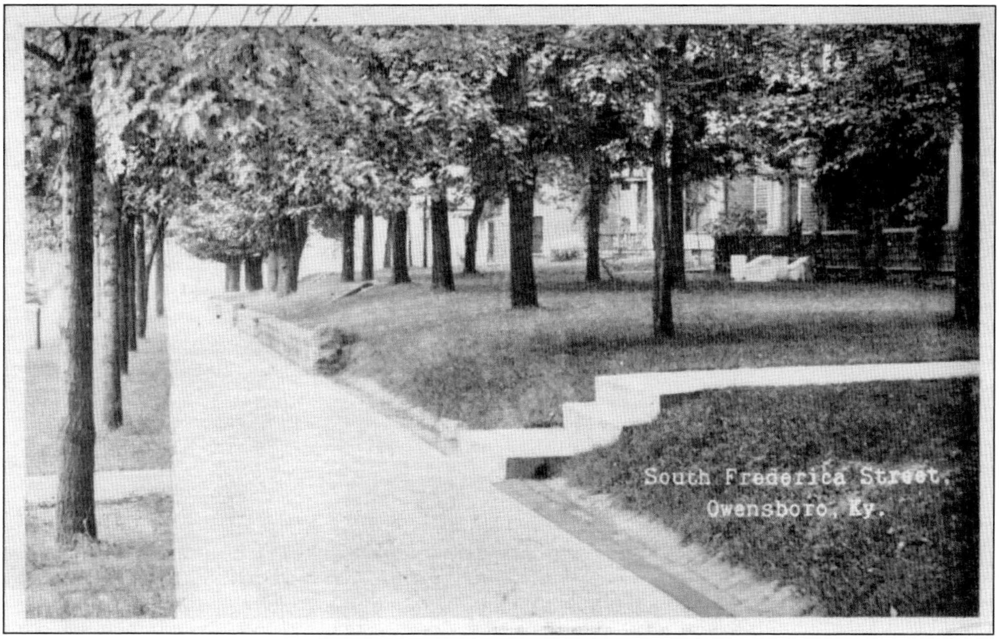


The original 1816 city plan for Rossboro, renamed Owensborough 35 days later, allowed for one north-south street to be wider and more important than the others. Frederica Street was originally designed as the city's premier residential street. For homeowners, a Frederica Street address projected a level of social eminence and stature. The term "South Frederica" indicated a newer area of town, not just the street, which included the city's newer grand homes. These postcards were created to showcase the community's residential amenities built under a canopy of mature trees. Today things have changed, and Frederica Street is the commercial hub of the community, the true main street.

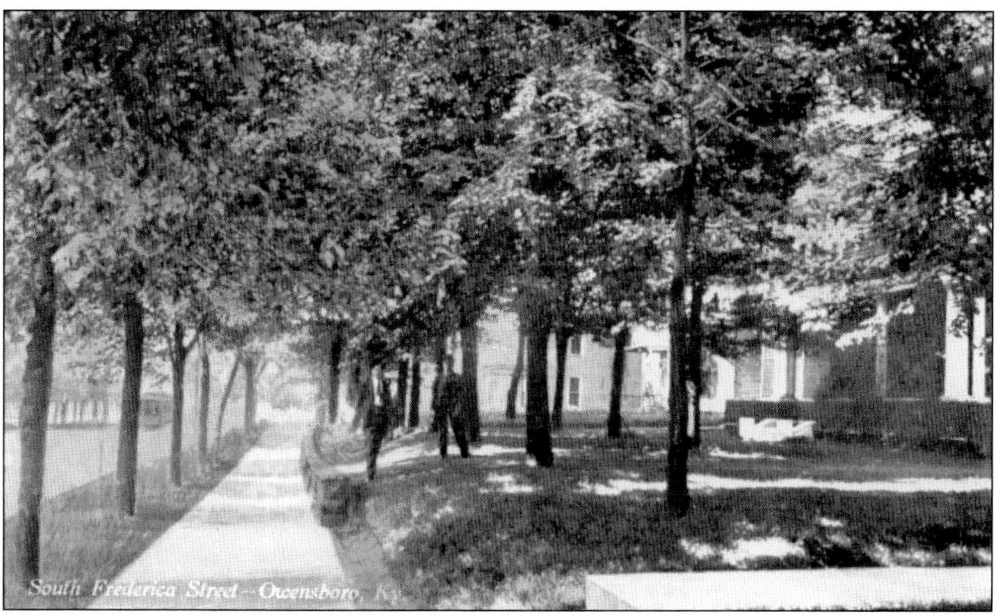

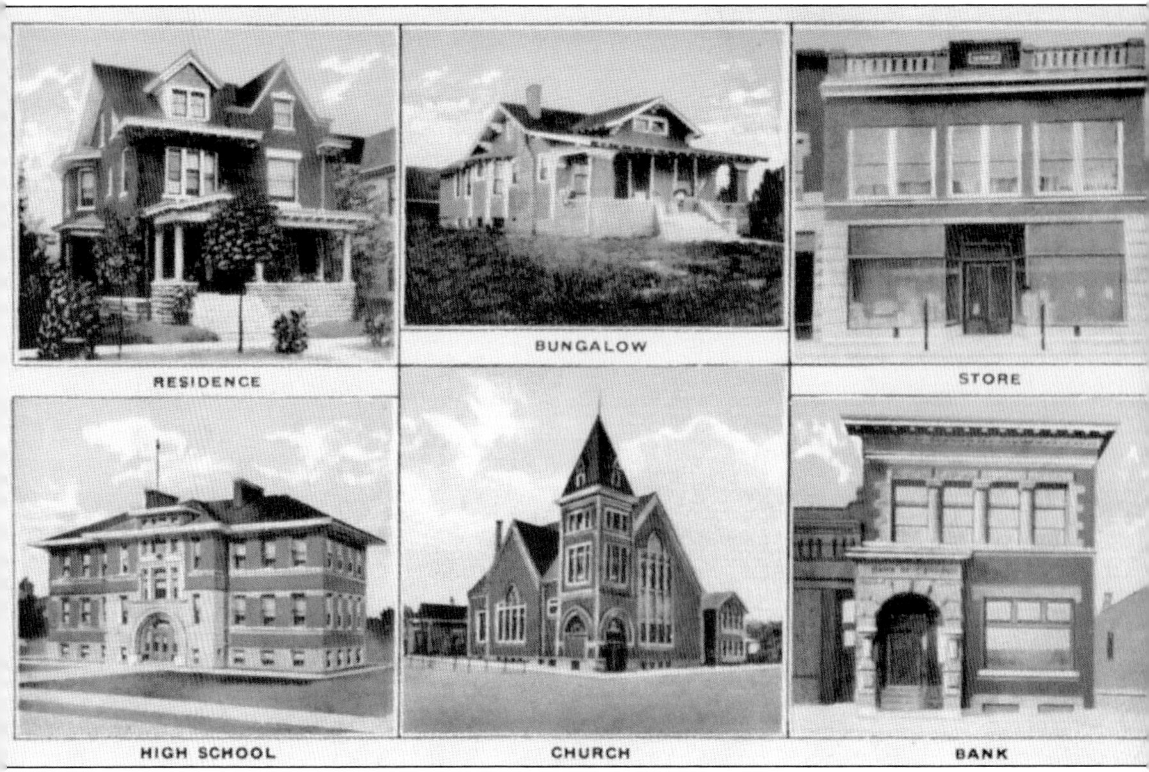


Owensboro architect Albert Killian advertised his services with this early postcard. It says on the back: "On the opposite side you will find a few of the modern buildings that I have designed. I will make special drawings in each case subject to your approval if a description of the character of the building you want will be furnished. I will give all the information that you may ask for." The residence shown above is still standing today on St. Ann Street in Owensboro.

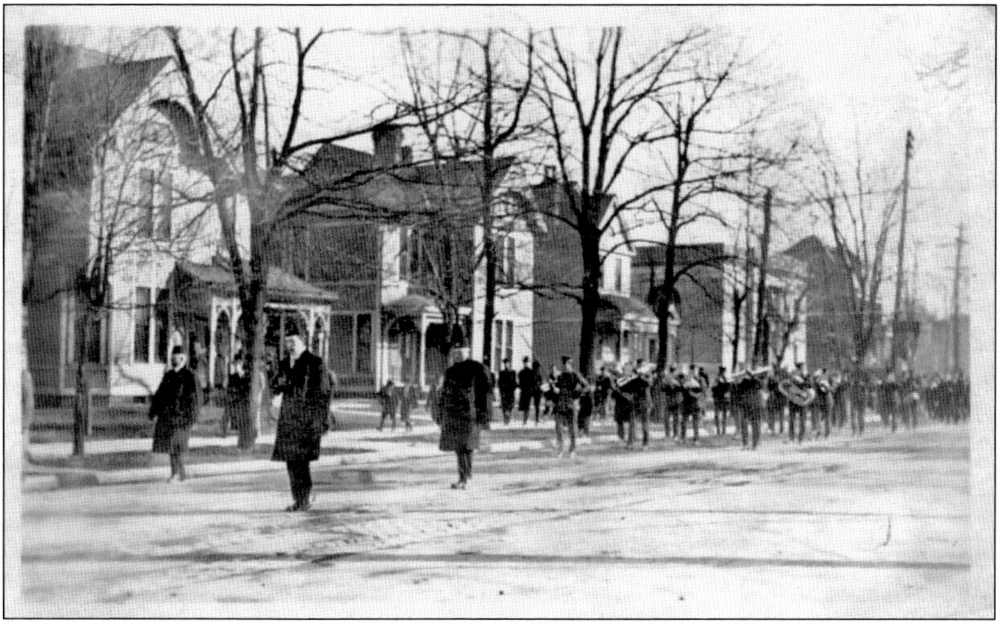

The above postcard shows a band marching north down Frederica Street in the winter of 1912. These east-side Frederica homes were located just north of Ninth Street. The brand-new Free Public Library is the fourth building visible from the left. On Valentine's Day 1927, Frank Sheehan crashed his new Kentucky Cardinal biplane into this intersection, killing him and his promising aircraft company. The location of the block of Frederica Street in the postcard below is unknown. Much of Frederica Street was lined with trees to help filter the dirt street's dust from entering the fine large houses along this main city artery.

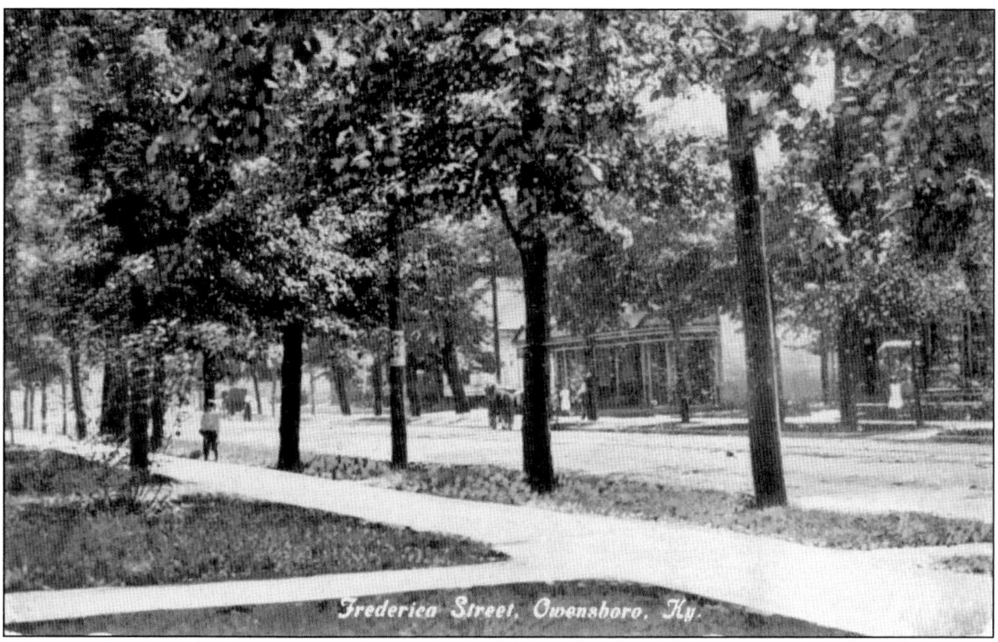

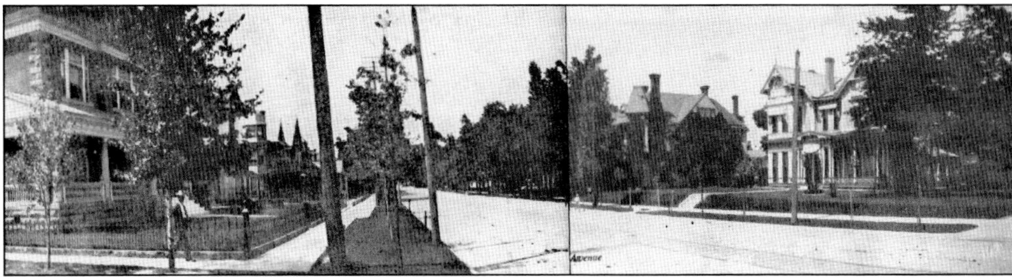

The real-photo postcards above represent two pictures overlapped to establish a pan view of Frederica Street looking north from White Street, now known as Seventh Street. The 1906 scene illustrates the prominent houses that lined Owensboro's principal street. Multiple views or pan shots were eventually developed by the postcard companies as foldout postcards and presented very rare views of many of our communities. C. W. Bransford's house on the left was purchased by the Knights of Columbus in 1922. Western Kentucky Gas later built its corporate office building on this site. That building is now part of Brescia University. Taken from the same spot, the 1914 postcard below shows a better view of the fine Frederica Street homes along the west side. As the downtown business center grew with the city, these houses were razed for commercial development.

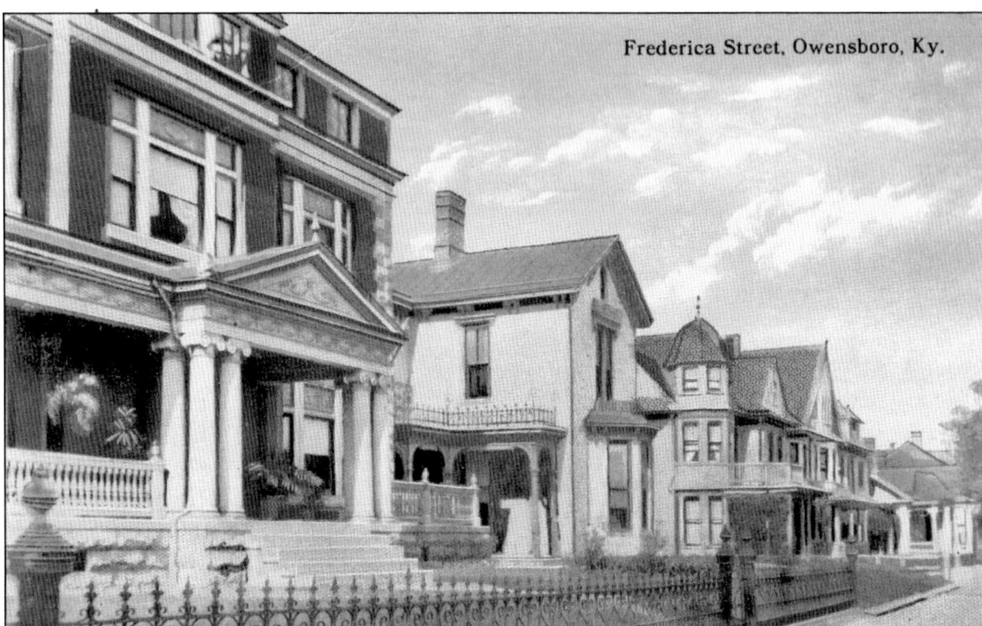

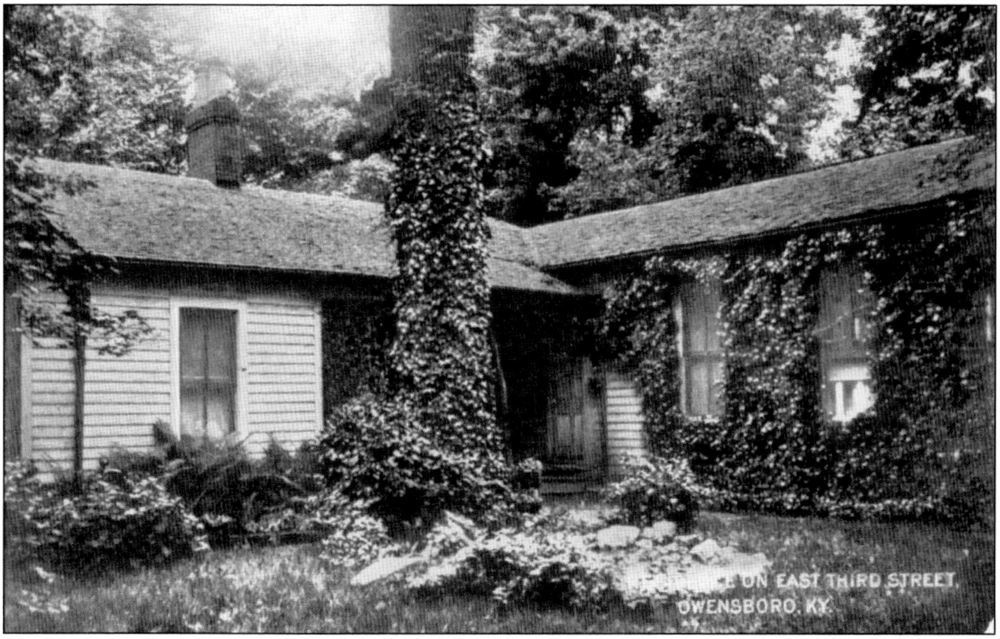


The postcard above, postmarked 1910, presents an unidentified residence on East Third Street. The scene's large trees and vegetation-covered house capture the density of the great woods that once existed around Owensboro. Below is a northward-looking view from Seventh Street, near present-day Brescia University. These houses still exist along the east side of St. Ann Street.

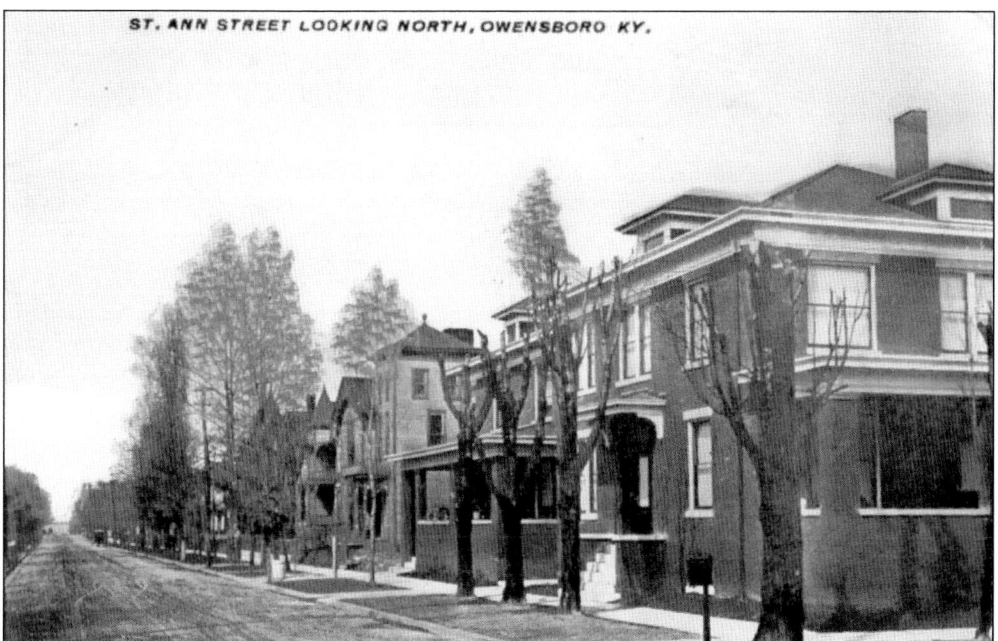

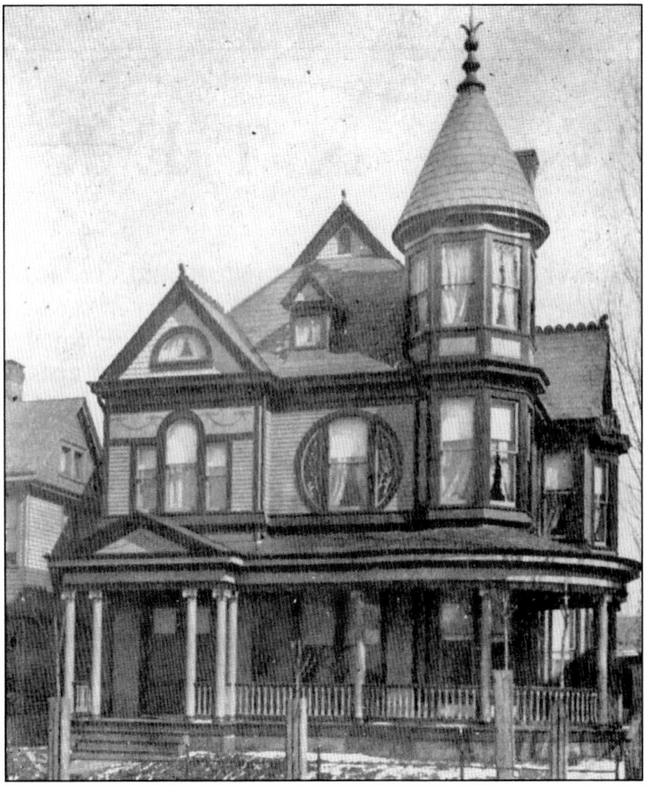

Above is a 1903 view of the Queen Anne home located at 521 St. Ann Street. Queen Anne is the most elaborate and eccentric of the Victorian architecture styles. Often called romantic and feminine, the Queen Anne approach ironically emerged in the 1880s and 1890s during the machine age. Wealthy industrialists pulled out all the stops building these lavish "castles," while country folks yearned for these fancy city trappings. Over time though, this styling began to look dated, and homeowners began remodeling to modernize appearances. The photograph below presents a current view of the Willard R. Bates house showing numerous substantial changes over the years.

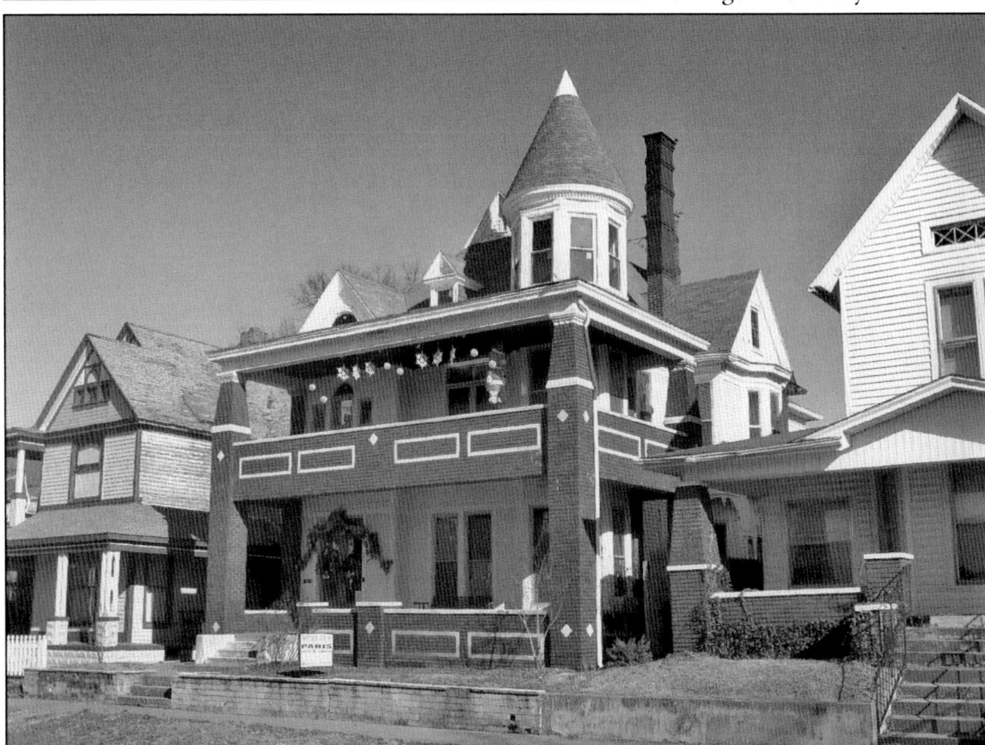

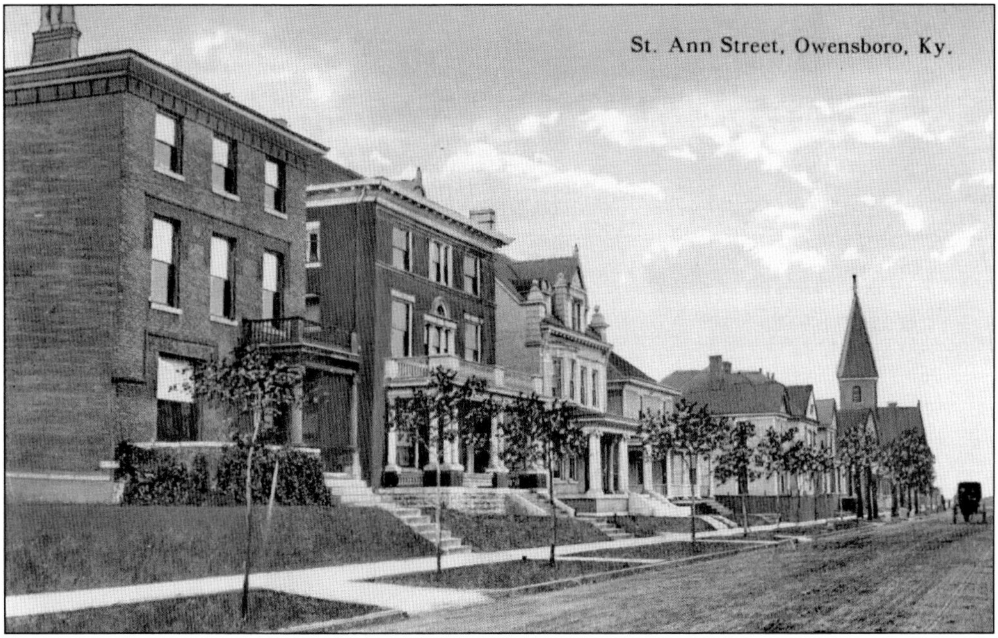


The postcard above presents a northward-looking view of the stately homes that once existed along St. Ann Street's west side. Central Presbyterian Church USA's steeple is visible at the end of the block. The postcard below is a southward-looking view of the same fine St. Ann Street homes. Unfortunately, all three of these structures have since been demolished. Brescia University's administration building now stands on the site across Seventh Street from the end of this block.

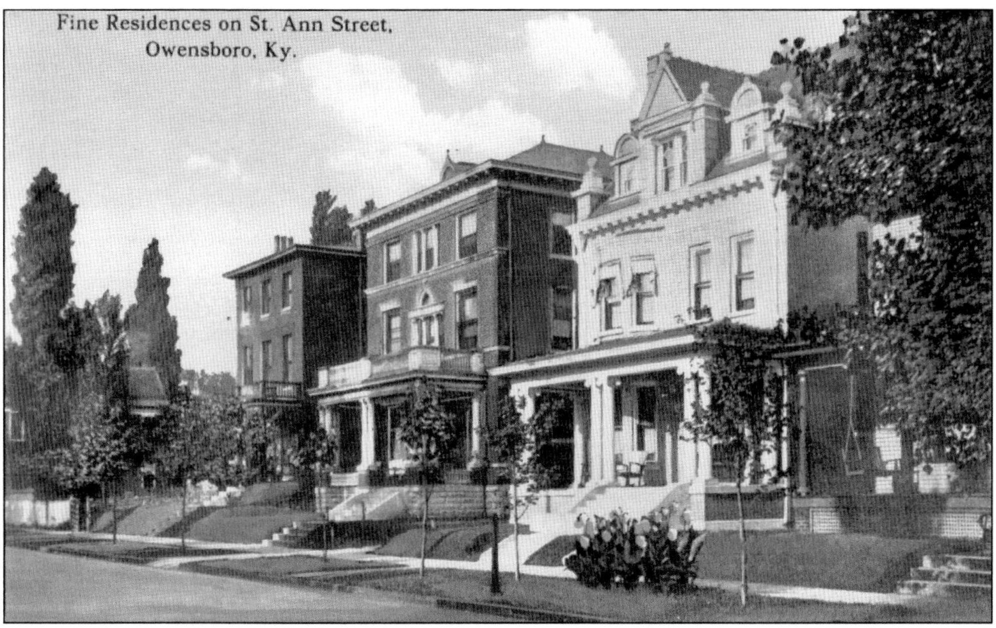

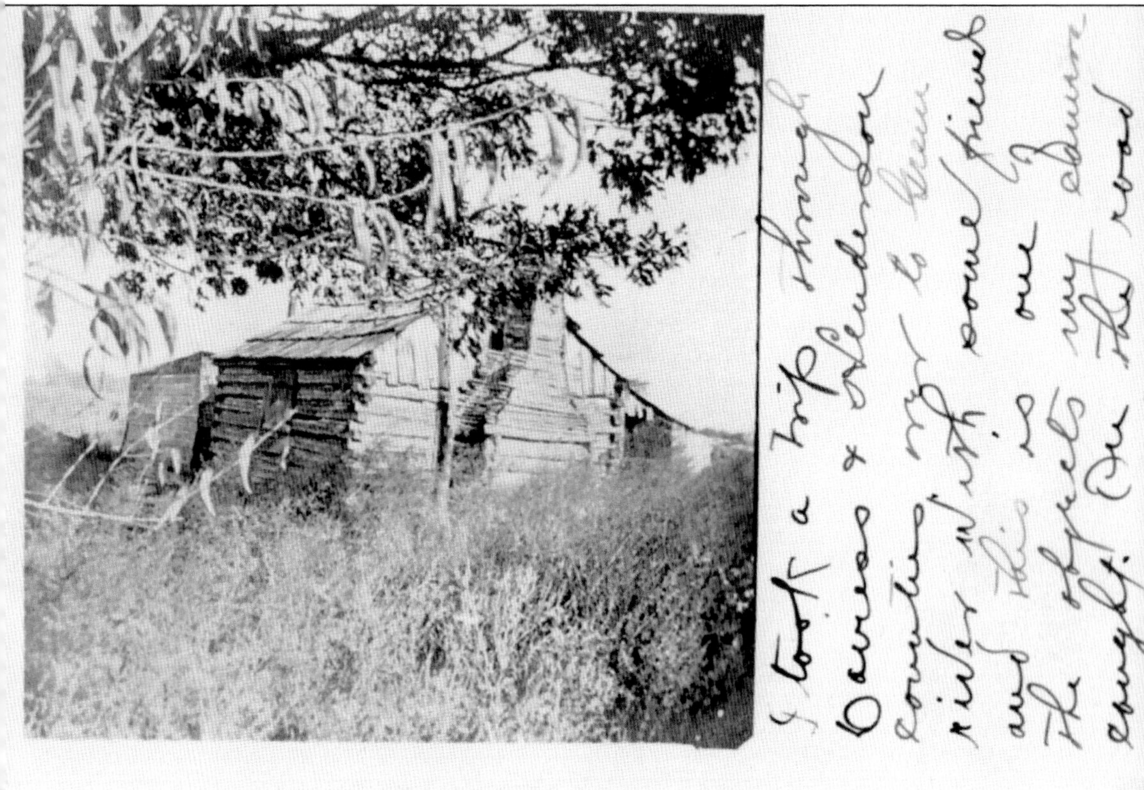

The caption on this real-photo postcard reads: "I took a trip through Daviess and Henderson Counties over to Green River with some friends and this is one of the objects my camera caught on the road to Owensboro, KY." The postmark date is 1906.

# *Ten*

# Communities

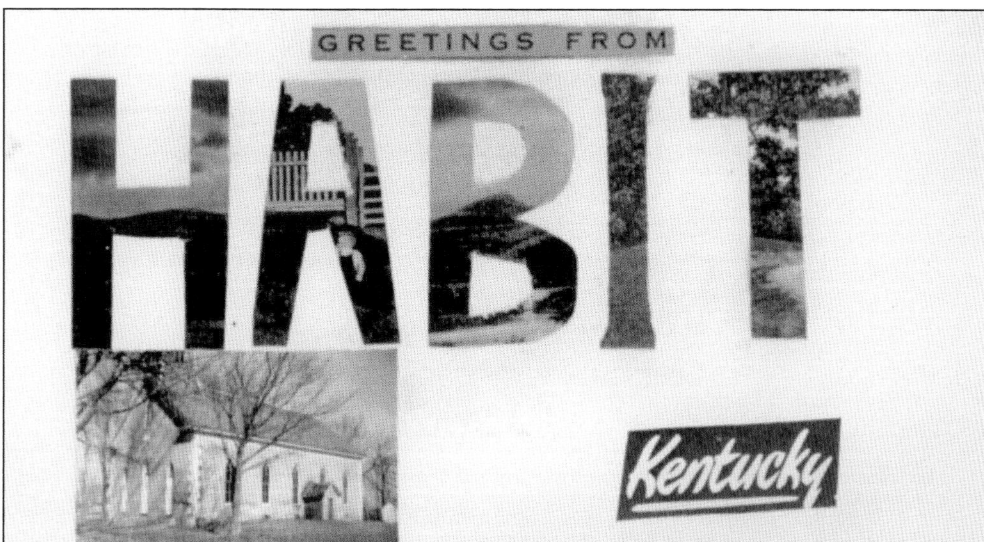


The postcard of Habit, Kentucky, is simply a way of documenting the existence of a community located southeast of Owensboro and directly south of Philpot, Kentucky. This important farming community exists at the intersection of KY 142 and Miller Mills Road.

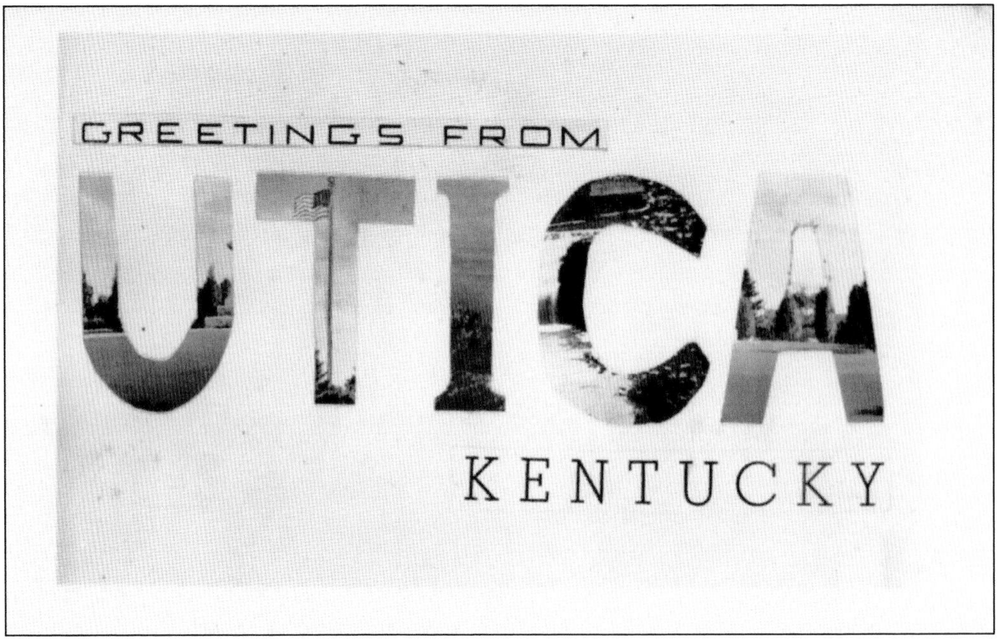


Utica, Kentucky, is a small town approximately 10 miles to the south of Owensboro, along the McLean County border. The postcard above reflects much of the area around the present-day Utica School. Below is a real-photo postcard of the Utica Deposit Bank. The bank building on the right remains today.

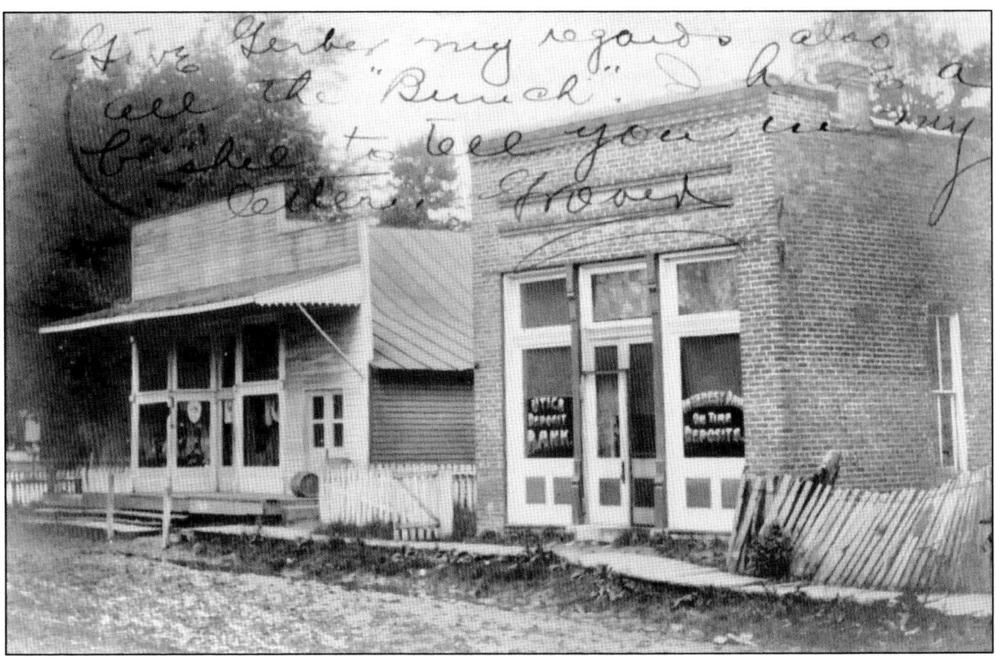

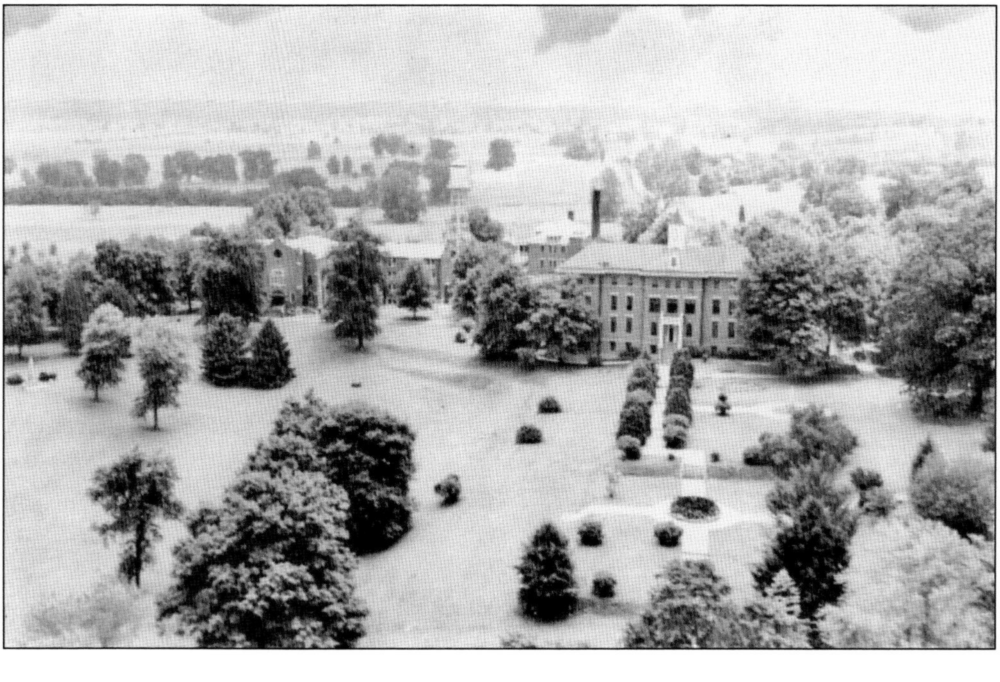

Mount St. Joseph was established on August 14, 1874, in the far western Daviess County community now known as Maple Mount, Kentucky. Fr. Paul Joseph Volk founded the ministry whose original purpose was "to form young ladies to virtue, ornament their minds with useful information, accustom them to early habits of order and economy, and to cultivate in them those qualities which render them both amiable and attractive, not only in the family circle, but in society likewise." These postcards showcase the beautiful campus of the school.

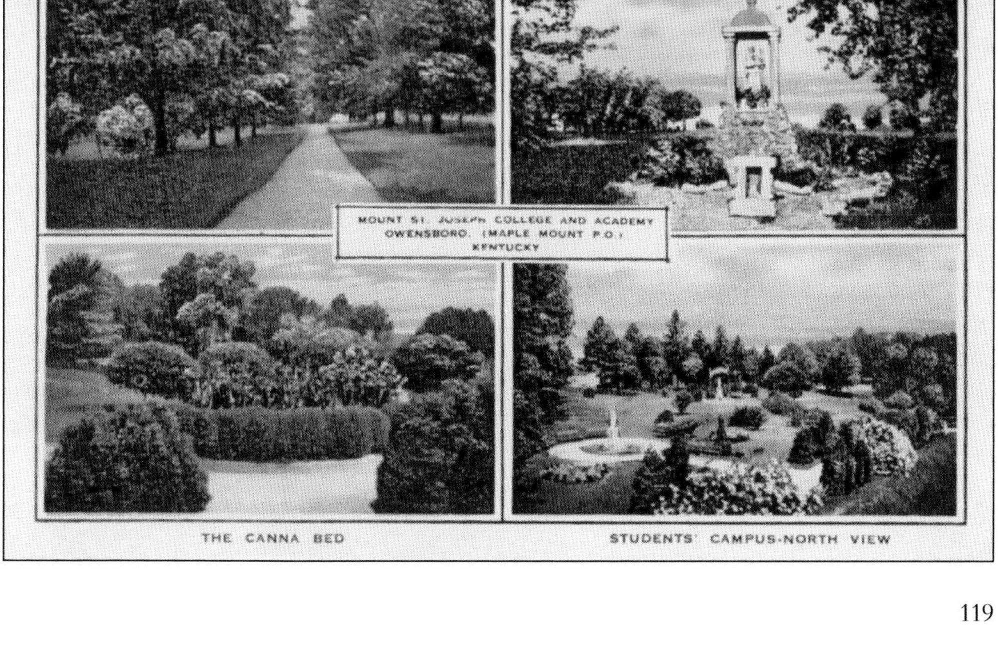

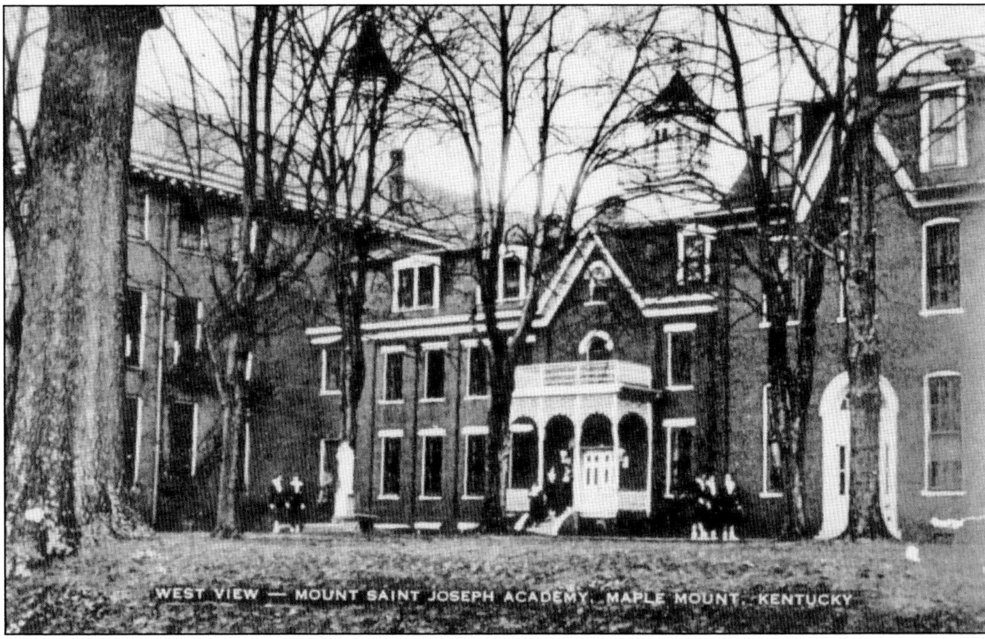


The postcards above and below show the first building at Mount St. Joseph was the first motherhouse for Roman Catholic Sisters in Kentucky west of Louisville and the oldest girls' academy in Daviess County. The Ursulines of Mount St. Joseph trace their origin to St. Angela Merici, who founded the first teaching order of women in the Catholic Church, the Company of St. Ursula, in Brescia, Italy, in 1535. Bishop Martin John Spalding invited the Ursulines from Straubing, Bavaria, to establish a foundation in Louisville, Kentucky, in 1858. From that order came the sisters to Daviess County 20 years later. At the request of Fr. Paul Joseph Volk, five Ursuline sisters came from Louisville in 1874 to establish a school in western Daviess County at the site that is now Maple Mount, Kentucky.

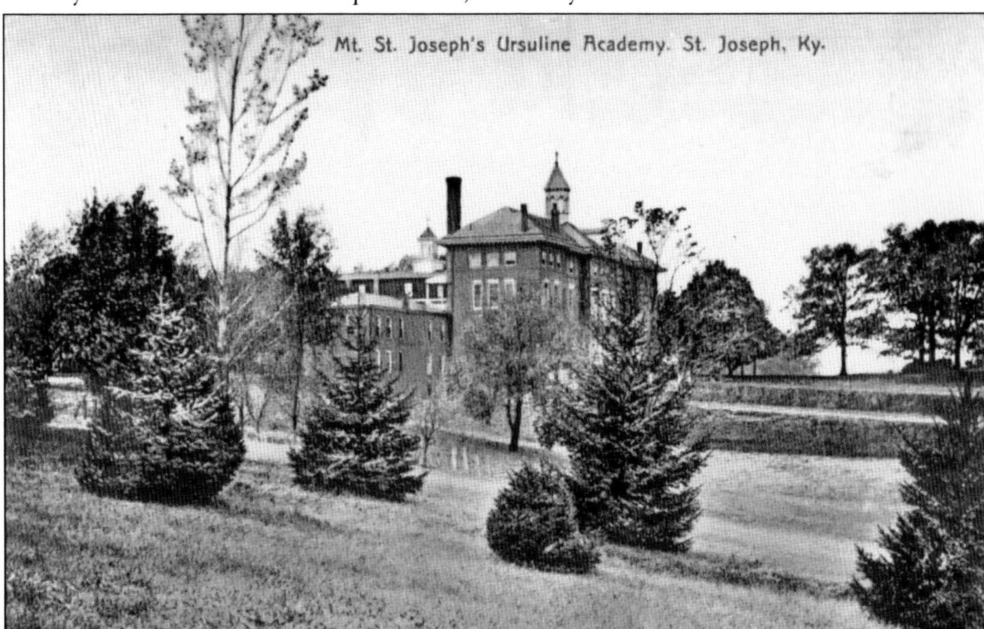

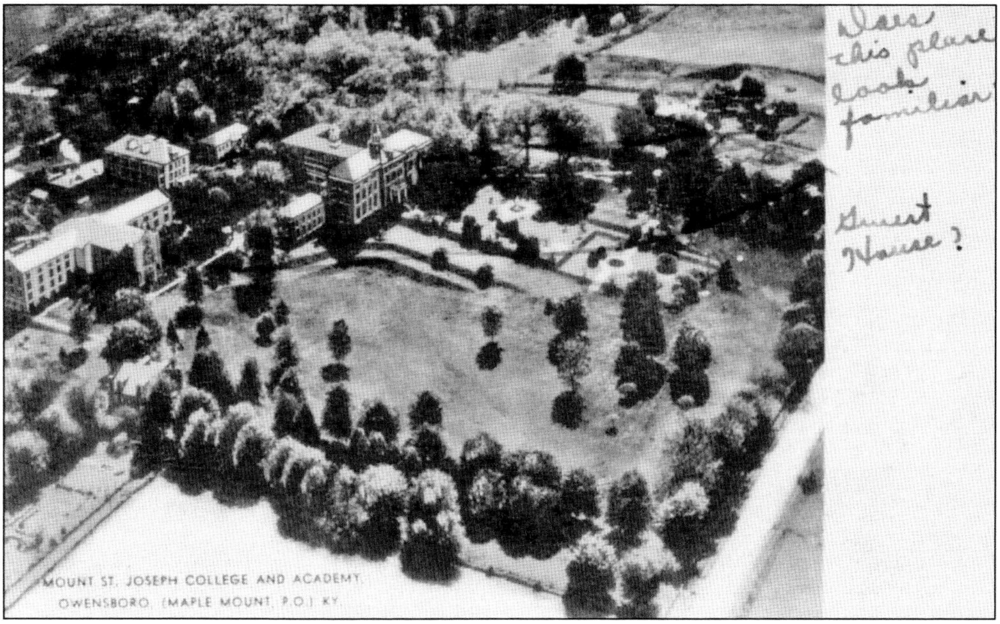


In 1880, the facility pictured above was incorporated by an act of the Kentucky Legislature as St. Joseph Female Ursuline Academy. The first graduate from the academy was Annie Johnson of Calhoun, Kentucky. By 1912, after 78 girls had graduated from the academy and 89 Ursuline sisters had lived and worked at Mount St. Joseph, the Ursuline Sisters of Mount St. Joseph became an autonomous congregation separate from the Louisville order. The Chapel, pictured below, was erected in 1929.

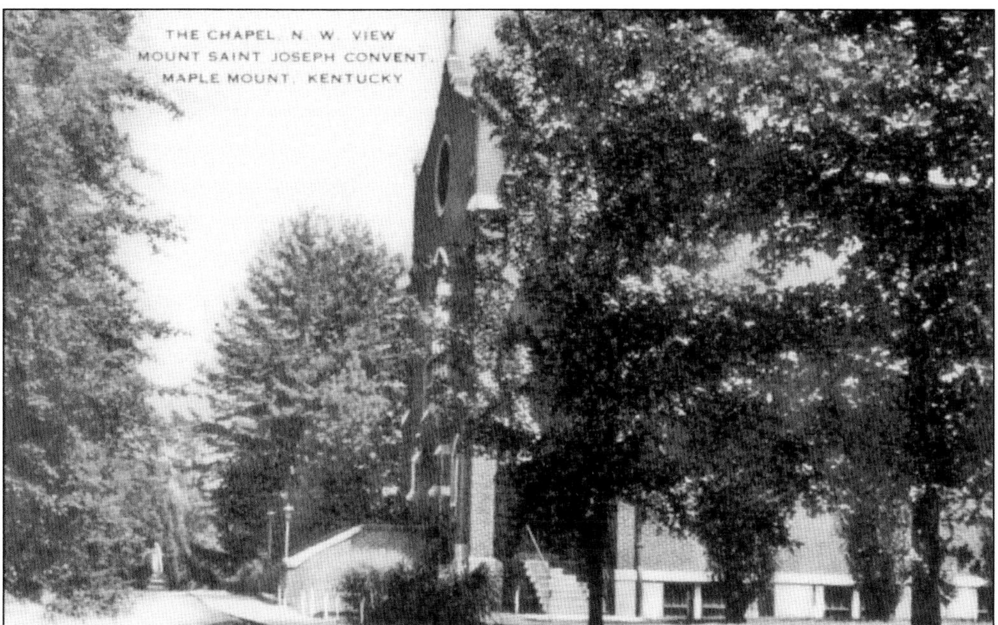

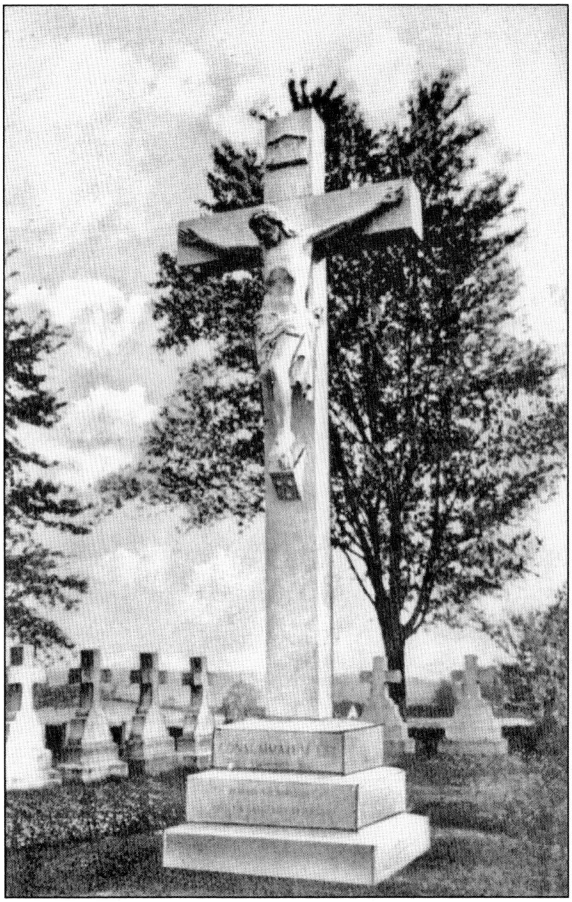

The postcards on this page reflect a portion of the rolling grounds that provide an important part of the beauty of Mount St. Joseph. The Ursuline Sisters are religious women who live an apostolic life supported by prayer and contemplation. They proclaim Jesus to all people through the ministry of education and Christian formation. By the time of the academy's centennial in 1974, more than 1,600 women had attended Mount St. Joseph Academy, but demands for services were changing. Guided by the advice of the Ursuline Sisters foundress, St. Angela Merici, "to make changes according to the times and needs," Mount St. Joseph Academy closed in 1983 after 109 years of service. The original buildings are still used today for the Mount St. Joseph Conference and Retreat Center, a center for spiritual, cultural, and educational enrichment.

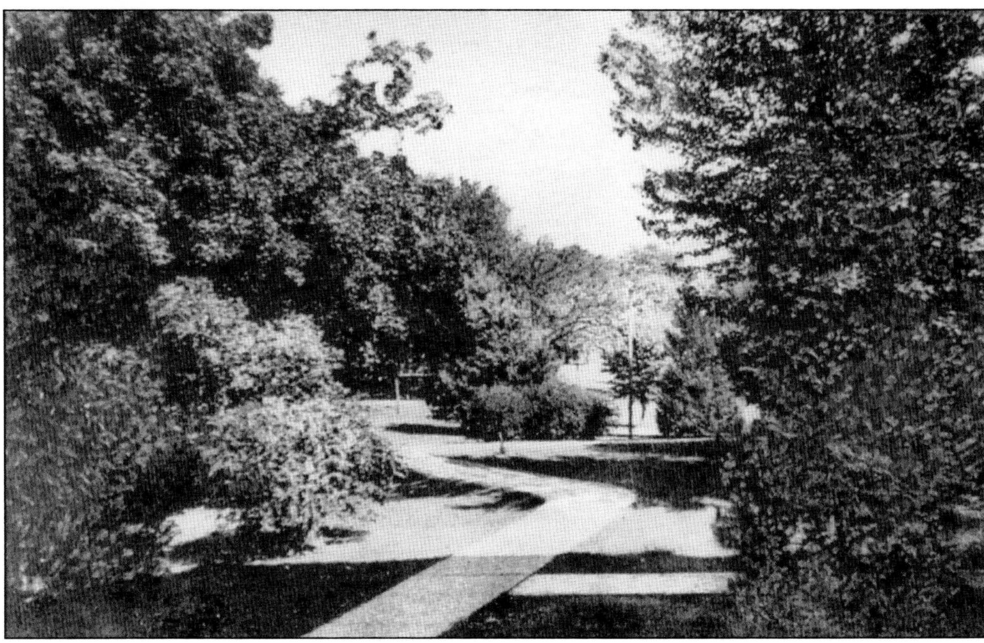

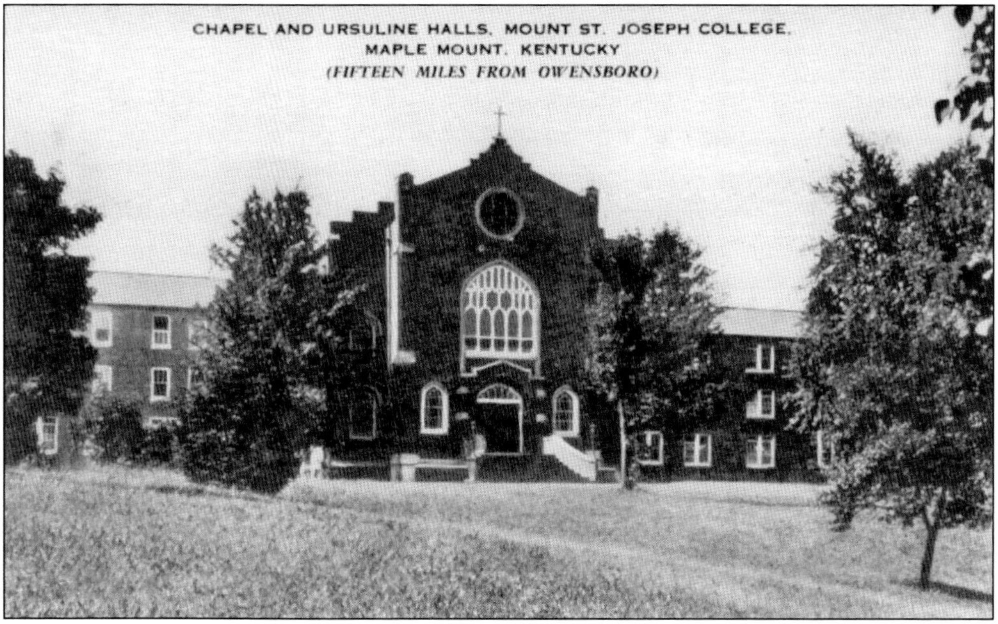


The Chapel, shown in the postcard above, remains active today as the primary place of worship for the Ursuline Sisters of Mount St. Joseph. The school and college have closed, but the Sisters have adapted to new programs of health care for the 90 sisters living at Mount St. Joseph. They have the latest environmentally controlled farm systems for the 750 acres of manicured grounds and farmland. The postcard below shows how the interior of the Chapel once looked. It has since been remodeled extensively.

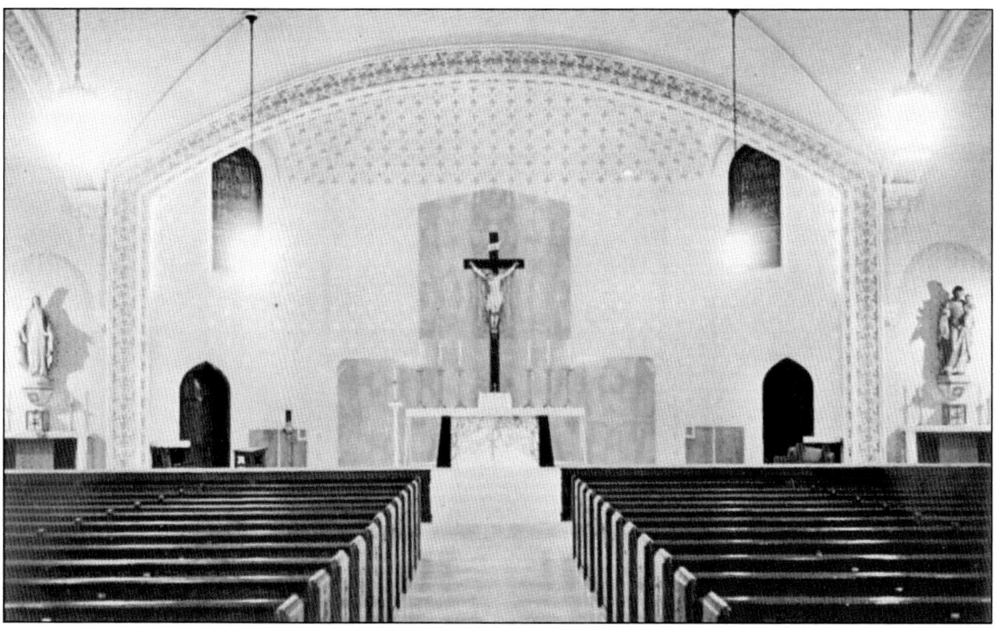

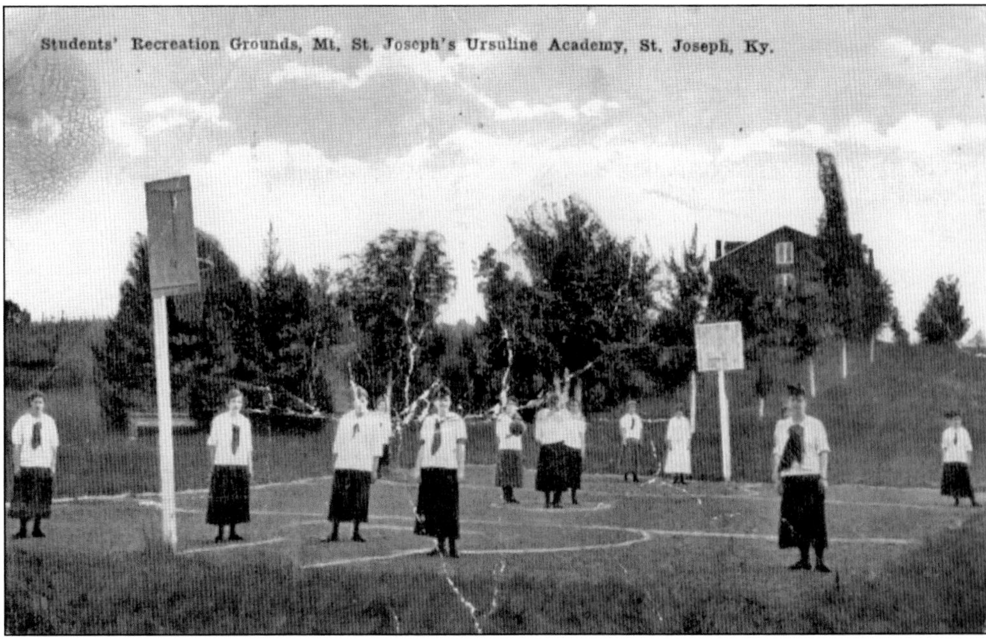


The 1925 postcard above shows the academy's female students playing basketball on their recreation grounds. That same year, the Ursuline Sisters continued their dedication to education by opening the Mount St. Joseph Junior College for Women. In 1950, the college became coeducational, moved to downtown Owensboro, and changed its name to Brescia College, now known as Brescia University. The all-female high school continued at the Mount to provided educational programs for girls from all around the world. The postcard below shows a Mount St. Joseph Academy graduation day in the mid- to late 1950s.

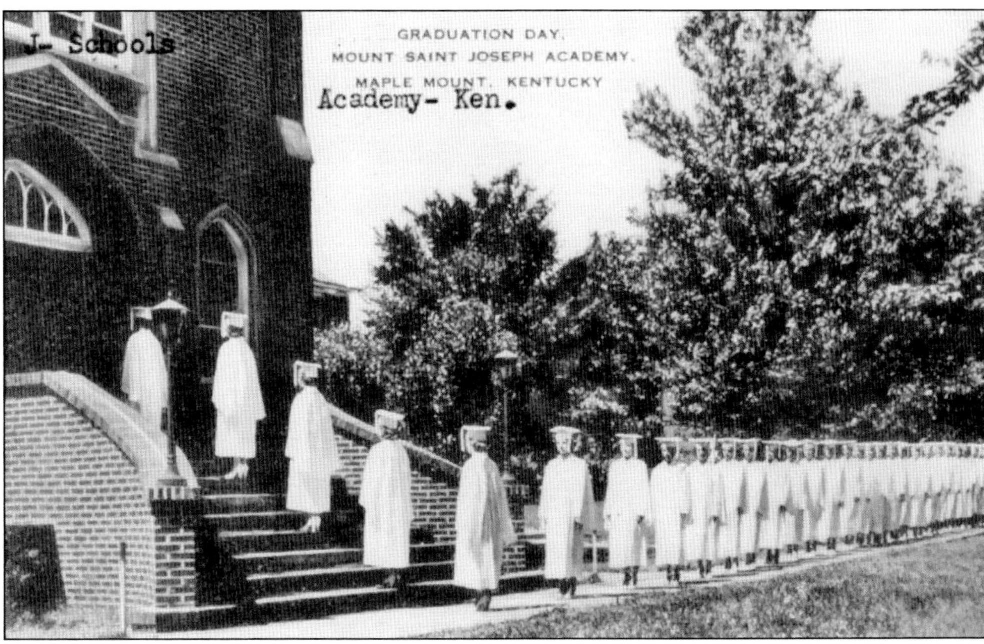

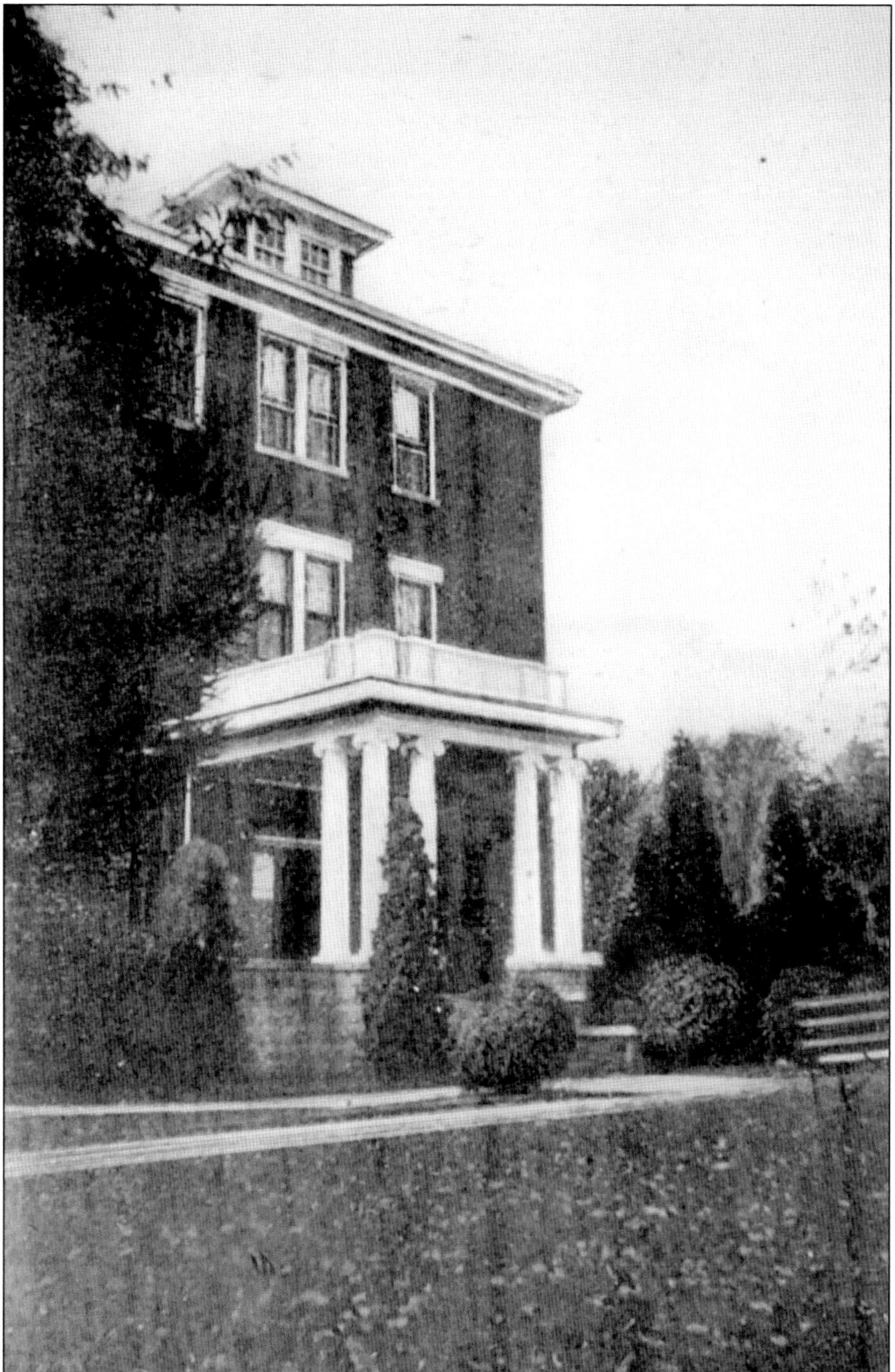

St. Angela Hall, pictured in the postcard above, was constructed in 1913. The Mount St. Joseph Ursuline Sisters, currently numbering over 170, minister in Kentucky; Illinois; Louisiana; Minnesota; Missouri; New Mexico; Tennessee; Washington, D.C.; and Chile, South America.

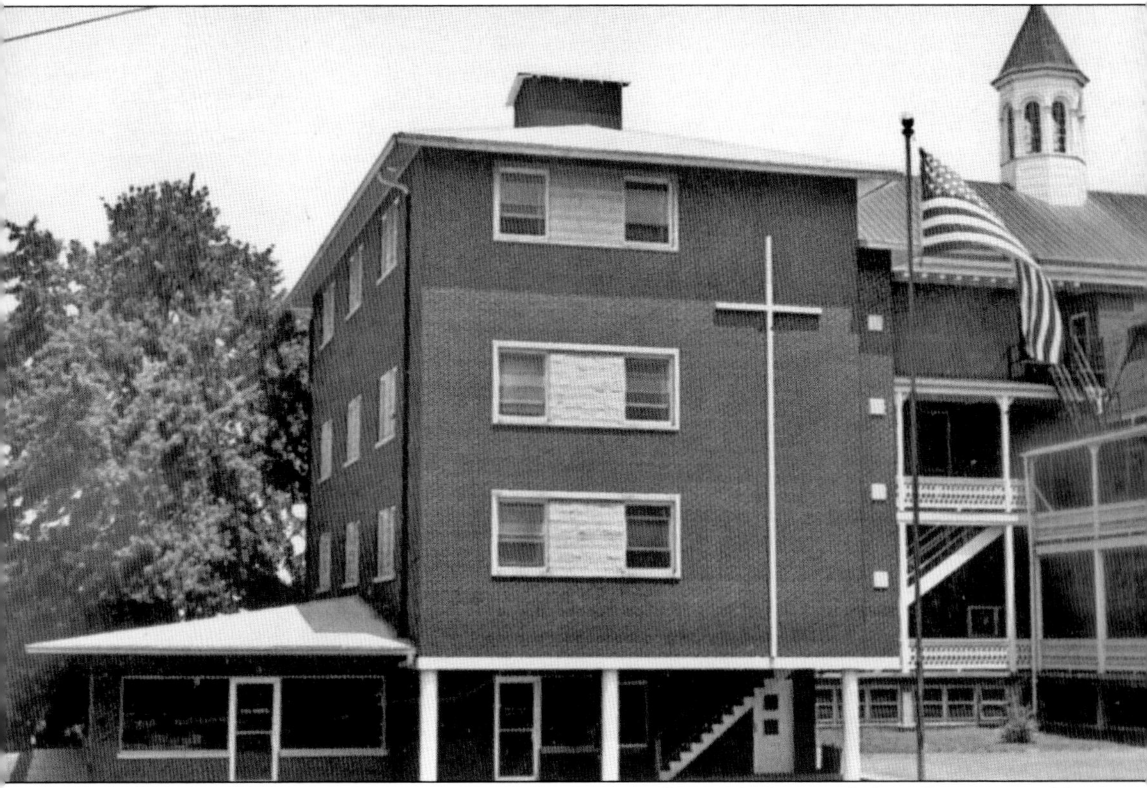

The most unusual Mount St. Joseph postcard is the card above of the Bloemer Building erected in 1962. The unique quality about the real-photo postcard is the fact that it is printed backwards. Probably only the visitors to the current Mount St. Joseph Conference and Retreat Center would catch this mistake.

# BIBLIOGRAPHY


Central Presbyterian Church. *The Birth of a Church 1839–1989.* San Angelo, TX: Newsfoto Yearbooks, 1989.

City of Owensboro. *A Brief General Outline of Its Past, Present and Future.* Publisher unknown. *c.* 1892.

City of Owensboro Parks Department. *1994 Owensboro Parks Community Calendar Celebrating the 100th Birthday of Legion Park.* Owensboro, KY: Progress Printing Company, 1993.

Dew, Lee A. and Aloma W. *Owensboro: The City on the Yellow Banks.* Bowling Green, KY: Rivendell Publications, 1988.

First Christian Church. *Church Directory.* Owensboro, KY: Messenger Job Printing Company, Inc., 1939.

First Presbyterian Church. *An Imperfect People Seeking the Perfect Will.* Owensboro, KY: Messenger Job Printing Company, Inc., 1951.

Hayes, William Foster. *Sixty Years of Owensboro, 1883–1943.* Owensboro, KY: Messenger Job Printing Company, Inc., 1944.

*Historical Churches of Daviess County 1776–1976.* Owensboro, KY: Owensboro Daviess County Ministerial Association and the Owensboro Junior Womens Club, 1976.

Jeffrey, Jonathan. "A Century of Change from Carnegie to Gates." *Kentucky Libraries* 70, no. 3 (2006).

Jones, Robert Ralston. *The Ohio River.* Washington, D.C.: Government Printing Office, 1916.

Mount St. Joseph Ursuline Sisters. *An Outline History of the Ursuline Sisters of Mount St. Joseph, 1874–1974.* Maple Mount, KY: Maple Mount Press, 1975.

Owensboro Bar Association Members. *Proceeding of the Owensboro Bar Association, in Memory of the Honorable Glover H. Cary.* Owensboro, KY: Messenger Job Printing Company Inc., 1940.

*Owensboro City Directory, 1911–1912.* Owensboro, KY: Messenger Job Printing Company, Inc., 1912.

Owensboro Chamber of Commerce. *Owensboro, Kentucky.* Chicago: Windsor Publication, 1967.

Potter, Hugh O. *Daviess County Sesquicentennial Historical Factbook.* Owensboro, KY: Radio Station WOMI, 1965.

———. *A History of Owensboro and Daviess County, Kentucky.* Owensboro, KY: Daviess County Historical Society, 1974.

———. *A History of Settle Memorial Methodist Church 1936–1966.* Owensboro, KY: Official Board of Settle Memorial Methodist Church, 1967.

Rone, Wendell H. *Daviess McLean Baptist Association 1844 to 1943.* Owensboro, KY: Messenger Job Printing Company, Inc., date unknown.

———. *Owensboro's First Church 1835 to 1985.* Owensboro, KY: Progress Printing Company, Inc., 1985.

Russell, Evan Ray. *History: Owensboro Parks and Recreation: 1815–1990.* Owensboro, KY: Progress Printing Comany, Inc., 1990.

Way, Frederick Jr. *Inland River Record 1956.* Sewickley, PA: Sewickley Printing Shop, Inc., 1956.

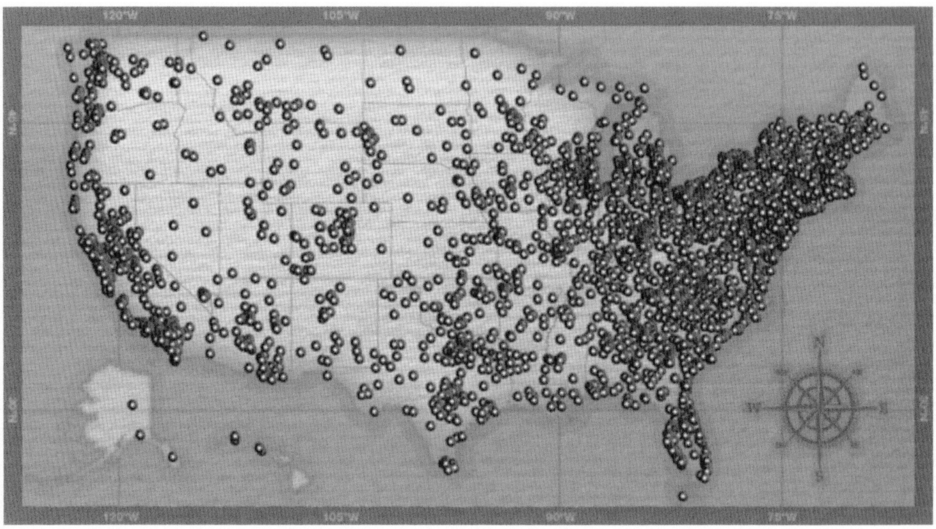